Outside
in the
Interior

Outside in the Interior

AN ADVENTURE GUIDE FOR CENTRAL ALASKA

More than 50 hikes, bikes, skis, strolls, and floats
for all levels of outdoor enthusiasts

Kyle Joly

University of Alaska Press
Fairbanks

Snowy Owl Books
an imprint of the University of Alaska Press

© 2007 University of Alaska Press
P.O. Box 756240
Fairbanks, AK 99775-6240
Second printing, 2008

Library of Congress Cataloging-in-Publication Data

Joly, Kyle.
Outside in the interior: an adventure guide for central Alaska / Kyle Joly.
  p. cm.
Includes bibliographical references and index.
ISBN 978-1-889963-99-0 (pbk. : alk. paper)
1. Outdoor recreation—Alaska—Guidebooks. 2. Alaska—Guidebooks. I. Title.
GV191.42.A4J65 2007
796.509798–dc22
            2007004149

This publication was printed on paper that meets the minimum requirements for ANSI/NISO z39.48–1992 (Permanence of Paper).

Cover and interior design: Dixon J. Jones, Rasmuson Library Graphics
All maps and photos are by the author unless otherwise credited.

Funding for this book was provided by the Dr. Terris and Katrina Moore endowment fund.

Contents

Author's Note . . . . *vii*
Acknowledgments . . . .*viii*
Introduction . . . . *ix*

Fairbanks Region

1	Creamer's Field	2
2	UAF, Skarland, and Pearl Creek Trails	4
3	Goldstream Valley Trails	10
4	Birch Hill	15
5	Ester Dome	18
6	Murphy Dome	21
7	Lower Chena River	24
8	Middle Tanana River	28
9	Chena Lake	32
10	Chena and Piledriver Sloughs	36
11	Isberg	40
12	Mount Healy via Bison Gulch	43
13	Nenana River	46
14	Kesugi Ridge	50

Chena River State Recreation Area Region

15	Upper Chena River	58
16	Compeau and Colorado Creek Trails	62
17	Twin Bears Trails	67
18	Stiles Creek Trail	70
19	Granite Tors Trail	74
20	Angel Rocks and Angel Rocks to Chena Hot Springs Trails	79
21	Chena Dome Trail	83
22	Angel Creek Trail	88
23	Trails of Chena Hot Springs Resort	91
24	Far Mountain Trail and Traverse	95

Steese–White Mountains Region

25 Chatanika River 102
26 Table Top Mountain Trail 106
27 Beaver Creek 109
28 Quartz Creek Trail 115
29 Mount Prindle 119
30 McManus Mountain 124
31 Birch Creek 127
32 Pinnell Mountain Trail 131
33 Mastodon Dome 136
34 White Mountains 139
35 Wickersham Dome and Summit Trail 144
36 Grapefruit Rocks 149
37 Tolovana Hot Springs Trail 152

Delta Junction Region

38 Highway Lakes—Harding, Birch, and Quartz 158
39 Clearwater and Tanana Rivers 161
40 Donnelly Dome 165
41 Castner Glacier 168
42 Rainbow Ridge 171
43 Fielding Lake 175
44 Delta River 178
45 Gulkana River 182

Fortymile Region

46 Eagle Trail 188
47 Tok and Little Tok Rivers 192
48 Upper Tanana River 196
49 Mount Fairplay 201
50 Fortymile River 204
51 Yukon River 209

Arctic Region

52 Finger Mountain 216
53 Marion Creek Falls 219
54 Sukakpak Mountain 222
55 Chandalar–Atigun Traverse 225
56 Atigun River Gorge and Sagavanirktok River 229

Appendix A: Expert Interior Favorites to Discover on Your Own 232
Appendix B: References, Contact Information, and Suggested Reading 234
Appendix C: Trip Locator Table 238
Index 239

Author's Note

I have tried to make the information in this guidebook as accurate as possible. The Interior is facing rapid changes from human development and climate change. Trail routes and conditions, as well as their existence, are likely to change. If you find any errors or note any changes, please send them along to outside-interior@hotmail.com so that I may incorporate them into future editions. If you love your Interior trails and wild areas, get involved in protecting them—see Appendix B for contact information. Bear in mind, you are ultimately responsible for your own actions and safety. This book is only a guide and is no substitute for backcountry skills and common sense.

Acknowledgments

A book like this begins with great partners to share in the adventures, so I must thank Julie Lurman, Shawn and Megan Wiegand, Martin Robards, Julie Morse, Nancy Fresco and Jay Cable, James Jackson, Brett Joly and Tete Diaz-Faes Zuniga, Lou and Judy Joly, Becky Joly, Adrian Gall and Dan Rizzolo, Nalon Smith, Ben and Karma Roth, Nikki Guldager and Ed Mallek, Jason Stahl, Collin Cogley, Dave Esse, Jason Thomas, Erika Ammann, Andy and Lili Ramey, Amy Lewis, Tom Dilts, Kyle Davis, Jason Geck, and Jenna App. Many thanks for all the smiles and company provided by my most faithful hiking partner, my mutt Spruce. I thank my parents for piquing my interest in the outdoors at a very early age on many memorable trips. I thank the Fairbanks BLM Recreation crew, especially Collin Cogley, Tim DuPont, Randy Goodwin, and Eric Yeager, for sharing their decades of experience in the Interior with me. The Alaska Public Lands Information Center and the Alaska Department of Natural Resources provided tons of useful information, for which I thank them as well. Maps were created using DeLorme's Topo USA (www.delorme. com). Plenty of my fellow outdoor enthusiasts helped me out along the way and provided lots of helpful information. Danny Kost provided inside information on guidebook publication. I thank Eric Troyer, Randy Goodwin, and Tim Stallard for suggestions and comments on an earlier draft that helped improve this guidebook. I thank the staff of the University of Alaska Press, especially Erica Hill and Sue Mitchell, for editorial reviews and seeing this project through. Lastly, I thank Julie for putting up with me and my efforts to complete this book and for her encouragement to do just that.

Introduction

This book is intended to guide outdoor enthusiasts of all ability levels to find ways to get out and explore Alaska's Interior. From pushing the stroller down paved paths to bagging rugged peaks to packrafting arctic rivers to skate skiing groomed trails, this guide is intended to reveal most of what the Interior has to offer for self-powered activities. This guide does not cover snowmachines, ATVs, or dog mushing (though they use some of the same trails). I specifically note which trails are nonmotorized and those that must be shared with motorized trail users. I point out where skijoring is allowed, because it is only assisted travel and there are few easily accessible trails to ski with dogs, harnessed or not. Due to the extreme cold and short days of winter, some people like to use snowmachines to haul gear to make skiing trips more fun, easier, and safer. I do not recommend or disdain this practice; it is simply part of the fabric of life in the far north. I have intentionally omitted hikes that originate within the Interior's most popular hiking destination, Denali National Park and Preserve. Hikes and treks in this spectacular area are documented well in other popular guides (see Appendix B). I have also included trips that may fall outside the bounds of what is normally considered the Interior if they are popular with Interior residents.

Interior roads used to reach trips in this book include Chena Hot Springs Road and several highways: Steese, Parks, Richardson, Elliott, Taylor, Denali, Dalton (the "Haul Road"), and Alaska ("Alcan"). (See overview map on page xxix.) Each adventure starts and ends along the relatively sparse road system. The number of trips in the Interior accessible by plane, even for just a drop-off or pickup, is almost infinite. As well as being more expensive, these trips are usually more remote and offer more solitude. For these reasons, I did not want to highlight any such trips and thus possibly diminish their unique value.

Any guidebook will likely increase use of described areas, so I feel responsible for educating users of this guide in the ethical use of this beautiful region and encouraging them to protect it. Future generations should enjoy it as much as I have; please review the Backcountry Travel section below. It is my solemn hope that any damages from increased use to areas due to this guidebook are at least offset by more people becoming familiar with these wild land resources and advocating for their protection.

Information about trails in the region has been diffuse. Some guidebooks cover a few of the most popular trails, such as Pinnell Mountain, Granite Tors, Angels Rocks, and Chena Dome. A few websites, such as those of the Alaska Department of Natural Resources and federal Bureau of Land Management, have trail information. The Alaska Public Lands Information Center also has a number of maps and pamphlets. (See Appendix B for useful places to get trail information.) But it seems that the best way to find out about Interior trails is to have lived and explored in the region for twenty years. Even so, I still hear about outdoor enthusiasts who have lived in the Interior for years and are surprised to learn of trails they never knew existed. It is one of the many idiosyncrasies of the Interior, especially the Fairbanks area. My motivation for writing this book is to let newcomers, as well as old-timers, know what there is to do in the region and dispel the myth about the Interior's paucity of trails. Of course, it was also a great excuse to do what I love most, explore the wild expanses of Alaska.

Using This Guide

The trip descriptions are designed to be packed with useful information, yet easy to use at a glance. I did not give step-by-step descriptions, because I feel that discovering the place on your own adds to the experience. I tried to give enough details for you to decide whether a particular adventure is suited to your ability, timetable, and mood. I also pointed out places where you might have difficulties. Each trip description is broken into five components: statistics, narrative, cautions ("Be Aware"), alternative trips for the more adventurous ("More Adventurous?"), and driving directions to the trip start. The statistics include distance, duration, high point, total elevation change, difficulty, route type, best season, USGS maps, and land manager.

"R/T Distance" is the round-trip distance covered by the adventure. "One-Way Distance" is noted for trips that have different start and finish locations (such as a river trip).

"Duration" is difficult to estimate because several factors come into play, such as fitness. Certain uber-athletes are capable of running 30 miles (48 km) of mountain trails in five hours, while others struggle to do it in three days, if at all. Pace is another factor. Some people like to see how fast they can cover ground, while others enjoy taking their time. Weather is another key component. For example, float times can vary dramatically due to water level, route choice, winds, number of obstacles (such as logjams), and the amount of paddling you do. The key to this statistic is that I tried to be consistent when determining the duration of the trip. Learn how your times fit against mine and you will soon be able to judge what the "real" duration should be for you.

"High Point" lets you know the highest elevation, above sea level, that the trip reaches. A steady climb to 4,000 feet (1,200 m) is a lot easier than going up and over several peaks. Those ups and downs can wear you out.

"Total Elevation Change" is an attempt to capture how much up and down there is between the start, high point, and finish of a trip. Imagine a hike from the south to north rims of the Grand Canyon as an example. Some guidebooks would have the total elevation change be 1,000 feet (305 m), as the north rim is at 8,000 feet (2,437 m) and the south is at 7,000 feet (2,132 m). My methodology captures the work required to go down to the river and back up. That hike would be 13,000 feet (3,960 m) of total elevation change in this guidebook, because it includes the 6,000-foot (1,827-m) descent to the river and the 7,000-foot (2,132-m) ascent back up to the north rim.

The same relativity in "Duration" is also seen in "Difficulty." Outdoor enthusiasts come in all ability levels; what I find "easy" you might find "difficult" or vice versa. Try a couple of trips you are comfortable with to get a feel for this rating system. A rating of "expert" means that only people with excellent physical condition and extensive wilderness experience in the mode of proposed travel should attempt this trip. These trips should be done with at least one other person and include a way of contacting help (satellite phones work best and can be rented—see Appendix B). Of course, you should always file a trip plan (see below) with a responsible person before heading out on any adventure.

"Route Type" lets you know what to expect from the trail (or lack thereof). Trips in this book use everything from paved bike lanes to unmarked wilderness routes, and include dirt roads, ATV and snowmachine trails, classic nonmechanized footpaths, and social trails. Social trails are paths that are not as obvious as established trails and can have numerous spur trails that make it easier to go the wrong way. They develop when people and animals use the same route over and over, eventually turning the route into a trail. With social trails, basic route-finding abilities are often required to avoid heading down the wrong rabbit trail. For trips where you must find your own way, I use the term "route." People attempting routes need to be skilled in orienteering, map reading, visualizing the lay of the land, and determining terrain types. People not confident with these skills should not attempt trips designated as "routes."

"Best Season" is somewhat subjective. Lowland trails in the Interior are notorious for being very wet in late spring and early summer and should be avoided so that they are not damaged and you do not sink up to your armpits in mud. Many summer trails are avoided during midwinter because of short days, extremely cold temperatures, and a lack of places to plug your vehicle in for days on end. I can tell you from experience that it is no fun to finish a trip by coming back to a frozen truck. At that point, another adventure might just be beginning.

"USGS Maps" let you know which topographic maps cover the area described by the trip. I recommend getting, studying, and bringing USGS maps on all trips outside of day trips in Fairbanks. Even close to town it does not hurt to use them, if just for practice.

The final component of statistics is "Land Manager." This lets you know which agency or agencies have management jurisdiction over the area covered by the trip. It is always a good idea to contact land managers before embarking on a trip to get the latest information about the area. There may be important trail information or news that they can share with you, such as a wildfire or grizzly bear alert, a closed road, or a washed-out bridge. It is always best to learn that a trailhead is closed before leaving home rather than after a two-hour drive to get there.

Following statistics is the trip narrative. The narrative should give you a good feel for the trip, identify important landmarks, and pique your interest. I do not describe every nuance of the trip; exploring is part of the adventure. I have attempted to give enough information so that you can prepare properly for your adventure and not lose your way. In other words, enough information so you do not pack two days worth of food and a life jacket for a seven-day hiking trip or seven days worth of food and no life jacket for a two-day packrafting trip.

There are inherent dangers in all outdoor adventures, though they certainly vary throughout the course of the year. In the "Be Aware" section I try to highlight possible dangers specific to each trip. More general warnings can be found in the "Environment" and "Backcountry Travel" segments that follow below.

In the "More Adventurous?" section, I give suggestions for additional exploration. Some simply suggest going a bit farther, while others hint at epic routes. So, while I describe more than fifty Interior adventures in the book, there are an additional hundred or so trip ideas embedded within this section. The idea was not to conclusively describe all trip possibilities but to whet your appetite and get you thinking about your own ideas for exploring the Interior.

The final section of each trip description contains driving directions to reach the start and finish locations. I have tried to make the directions clear and simple. Road naming and numbering conventions in the Interior are a bit muddled, so I try to give both to help clarify matters. For example, someone driving into Alaska from Canada starts by heading west on the Alaska Highway (Alaska 2), also known as the "Alcan." At Delta Junction the highway becomes the Richardson Highway, although the driver has not exited or even changed lanes. The

Richardson Highway to the south of Delta Junction is Alaska 4, but the driver is on Alaska 2 from Delta Junction to Fairbanks. Upon entering Fairbanks, again without leaving the highway, the driver ends up on the Steese Highway, heading north. If the driver turns right in Fox, just north of Fairbanks, the car would remain on the Steese Highway (Alaska 6) heading toward the town of Circle. If the driver continues straight, the car would be on the Elliott Highway (Alaska 2). To remain on the Elliott Highway the driver would have to turn left at milepost 73 shortly after the town of Livengood; going straight would put the driver on the Dalton Highway (Alaska 11). The Dalton Highway, which ends at Deadhorse just shy of the Arctic Ocean, is commonly referred to as the Haul Road. Clear as mud? Hope I do better. Many directions are based on highway mileage markers. As these signs and almost all car odometers are only in miles, I do not include conversions to metric distances for them.

I have included maps in the book to give you a rough idea of where you are heading and what you might be getting into. Red lines depict the described routes. For most trips "P" stands for parking, but it also means put-in for float trips. Look for a "T" for take-out locations. The symbol "P/T" means the location can be used for either a put-in or take-out. These maps should not take the place of USGS topographical maps.

Environment

There are many different ideas about what constitutes the Interior. For this guide, I define the Interior as the drainages that flow into the Yukon River and that are accessible from the contiguous road system. In the Interior, seemingly endless expanses of black spruce stands are intermingled with willow-encircled ponds left on the floodplains of a mighty river's younger course. This landscape is called the taiga or boreal forest; it is the singular image that many have of the Interior. In contrast to the rugged and spectacular scenery of coastal Alaska, the Interior's beauty is sublime and austere. However, the Interior is deceptively diverse. The Alaska and Brooks ranges stand in towering contrast to the taiga. The Delta River, which drains the southern slopes of the Alaska Range, cuts northward through the mountains and eventually joins the Tanana River, which then joins the Yukon River. Thus, trips in the rugged and spectacular Delta River headwaters are in the Interior. Less dramatic mountain ranges can also be found in the Interior and offer excellent alpine hiking or scenic backdrops to float trips.

TAIGA: Even within the taiga there is diversity. The taiga, though dominated by black spruce, has stands of birch, aspen, and white spruce trees. Black spruce reign in lowlands, muskegs, and other wet areas because these hardy trees are about the only tree that can grow in the wet and frigid land dominated by permafrost. Muskegs, which are low-lying wet areas dotted with small ponds lined with black spruce, are a distinctive characteristic of the taiga. Aspen and birch, which are hardwoods, require drier soils than black spruce and are a good indicator that permafrost does not underlie the area. Quite often, just a small environmental change can make a big difference. Cruising through the Interior, you will often see extensive birch stands on the south-facing side of a low hill. At the bottom, diminutive black spruce take over and may well be on the north face of that same hill. The sun's warmth in the short northern summer can be enough to make that south slope favorable to the hardwoods. Mixed forests—stands with both spruce and hardwoods—are common within this ecosystem.

The taiga hosts a wide array of wildlife including moose, black bears, grizzly bears, wolves, overwintering caribou, American (pine) martins, porcupines, lynx, red fox, snowshoe hares, red squirrels, and voles. This ecosystem also supports a wide range of birds including ravens, gray jays (camp robbers), owls, woodpeckers, chickadees, spruce grouse, goshawks, and many, many songbirds during the summer.

RIPARIAN CORRIDORS: White spruce trees grow much larger and taller than black spruce, though they can be difficult to tell apart and can hybridize. White spruce are most commonly found along high riverbanks, also known as riparian corridors, which tend to be drier than black spruce habitat. Thickets of alder and willow often line waterways. Moose love these large patches of willow. You can often see them as you float down a quiet river. Riparian corridors are just that—corridors. All manner of wildlife use riparian corridors for traveling. Humans also use these corridors for travel and have for thousands of years. Beaver, river otter, muskrats, and mink are animals that specialize in using riparian areas. Look for kingfishers, pintails, mallards, mergansers, dippers, lesser yellowlegs, and bank swallows. Both black and grizzly bears are commonly found in riparian areas because of the fish found there. Use extra caution while traveling in riparian corridors, because thick brush reduces visibility and increases your chances of encountering a bear.

SHRUB: Shrub habitat is found in transition zones between forested and nonforested areas. This transition can be due to altitude or latitude. Altitudinal transitions occur as you head from the taiga into alpine areas. Between these two ecosystems a band of shrub typically occurs. Sometimes this band is mercifully narrow and easy to pass through; in other places it can be wide and seemingly impassable. Good routes around these areas, though longer, may save lots of time and energy. Numerous songbirds enjoy the relative safety of this zone, but most wildlife just pass through. The latitudinal transition shrub zone generally offers a different suite of species than the altitudinal one. Moving north, trees get smaller and smaller and then vanish entirely. In this zone, dwarf birch (also known as resin birch), blueberry, willow, Labrador tea, and wild rose are common.

TUNDRA: Altitudinal and latitudinal differences between shrub communities are also reflected in two widely disparate tundra types: alpine and tussock tundra. Alpine tundra is found only at high elevations. Just what constitutes high elevation depends on how far north you are, as well as other factors. Low-lying vegetation such as low-bush cranberry, crowberry, willow, heather, bearberry, grass, dryas, and a slew of lichens dominate alpine tundra. Shortly after the snow recedes in summer, alpine tundra is a spectacle of wildflowers, like the wooly lousewort, mountain harebell, alpine azalea, paintbrushes, and bistorts. Alpine tundra is a good place to spot Dall sheep, caribou, grizzly bears, marmots, ground squirrels, and the elusive wolverine. Ptarmigan and ravens are the birds you will most likely see.

Tussock tundra is a completely different community. Tussocks, those mini-towers of vegetation that making walking so difficult, are formed by cottongrass. Tussock tundra is common north of tree line and in wet and low-lying areas. Sedges and dwarf shrubs are important components of this ecosystem. Lichens can also be productive. Lichens and freshly sprouted cottongrass attract the tundra's most commonly seen critter, the caribou. Grizzly bears and wolves can also be seen. Waterfowl are attracted to this ecosystem's numerous water bodies.

WILDFIRE: In 2004, a record-setting 6.5 million acres (2.6 million hectares) of forest burned. Wildfire is the most important ecosystem driver in the Interior. Fires can devastate some types of vegetative communities while rejuvenating others. Black spruce, with its low-slung canopy, is highly vulnerable to wildfire but also very well adapted to it. Lichens, commonly associated with black spruce stands, are easily consumed by wildfires. They can take fifty to two hundred years to recover after a severe burn, especially those preferred as winter forage by caribou. Therefore, wildfires are detrimental to wintering caribou herds until the lichens have recovered. On the up side, willows, grasses, and forbs quickly establish themselves after fires, providing excellent habitat for moose. Also, for the mushroom lovers, morels tend to spring up in areas that burned the previous summer. Know your mushrooms before picking—some species can make you ill or worse.

Since wildfires are common almost every summer in the Interior, outdoor enthusiasts should know what problems they present. Wildfires in the Interior can get very large (one million acres [400,000 hectares] or more), closing major roads and causing the evacuation of entire towns. Smoke that billows from these fires presents two additional problems. First, smoke can get so thick that it seriously diminishes visibility, making navigation difficult. Second, breathing in smoke, especially while exerting yourself, is unhealthy. You should take smoke inhalation seriously, keeping it in mind when making decisions about which trip to take. Check with the land managers and the Alaska Fire Service (see Appendix B), which coordinates fire operations in the Interior, before leaving on a summer trip. Driving for hours only to find the road closed because of a fire is no fun, but being stuck in one could be deadly. Fires from previous years present two problems as well. They often leave stands of black spruce poles, which can fall very easily, so beware. Wildfires can denude slopes of vegeation, making them more prone to landslides that can take out trails and even change river courses. Always keep your eyes open when entering a burned area.

MOSQUITOES: Sometimes known as the Alaska State Bird, mosquitoes are a force to be reckoned with in the Interior. Thick smoke from wildfires can keep their numbers down in some years; however, the extensive wetlands in the Interior serve as spawning grounds that make mosquitoes almost ubiquitous during the height of their season (May through July). Insect repellent (bug dope) is an essential item for every trip during this time. You might not always need it, but you should always bring it. Mosquitoes can be found at all but the very highest elevations of trips described by this guide. DEET, an insecticide rather than a repellent, is the only ingredient that works effectively. It comes in a variety of applications, such as spray, cream, or liquid, and in concentrations from 5 to 100 percent. Even 15–20 percent DEET spray works well for a short time. Use it as sparingly as possible on children. Some parents put it on their children's clothing only. If your travels take you through prime mosquito habitat (lowlands, muskegs, and river bottoms), you will want pants and long-sleeved shirts. Mosquitoes can drill right through thin layers, especially synthetics. I also strongly recommend head nets and bug jackets in these habitats. All this clothing can make you overheat. Interior temperatures can shoot up past 90°F (32°C) in the summer. Be sure to keep well hydrated.

BEARS: Bears leave their winter dens just before the arrival of the mosquitoes. The Interior has grizzly and black bears. Salmon runs in the Interior are smaller and more spread out than they are along coastal Alaska, and thus grizzly bears are typically much smaller than their coastal cousins, the brown bear. The lower concentrations of easily accessible food also leads to lower densities of bears in the Interior than in coastal ecosystems. A low density of bears means that they are less social, and therefore less socialized. Bears that are fed and socialized well, such as those in Katmai National Park on the coast of the Alaska Peninsula, tend to have smaller "personal space" needs. People or other bears can be relatively close without alarming them (i.e., they are more tolerant). Interior grizzly bears, being less well fed and socialized, tend to require a larger buffer. A safe viewing distance in Katmai may be 50 yards (meters), whereas in the Interior the distance is recommended to be about a quarter mile (0.4 km). The good news is that since the density is so much lower, the likelihood of encountering a bear is lower. The number of bear sightings that turn into attacks on people is extremely low, even in the Interior. So there is a low probability of seeing a bear and even much less chance of being attacked—but there is always that chance when you go out adventuring. A serious bear attack happens most every year in Alaska.

There are many simple ways to reduce your chances of encountering a bear and reduce the chance of a bear encounter turning into a bear attack. The most effective method of avoiding a bear encounter is to travel in groups and be alert. The rate of bear attacks drops precipitously with larger groups. The vast majority occur on people traveling singly or in pairs. Another important avoidance tactic is to make plenty of noise, especially talking or singing loudly. Most bears will try to avoid people whenever possible, and the human voice is the best way to let a bear know you are in the vicinity. Some people use bells, but they are probably not as effective as the human voice. The ring of bear bells can alert a grizzly that something is in his personal space, but the bear may not realize that sound is coming from a person. Also, the sound of bear bells does not carry far. Some guides suggest shouting "Hey bear!" frequently to warn bears of your presence. I recommend against using the word "bear" unless you actually see one. If you have been shouting "Hey bear!" for two hours and then shout "BEAR!!!" when you actually see one, members of your party and even other people in the area may not immediately recognize the danger. Save the word "bear" for those rare occasions when you actually see one. Try "Hey moose!" as you are much more likely to see one of them, and they can be dangerous as well (see next section).

Call out more frequently when your field of vision is reduced, such as in thick brush or near streambeds. In open alpine country, you may want to call out only when cresting a knoll where a bear could be camped out on the other side. While the visual acuity of bears is highly variable, not characteristically poor as reported in some older guidebooks, all bears have a highly developed sense of smell. If the wind is at your back, you will not need to call out as frequently, because the bear will likely smell you long before it hears you. With this in mind, it is particularly important to call out louder and more frequently if you are headed into the wind. Your scent will not alert a bear in this scenario and your voice will not carry as far. To make matters worse, bear spray (a type of pepper spray) has a very short effective range shooting into the wind (practically nil) and will probably incapacitate you rather than the bear. Bear spray has proven its effectiveness in many cases (though not all), but you still need to have the wind at your back! Even a hint of breeze is enough to drastically reduce the range of the spray. Be sure to get "bear" spray as it is much stronger than sprays designed to defend against people (personal defense sprays).

If you do have a bear encounter, do not rely on climbing trees to escape. Both black and grizzly bears can climb trees, though black bears are much better at it. Finding a suitable climbing tree in the Interior is often difficult anyway. Only attempt this kind of retreat if there is plenty of time and you can get at least 15 feet (5 m) above the ground. Also do not think you can outrun a bear. They can run 35 mph (55 km/h) for short stretches, much faster than Olympic sprinters. Hold your ground. DO NOT RUN—fleeing triggers a chase response in predators. A large percentage of grizzly bear charges are bluffs. Hold your ground to let the bear know you are not prey. Talk to the bear in a calm, deep voice to let it know where and what you are. Bears will often stand up to get a better smell of the situation. This is not an aggressive display. Raise your arms and wave them slowly to appear larger. Holding a jacket between two people can also have this effect. Try to back away slowly to diffuse the situation. Avoid eye contact with adult bears as they consider this a threat display. If the bear continues to display interest, keep talking and appearing as large as you can.

Even if you have done everything correctly, there is still a slim chance the bear will come closer. If contact between you and the bear is imminent, drop to the ground and try to protect your vital areas. The best position is to be face down with your legs spread (to make it more difficult to flip you over) and your hands across the back of your neck to protect it. Leave your pack on! This will give you extra protection. Most attacks by grizzly bears stem from people not giving them enough personal space. An attack usually is the bear's way of showing you who is boss. Typically, once you have shown that you are not a threat, the attack ends swiftly, though a grizzly can inflict substantial, if not mortal, damage in that short period. Wait until you are sure the bear has left the area before you attempt to get up. Getting up prematurely may prompt round two. If the attack is prolonged, it may be the extremely rare predatory attack. Fight back anyway you can: rocks, sticks, pocket knife, whatever.

Black bears are thought to be more predatory than grizzly bears, thus it is recommended that you NOT "play dead" when a black bear attacks. Fight with whatever means you have available. Attacks of this nature are extremely rare for either species. Learn to differentiate black and grizzly bears. Color is not a reliable indicator. Grizzly bears have a large shoulder hump, long visible claws, and a concave facial profile. Black bears do not have the larger hump, their claws are smaller, curved, and can be hard to see, and the facial profile is straighter (flatter).

A couple of special cases of bears should be noted. Young bears are curious and often inexperienced with humans. If a young bear does not lose interest even as you try to slowly back away, you may need to use dominance displays to let it know that you know it is immature. However, you must be knowledgeable about bear behavior if you attempt this. Incorrectly predicting bear behavior can mean death. Sows with cubs are probably the most dangerous, because sows are extremely protective. If you see a cub, do not spend time taking a picture. Get out of the area before mama comes. She will not be far away. Kill sites are another danger. Bears protect their food aggressively. If you see or smell a carcass, assume a bear is around. Circling ravens sometimes indicate a kill site might be nearby. Either head back the way you came or take a wide detour around the area through the most open terrain you can find. Stephen Herrero is a leading expert on bears attacks and their causes. Read his book *Bear Attacks* (see Appendix B) to get the best information to avoid bear encounters. His book and this guide (see "Backcountry Travel") give recommendations on how to set up a campsite to minimize the possibility of attracting bears. Will Troyer's book *Into Brown Bear Country* (see Appendix B) also provides useful information on venturing into bear country.

MOOSE: Moose are more numerous than bears and can be ornery as well. A big moose is generally larger than a big bear in the Interior. Incidents with moose are almost always about personal space. In general, spooking a moose is no big deal. Just make plenty of noise, and it will usually cede the trail. However, if the moose is in a particularly good patch of willow, it may take its own sweet time there. If you do not have the patience, make sure the moose knows where you are as you attempt to circle around it. Three types of encounters with moose require more concern. First, cows with calves, especially when they are young (May–August), can be very defensive. Despite their gangly appearance, moose can cover short distances very quickly. Cows defending their calves will charge people up to 50 yards (meters) away. The second occasion is with bull moose during the rut (late September–early November). The bulls work hard to keep competitors away from their harem. It is best not to have a bull think of you as competition. In both of these circumstances, unlike responding to a bear, the best thing to do is to retreat out of their personal space. Thirdly, be wary of moose on packed winter trails, especially in later winter. Stressed from the long winter, moose often do not want to give up the trail and can be aggressive.

WOLVES: Although occurrences are very uncommon, wolves can become interested in people. In most cases, when humans feed wolves the animals lose the fear that they generally have of people. A few attacks have been reported over the years. If confronted with the extremely rare circumstance of an attentive, unfrightened wolf, do not run. Running can elicit the predator's chase response. Stand your ground and make noise to scare it off.

LAND OF EXTREMES: Extreme variability is the hallmark of the Interior. Official daylight can range from zero to twenty-four hours a day, depending on whether it is December 21 or June 21, at the Arctic Circle. The sun still provides three to four hours of light to the Interior at winter solstice, and, while the sun does set in Fairbanks area on summer solstice, there is enough twilight on a clear night to get around. There are twelve hours of official daylight during the spring (March) and fall (September) equinoxes. Because of these radical transitions, the amount of light in a day can be as much as seven minutes more or less than the previous day. Keep track of the length of the days, so you do not attempt a twelve-hour hike with only seven hours of available daylight. These radical shifts in day lengths are mirrored by variability in temperature. The Interior experiences some of the most dramatic swings of temperature in the world. More than 150°F (80°C) can separate summertime highs that get past 90°F (32°C) and wintertime lows down to –60°F (–50°C) or more. Differences between high and low temperatures within a single day can be dramatic as well. Temperature shifts occur altitudinally as well as seasonally and daily. Often as you climb higher in the summertime, temperatures drop. In wintertime, however, temperature inversions are common and hilltops stay warmer than low-lying areas. Snowstorms can occur even in summer up in the mountains. Spring and fall weather can be especially hard to predict. One mid-May I clipped off the miles on a barren ridgeline; the following May the snow was waist deep in the same area. Plan accordingly!

WINTER: Cold, dark, and snowy; that is just winter. But here in the Interior the extreme cold and short days of winter go to a different level. The right equipment can make the difference between a good adventure and a disaster. Even minor injuries can create serious situations in the cold and dark. See the "Backcountry Travel" section for ideas to help deal with the cold. Many Interior residents use –20°F (–29°C) as a cutoff point for deciding whether to go out and enjoy winter. At –40°F (–40°C), strange things start to happen, such as metal getting brittle and oil freezing quickly. Only experienced people with the right equipment should start an adventure at these temperatures, but everyone going on winter trips should be prepared for such temperatures. The high-pressure weather systems that typically bring these extremely cold days may last days or even weeks since the winds needed to move new systems into the area are scarce at this time of year. On the bright side, the aurora borealis lights up the sky frequently with spectacular displays.

Backcountry Travel

Backcountry travel that is successful and environmentally friendly has many facets. I will briefly address them, but see Appendix B for books that deal entirely with this subject. Environmentally friendly travel stems from a conservation ethic. Get to know how the lands you explore are protected. If an area is unprotected, contact conservation groups to learn how to help protect it. You respect the land, usually, by treading lightly on it. Successful backcountry travel is based on preparedness, experience, and determination. Often preparedness is based on previous experience. The key is to get out there and explore. Start small, and work your way into more advanced trips. If possible, tag along with more experienced friends or groups. To help you prepare for your travels, I have included advice in the paragraphs below gained from my own experience. I have also included information in the Environment section (above) and in the trip descriptions. Please do all you can to be prepared. Emergency medical help is often very far away. It could be days away if nobody knows you are in trouble.

FILING A TRAVEL PLAN: One of the most important ways to prepare for a trip is to file a travel plan. Simply tell a responsible person your destination, trip partners, route, means of travel, departure time, and expected return time. Give that person a specific time and date when he or she should initiate a formal search if you do not return. This last bit is crucial; do not make the person guess when they should call the cavalry. However, you should allow some cushion between the time you expect to return and when you think a search should be started. How great a cushion depends on your comfort level, the duration of the trip, and your availability to communicate with your contact person. You must let your contact know when you are back. Also, tell your contact to call you first before calling for a rescue, just in case you forgot to check in. Searches can be expensive and dangerous for the rescuers; take them seriously. Cell phone coverage is limited in the Interior, so do not rely on your cell phone. Satellite phones are much more reliable and can be rented if you can not or do not want to buy one. For frequent adventurers, a satellite phone is a wise investment. Another option is to buy an emergency personal locator beacon (EPIRB). When activated, EPIRBs send out a signal that can be traced by rescuers.

LEAVE NO TRACE: The basic premise of the "leave no trace" wilderness travel ethic is simple. "Take only photos, leave only footprints," as the saying goes. The motto should be remembered and applied widely. The central tenets of "leave no trace" are that you travel and camp on durable surfaces, pack out what you pack in, dispose of waste properly, leave historic and natural artifacts (e.g., fossils) so that others may enjoy them, minimize campfire impacts, respect wildlife, and be considerate of others.

Traveling on durable surfaces is simple when trails are present. Use them to keep wear and tear to a single path. You may need a lot of discipline not to cut corners on moderate slopes that seem to have too many switchbacks—but try. These short-cuts widen trails, denude vegetation, increase erosion, and invite others to develop shortcuts on other switchbacks. Stay on trails even where they are worn into ruts that collect water. Where wet trail conditions exist people often avoid the main trail and instead create a braided trail with each braid as muddy and wet as the first. Again, try to avoid the temptation. Wear waterproof boots and stay on the trail. If there are no existing trails, try to fan out in order to prevent one from being established. Try to avoid using trails during breakup and after wet spells, as trails are especially vulnerable at these times—this goes especially for bikers.

Fires should be limited to established areas (e. g., fire rings, woodstoves) or below the annual high-water mark on riverbanks and lakeshores, where spring floods will wash away signs of your presence. Burn only down or dead wood. Put only paper in campfires. Pack out garbage that can not be completely burned. Bury human waste at least 6 inches (15 cm) deep and at least 100 feet (30 m) from water. Always check with the land manager of the area you are going to to learn the area's fire danger and to see if campfires are allowed.

CAMPSITES: The following are important campsite guidelines so that you can minimize the chance of bear problems. First, avoid areas that show signs of bear use. Often you will be able to spot trails or tracks. If any sign of a kill is around, move far away from the area. Rivers are usually travel corridors for all sorts of wildlife. Camp far enough away from waterways so that wildlife can travel by without disturbing your camp. Try to camp on durable surfaces, such as bare ground. Sand is comfortable to sleep on, but it gets into everything, making a mess, especially if it rains. Fine-grained, smooth gravel is always the best surface if available. Your camp should have a triangular shape. Tents make the top corner of the triangle. Put your kitchen, where you cook and eat, about 50 to 100 yards (meters) away and directly downwind from the tenting area. Tents should not be downwind of the kitchen to avoid bears coming by the tents if they are attracted by the food smells. The final corner of the campsite triangle is the food storage area. It should be in line with the cooking area but 50 to 100 yards (meters) away. Store your food and any odoriferous items there. If large trees are present, hang your storage bags in them. The bags should be at least 10 feet (3 m) above the ground and 4 feet (1.3 m) from the tree trunk. Unfortunately, the Interior has few trees that fit these requirements. Your best bet is to buy, borrow, or rent bear-resistant containers (bear barrels). These are containers specially designed to foil bears. If they work once in your life, the money was well spent on your protection, as well as the protection of the bear. Bears that associate humans with food often end up being killed.

MAP READING: I am an unabashed supporter of the "old school." The ability to read terrain and a map is becoming something of a lost art form. Backcountry users need to know how to use a compass and follow a map, especially in a remote Alaska setting. Bring a geographic positioning system (GPS) unit for backup if you want, but you (not a gadget) are ultimately responsible for you and your party's safety. Therefore, I have avoided using or providing GPS data. GPS units are becoming ubiquitous and are useful for locating where you are and determining routes for where you want to go. However, they have made it easier for people to go into the backcountry without maps and compasses or the ability to use them. I enjoy getting away from cities, gizmos, technology, and the buzz of modern life. Therefore, while I accept the utility of the GPS, I mostly have forsaken the device for the oldschool map and compass. GPS units have their down sides. They add extra weight, their batteries can die, and sometimes they get broken. Even if you will not leave home without a GPS, I strongly recommend that you bring maps and a compass. Blind reliance on technology is not a good thing in my book. Go practice the essential skill of map reading and tuck your GPS deep in your pack with your satellite phone in case of emergency.

WATER HAZARDS: River crossings in Alaska are inherently dangerous, as the currents can be strong and the water extremely cold. The Interior, in general, has fewer and less dangerous river crossings than other regions of the state, such as southcentral Alaska. There are plenty of glacial rivers in the Interior, such as the Tanana, Delta, and Nenana, but few hiking trails cross them. Still, the Interior has river crossings. Rivers should be crossed where water levels are lowest. Look for riffles, as they usually indicate shallow water, and try to work your way between the islands of gravel dotting the channels of braided rivers. Wide spots in the river often are shallower than narrow spots. Cutbanks should be avoided as they are sure signs of relatively deeper water. To test a river for depth, toss a rock into the water. A crashing of rocks signals shallower water, whereas a "kerplunk" reveals deeper water. Use caution when choosing a river-crossing route. The shortest is often not the best. Do not attempt to cross rivers that are deeper than mid-thigh, as they will likely be too powerful and the chances of being swept downstream are great.

Always unfasten your backpack belt strap before attempting to cross. If you lose your footing, the additional weight of your pack will make it very difficult to get back up. With the belt strap unfastened you can shed your pack much easier. Soaking or even losing a backpack is better than drowning. Groups of people should cross strong rivers together, arms locked, with the strongest member being the furthest upstream. Some people prefer that the group be in a straight chain while others like a pyramid shape. Either technique is fine. Both break the force of the current for people below the strongest member and add stability for everyone. Weaker and shorter people should be in the middle with the second strongest person at the trailing end. I prefer breaking large groups into smaller ones so that each has no more than about four per crossing group. More than five people in a group make it unwieldy.

Packrafting is an ideal way to cross powerful or large rivers. New packraft models are extremely light, weighing just 4 pounds (2 kg). They are small enough to fit in a pack, yet they can fit a single occupant with some gear and are very durable. They take just a couple of minutes to inflate. In addition to crossing rivers, packrafts can be used to travel down them. These devices open a wide array of routes, increase safety of river crossings, and increase the distance you can cover in backcountry adventures. Personal flotation devices (life jackets) should always be worn while packrafting, as well as doing other types of boating.

As noted above, rivers in Alaska can be dangerous. Besides the frigid water temperatures, boaters need to be mindful of sweepers, rapids, and environmental factors (see next subsection). Sweepers are trees that overhang a river channel just above the surface of the water and can completely span the channel. They are created by river currents that typically erode into the outside bank. This erosion creates steep embankments and undercuts trees, which tilt toward the river and eventually fall in. Sweepers are the most common cause of boaters becoming swimmers. Aside from knocking boaters into the water, sweepers can be dangerous because the force of the river's current can easily pin someone against them. Logjams and, early in the season, ice also present problems as both can span entire river channels. Try to stay in wider channels that have more water. Avoid channels that look new, as they often have hazards that are unavoidable and dangerous. Winds are less dangerous, but should be treated with respect. They seemingly arise from nowhere, rocking canoes and greatly slowing progress. Often, it is best to take a break on shore until strong winds die down.

As with many things, experience is the key to becoming more proficient with any watercraft. Begin with easy floats and lake trips. Slowly build up to rapids, go with experienced paddlers, and consider taking a paddling course. The difficulty of rapids is characterized by a class system. Class I is flat water that requires little maneuvering, whereas class V is all but impassable even for highly experienced paddlers. Class III is probably the limit for using canoes and small rafts, such as the packraft. Only experts should attempt to run rapids rated class III or above.

Throughout winter, unfrozen water can be on top of river or lake ice, often hidden under snow, as ice settles or rivers percolate. This condition is known as overflow. It can be dangerous for travelers—if you get wet from overflow, dry off and put on spare clothing. Keeping moving is often the best and only way to keep warm before reaching or creating shelter.

GIARDIA: Giardia lamblia is a different type of water hazard. It is a waterborne protozoan parasite present throughout interior Alaska and can cause serious fever, nausea, diarrhea, and cramping. The illness, often known as "beaver fever" because of the parasite's association with beavers and other rodents (though all Interior mammals are potential carriers), can cause severe dehydration due to extensive water loss. These symptoms usually arise about seven to fourteen days after exposure. The illness is not easy to diagnose, but for the majority of people treatment is relatively easy and available at most medical facilities. Still, it is best to avoid this illness and others caused by microscopic organisms. Treat water before drinking it by either boiling it for three to five minutes, adding iodine tablets, or filtering it.

ENVIRONMENTAL FACTORS: Blizzards in July or 45°F (7°C) days in March, Mother Nature can throw all sorts of conditions at you. Be prepared for all conditions at any time of the year. The possibilities are endless, so I will touch on a few issues that commonly occur. Most summer hiking trails avoid soggy bottomlands in favor of upland ridges. The majority of these ridges have sparse supplies of water, and they become drier later in the season as remnant snow patches melt. Stay hydrated. Temperatures in the summer can soar past 90°F (32°C). Lack of water can lead to weakness, heat stroke, and even death. Make sure to plan for your water needs.

Hiking on ridges can present other problems. Higher elevations get fogged in sooner than lowlands. You can easily lose your orientation in thick fog. The abilities to use a compass and read maps are essential. Storms can arrive swiftly, bringing cold temperatures, driving winds, rain, sleet, snow, and lightning. Most ridges described in this book are above tree line, making a hiker the tallest object—a natural lightning rod. Get off the top of the ridge during a thunderstorm. Lightning also ignites a large percentage of forest fires in the region, so keep on guard for new fires if you see lightning.

Summer hikes have the benefit of extremely long days, making headlamps mostly unnecessary in the middle of summer. Still, keep in mind that day length changes constantly and differs greatly between the northern and southern extents of the Interior. As the days get shorter, they also get colder. Hypothermia cases typically happen in the spring and fall. Hypothermia is a life-threatening condition in which a person's core body temperature drops dangerously. Hypothermia can occur in the summer, though usually at high elevations; in cool, rainy weather; or after an unexpected dip into cold water. To avoid this condition stay dry and warm. If you do get wet, put on dry clothes, insulate yourself, and drink warm beverages. If possible, keep moving to help your body warm itself.

Spring is the wettest time of the year and when floods are most common. Boaters need to be aware, as rivers can rise 10 vertical feet (3 m) or more above their normal levels when the snowpack melts in the spring.

Winter brings extreme cold. Interior residents like to brag about what temperature they can endure and still go outside to ski, work, or whatever. Everyone should be wary doing outdoor activities in temperatures –10°F (–23°C) and colder. Proper gear is essential, as is being prepared for temperatures to get much colder. Frostbite can occur at any temperature below 32°F (0°C). I strongly recommend forgoing expeditions if the temperature is below –20°F (–29°C) before leaving the house. The smallest injury or mishap can be life-threatening at those temperatures. An additional problem is that vehicle liquids can freeze or gel quickly in extreme cold. Dealing with a frozen vehicle far from town at the end of a trip is no fun. The following should be in your vehicle on all winter trips outside of town: warm sleeping bag, snow shovel, food, fire-starting equipment, flare, and some means to thaw your vehicle. A satellite phone is a good idea too—if you can keep the batteries warm.

AVALANCHES: The Interior has many characteristics that decrease the likelihood of avalanches. The terrain is typically gentle, winter temperatures are usually below freezing, and the wind is usually mild. Still, the Interior has avalanches and not just in the Alaska and Brooks ranges. Backcountry travelers should be familiar with conditions that often accompany avalanches. Avalanches are more likely after a storm, in warmer spring weather, on days with large changes in winds or temperatures, on lee slopes where wind has deposited snow, and on moderately steep slopes (30–45 degrees). Snow conditions, weather, and terrain all factor into whether an avalanche is likely. Backcountry users traveling on snow should be constantly evaluating avalanche conditions; look for "nature's billboards." Can you spot previous avalanche activity? If there have been recent avalanches, have they been on slopes with similar aspects and angles as the one you are considering to cross? If so, do not travel that way. Does the snowpack fracture when you jump on it? Does it make a hollow "woomf" sound? If so, stay off that slope. If you know about snowpack structure, bring a snow shovel to look for weak layers. There are classes and books on avalanche safety, of which Fredston and Fesler's *Snow Sense* is one of the best (see Appendix B). Learn these skills if you are going to be traveling on snow. If you do not know how to assess the risk of crossing a snow-covered slope, do not try it until you learn how.

TRIPS WITH CHILDREN: Instilling the love of the outdoors in the next generation is critical. If they love getting outside, they are more apt to protect it. Please take them on wilderness trips. Teach them backcountry skills and how to identify wildlife and wildflowers. Convey to them your love of the outdoors. However, while backcountry trips with children are important and rewarding, they require certain accommodations. Children generally travel at a slower pace. Plan to travel fewer miles, make more stops, and carry more stuff. Experience will dictate what adventures are right for you and them. Start small and work your way into bigger trips. Also, many kids can be fearless, careless, or clueless, making accidents more likely—all the more reason to bring a satellite phone. Be especially careful with children around animals. Predators such as bears tend to focus on weaker and smaller members of a group of prey. Do not let children wander too far from the main group. If you do have an encounter with a predator, lift children up into your arms to keep focus away from them. (See previous subsection on bears for more information on avoiding or dealing with bear encounters.)

TRAIL ETIQUETTE: The basic rule of thumb is that more maneuverable trail users should yield to less maneuverable ones. In winter, hikers and snowshoers should yield to skiers, and all these should yield to skijorers. Everyone should yield to dog mushing teams. If you are traveling with dogs or young children, move them at least 5 feet (1.5 m) off the trail when dog teams approach. Dogs in teams will occasionally try to jump out and nip children and other dogs as they pass. Walkers, where allowed on groomed winter trails, should stay to the side so any holes they make are on the periphery. Especially try to avoid the parallel tracks set for classical skiers. In summer and all the year round, hikers and runners should yield to mountain bikers. Everyone should yield to horses. Yield the trail when you hear snowmachines or ATVs as well. Their drivers can not hear you, and sometimes they can be traveling too fast to maneuver out of your way in time. If you are traveling with a dog and you see another trail user with their dog leashed, you should leash or restrain your dog until you have passed. Always restrain your dog when around horses.

A young bull moose near Quartz Lake.

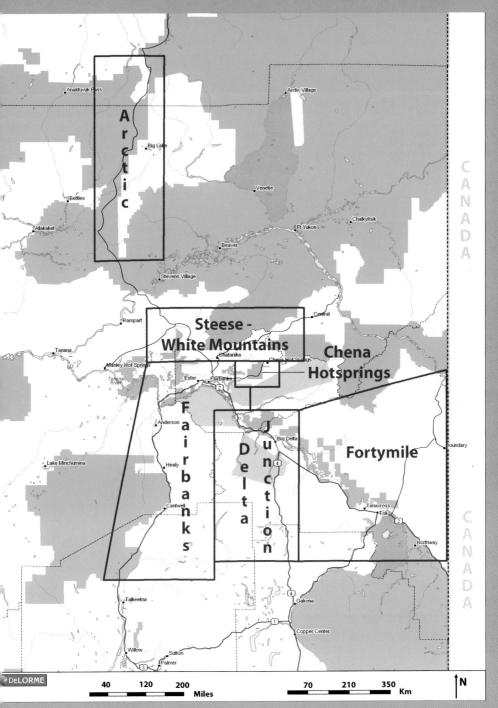

Overview map of interior Alaska trips.

40	120	200		70	210	350

Miles

Km

N

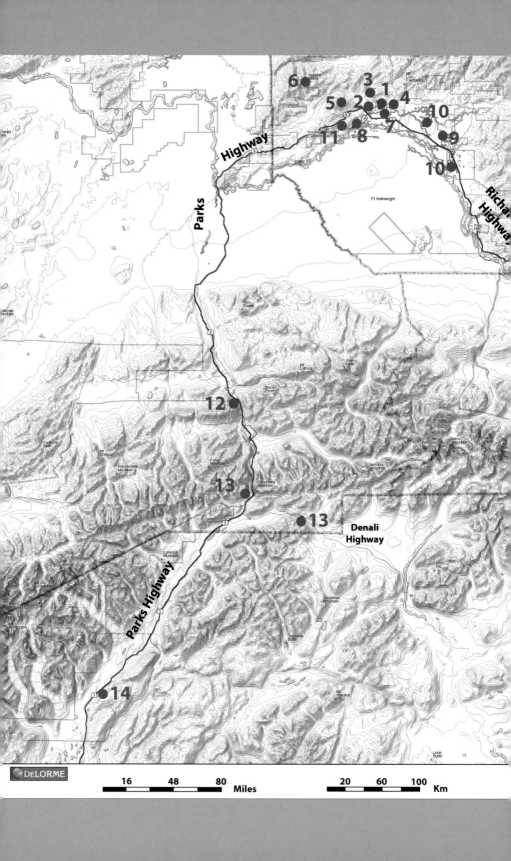

Fairbanks Region

Fairbanks is the largest city and the heart of the Interior. Centrally located, it is the only place in the region that has jet service. Because it is a hub for the entire region, it has more amenities than might be expected for a city of 85,000 people. The Fairbanks area is characterized by low rolling hills in a sea of boreal forest. Low-lying areas are dominated by muskegs, lakes, and black spruce. On drier slopes, you can find extensive groves of birch and aspen trees. White spruce and poplars are common along riparian corridors. Some of the best ski trails in the region are found here, but real mountains are an hour or two drive away to the south, east, or north. The Fairbanks area offers a ton of trails, even more than what I have included in the book. Go exploring and try them all! Kesugi Ridge (Trip 14) is not in the Interior as I have defined the region, but the hike is very popular with Fairbanksans, so I have included it.

1 CREAMER'S FIELD

R/T DISTANCE: 1.4–2.0 miles (2–3.2 km), longer loops in winter

DURATION: 1 to 2 hours

HIGH POINT: 440 feet (134 m)

TOTAL ELEVATION CHANGE: Less than 50 feet (15 m)

DIFFICULTY: Easy

ROUTE TYPE: Dirt roads and established trails (nonmotorized)

BEST SEASON: All year

USGS MAPS: Fairbanks D-2

LAND MANAGER: Alaska Department of Fish and Game (Fairbanks),
907-459-7200

Once a working farm, Creamer's Field now offers visitors a wide array of activities. One attraction is the Alaska Bird Observatory, which is on the migratory waterfowl range's 1,800 acres (730 hectares). The observatory runs all sorts of bird-related activities throughout the season and can help you check out birds close up. Finding migratory birds at Creamer's on your own is easy; geese, ducks, and cranes are plentiful during the spring and fall. The refuge provides nice trails for walking during summer and skiing and skijoring during winter.

Creamer's Field has three aptly named, pleasant, flat strolls. The Seasonal Wetland Trail is a 1.4-mile (2-km) round trip with interpretive signs. The trail takes you to a pond that appears in spring and dries up as the heat of summer progresses. The Boreal Forest Trail is a 2-mile (3.2-km) loop that winds through spruce and birch stands. Long segments of this trail are on boardwalk. The most popular trail is probably the 1.6-mile (2.6-km) Farm Road Trail. It is a simple and easy walk with the dog, kids, or grandparents. There are additional dirt roads that connect to this trail, which you can use to extend your outing. Biking is permitted on these roads.

During winter, miles of trails at Creamer's Field are groomed for skiing and skijoring. The trails are flat, making them a great place to learn to ski or skijor. Walkers and dog walkers are welcome on the ungroomed trails. Creamer's is a great spot to get out during a lunch break to bask in some sunlight during the short winter days.

BE AWARE: Parts of the area are closed during spring bird migration (April 1 to June 1) and fall migration (August 1 to September 15). During winter, serious skijorers use the groomed trails, so please follow posted instructions about proper etiquette and be watchful of racing events.

Large congregations of cranes, geese, and ducks can be seen in the fields.

MORE ADVENTUROUS? Skijorers can link up with the extensive Jeff Studdert Trails on the north side of Creamer's Field, so go ahead and extend that ski! Be sure to yield to dog teams anywhere, but especially on the Jeff Studdert Trails. The Alaska Dog Mushers Association asks that users pay a small daily use fee at Musher's Hall on Farmer's Loop. They also have season passes. Their trails, ranging from 1 to 27 miles (1.6–44 km) long, are mainly for mushers, but skijorers are welcome.

DIRECTIONS: Parking for Creamer's Field is directly behind the offices of the Alaska Department of Fish and Game at 1300 College Road in Fairbanks. Skijorers can reach the Jeff Studdert Trails from Mushers Hall at milepost 4 on Farmers Loop Road.

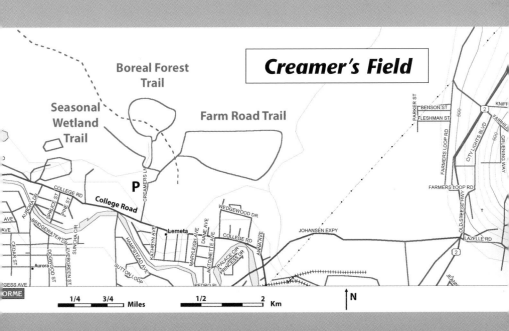

2 UAF, SKARLAND, AND PEARL CREEK TRAILS

R/T DISTANCE: Up to 6 miles (9.7 km) or more

DURATION: Less than 3 hours

HIGH POINT: 700 feet (213 m)

TOTAL ELEVATION CHANGE: Generally less than 500 feet (152 m); depends on route

DIFFICULTY: Easy to moderate

ROUTE TYPE: Established trails (nonmotorized)

BEST SEASON: All year

USGS MAPS: Fairbanks D-2; also see Nordic Ski Club of Fairbanks website (Appendix B)

LAND MANAGERS: University of Alaska Fairbanks (University Trails Club), 907-474-6027; Fairbanks North Star Borough, 907-459-1070; Nordic Ski Club of Fairbanks, 907-457-3572

University of Alaska Fairbanks Trail System

The University of Alaska Fairbanks has some of the best, easily accessible trails in town. Its trail system offers great biking, hiking, walking, and running opportunities in summer and beautifully maintained cross-country ski trails during the winter. Trail maps are at key positions throughout the trail system. The trails meander through typical Interior habitats, such as black spruce bogs, muskegs, towering white spruce stands, and groves of birch. The trails also take you by trees you will not find elsewhere in the Interior in the fenced Exotic Tree Plantation. Dogs are allowed on the trails all summer (until they are groomed after the first good snow) and on the unmaintained Pooch Loop year round. The skiers are finicky about the maintained trails, so walkers, runners, and cyclists are asked to stay off the trails once they have been groomed. Snowshoers are allowed somewhat grudgingly. In 2006, UAF started installing winter walking trails, which will be groomed. This is a

4

multi-year project. Runners, walkers, and snowshoers will be allowed on those trails as they are completed.

Some of the most challenging trails are in the southwest corner of the UAF system, including Midnight Express and Big Whizzy loops. Parts of the trails in this are lit during winter. Bicycle Bumps, just to the east of the Potato Field, is probably the most technical trail. It is a single-track trail that generally heads downhill but features several short, steep dips. The most single-track trails can be found in the northwest corner of the system, the area that has the remotest feel. Single-track trails, however, can be found scattered all over the UAF trail system.

Smith Lake is a great place for beginners to learn how to ski, both skate and classical styles. It is flat, and well-groomed trails circle the lake. There are nice views of Ester Dome when you have to stop to catch your breath. As you gain confidence you can branch out in three different directions. Many of the trails are lit, especially in the southwest corner, so you can ski that area at night.

Skarland Trail

Skarland Trail is a 6-mile (9.7-km) loop that encircles the UAF system. In winter, the entire loop can be used by classical skiers, but only sections on the UAF trails are groomed for skate skiers. Skarland Trail leaves the UAF system at the Large Animal Research Station (LARS) on Yankovich Road as a classical ski trail (dogs and walkers discouraged). After crossing Yankovich, follow the LARS fence to the east to pick up the trail. It heads uphill and northeast. The trail crosses Dalton Trail and Ballaine Road as it continues eastward winding through subdivisions and connecting to the Pearl Creek trails. In summer, Skarland Trail is great for walking, running, and mountain biking. (Bikers, please watch for slower trail users.)

Pearl Creek Nordic Park

The Pearl Creek Nordic Park was designed and is groomed for classical skiing, so walkers and dogs are discouraged in winter. The park is tucked between Ballaine Road and Auburn Drive, just to the northeast of the university. The park is a labyrinth of interestingly named trails maintained by local users. The tall, thick woods make for a nice, quiet getaway that is close to town. The trails can be used in summer but are generally pretty wet.

ALL ROUTES BE AWARE: Trail groomers have their engines revved just waiting for that first good snow. Once the grooming starts, skiers become possessive of the trails. Like Birch Hill (Trip 4), walking, biking, and dogs are not allowed on the groomed trails. You can snowshoe and walk your dog on UAF's Pooch Loop Trail. The trails dry out in spring at widely varying times depending on elevation, slope, vegetation, snow accumulation, and rainfall. Trails designated wet trails are too wet to use in summer

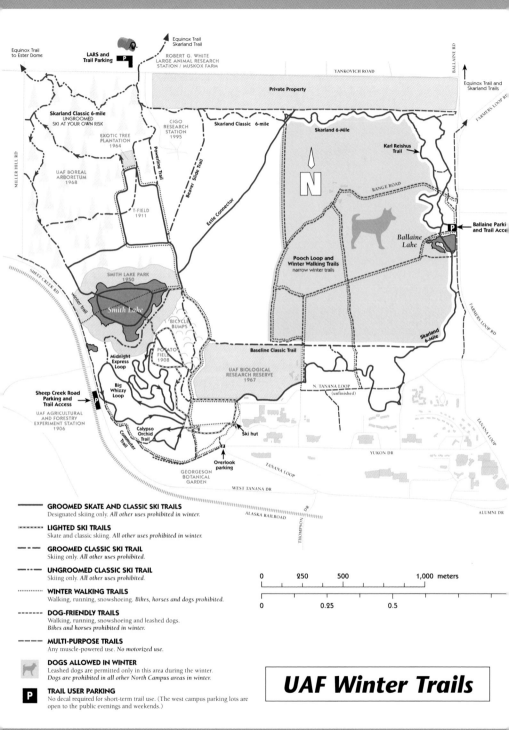

Equinox Trail
to Ester Dome

Equinox Trail
Skarland Trail

LARS and
Trail Parking

ROBERT G. WHITE
LARGE ANIMAL RESEARCH
STATION / MUSKOX FARM

YANKOVICH ROAD

BALLAINE RD

Private Property

Equinox Trail and
Skarland Trails

FARMERS LOOP RD

Skarland Classic 6-mile
UNGROOMED
SKI AT YOUR OWN RISK

CIGO
RESEARCH
STATION
1995

Skarland Classic   6-mile

Skarland 6-Mile

Karl Reishus
Trail

EXOTIC TREE
PLANTATION
1964

MILLER HILL RD

UAF BOREAL
ARBORETUM
1968

Powerline Trail

Beaver Slide Trail

N

RANGE ROAD

Ballaine Parki
and Trail Acce

T-FIELD
1911

Extle Connector

Ballaine
Lake

SHEEP CREEK RD

Winter Trail

SMITH LAKE PARK
1950

Smith Lake

BICYCLE
BUMPS

Pooch Loop and
Winter Walking Trails
narrow winter trails

FARMERS LOOP RD

Skarland
6-Mile

Midnight
Express
Loop

POTATO
FIELD
1908

Baseline Classic Trail

Sheep Creek Road
Parking and
Trail Access

Big
Whizzy
Loop

UAF BIOLOGICAL
RESEARCH RESERVE
1967

N. TANANA LOOP
(unfinished)

TANANA LOOP

UAF AGRICULTURAL
AND FORESTRY
EXPERIMENT STATION
1906

Calypso
Orchid
Trail

Commuter Trail

Ski hut

YUKON DR

Overlook
parking

GEORGESON
BOTANICAL
GARDEN

TANANA LOOP

WEST TANANA DR

ALASKA RAILROAD

THOMPSON DR

ALUMNI DR

GROOMED SKATE AND CLASSIC SKI TRAILS
Designated skiing only. *All other uses prohibited in winter.*

LIGHTED SKI TRAILS
Skate and classic skiing. *All other uses prohibited in winter.*

GROOMED CLASSIC SKI TRAIL
Skiing only. *All other uses prohibited.*

UNGROOMED CLASSIC SKI TRAIL
Skiing only. *All other uses prohibited.*

WINTER WALKING TRAILS
Walking, running, snowshoeing. *Bikes, horses and dogs prohibited.*

DOG-FRIENDLY TRAILS
Walking, running, snowshoeing and leashed dogs.
Bikes and horses prohibited in winter.

MULTI-PURPOSE TRAILS
Any muscle-powered use. *No motorized use.*

DOGS ALLOWED IN WINTER
Leashed dogs are permitted only in this area during the winter.
Dogs are prohibited in all other North Campus areas in winter.

TRAIL USER PARKING
No decal required for short-term trail use. (*The west campus parking lots are open to the public evenings and weekends.*)

| 0 | 250 | 500 | | 1,000 meters |

| 0 | | 0.25 | | 0.5 | |

UAF Winter Trails

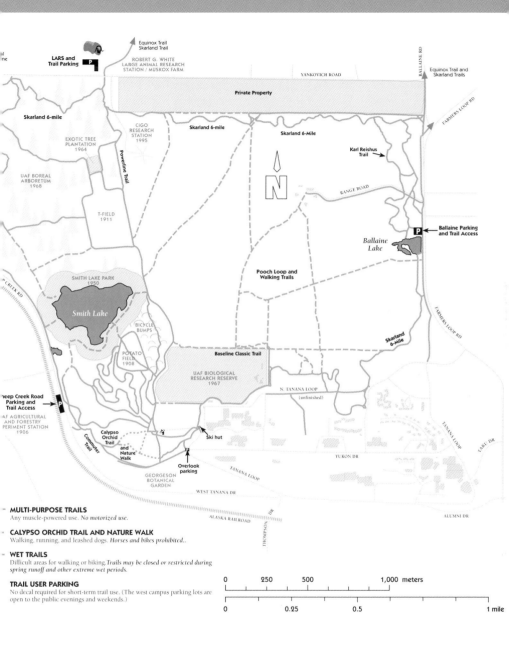

Equinox Trail
Skarland Trail

**LARS and
Trail Parking** P

ROBERT G. WHITE
LARGE ANIMAL RESEARCH
STATION / MUSKOX FARM

YANKOVICH ROAD

BALLAINE RD

Equinox Trail and
Skarland Trails

Private Property

FARMERS LOOP RD

Skarland 6-mile

CIGO
RESEARCH
STATION
1995

Skarland 6-mile

Skarland 6-Mile

EXOTIC TREE
PLANTATION
1964

Karl Reishus
Trail →

UAF BOREAL
ARBORETUM
1968

Powerline Trail

RANGE ROAD

N

T-FIELD
1911

FARMERS LOOP RD

Ballaine
Lake

P ← **Ballaine Parking
and Trail Access**

SMITH LAKE PARK
1950

SHEEP CREEK RD

**Pooch Loop and
Walking Trails**

Smith Lake

BICYCLE
BUMPS

Skarland
6-Mile

POTATO
FIELD
1908

Baseline Classic Trail

UAF BIOLOGICAL
RESEARCH RESERVE
1967

N. TANANA LOOP
(unfinished)

TANANA LOOP

Sheep Creek Road
Parking and
Trail Access P

AF AGRICULTURAL
AND FORESTRY
PERIMENT STATION
1906

Commuter
Trail

Calypso
Orchid
Trail
and
Nature
Walk

Ski hut

TAKU DR

YUKON DR

Overlook
parking

TANANA LOOP

GEORGESON
BOTANICAL
GARDEN

WEST TANANA DR

– **MULTI-PURPOSE TRAILS**
Any muscle-powered use. *No motorized use.*

ALASKA RAILROAD

THOMPSON DR

ALUMNI DR

– **CALYPSO ORCHID TRAIL AND NATURE WALK**
Walking, running, and leashed dogs. *Horses and bikes prohibited..*

– **WET TRAILS**
Difficult areas for walking or biking.*Trails may be closed or restricted during
spring runoff and other extreme wet periods.*

TRAIL USER PARKING
No decal required for short-term trail use. (The west campus parking lots are
open to the public evenings and weekends.)

0	250	500	1,000 meters

0	0.25	0.5	1 mile

UAF Summer Trails

Skiers enjoying the trails on Smith Lake.

in all but the driest years. Both the UAF Trails Club and the Nordic Ski Club of Fairbanks (NSCF) help maintain the UAF trail system and appreciate donations from frequent users of the trails. It is a great resource; help out if you can. (For information on where to donate, see Appendix B.) Local residents maintain the Pearl Creek Nordic Park Trails; check signs or with the NSCF if you want to help them out as well.

MORE ADVENTUROUS? A side trail off the northeast part of the Skarland Trail takes you all the way to the top of Ski Boot Hill Road (4 miles [6.5 km] from Ballaine) and onto the Skyline Ridge Trail. A popular choice is to drive to the top of Ski Boot Hill Road and either bike or ski down the side trail. Be careful driving, as the road is not regularly maintained. The trail has some steep ups and downs and rutted sections, as well as crisscrossing trails that can make navigation difficult. Learn the trails with someone who is familiar with them or be prepared to get a bit lost.

Runners should considering doing the Equinox Marathon. Run every September, the marathon uses parts of the UAF Trail System and the Skarland Trail and is one of the country's most difficult marathons (see Trip 5). Goldstream Valley (Trip 3) offers more, but less manicured, winter trails that are close to the UAF, Skarland, and Pearl Creek trails. Outside of town, volunteers maintain ski trails (sections of which are lit) at Two Rivers and Salcha elementary schools.

DIRECTIONS: The University of Alaska Fairbanks Trail System has several trailheads. On West Ridge (the very west end of campus) there is parking near the ski hut in several parking lots. During the week before 5 p.m. most parking spaces in these lots require a permit. Read the signs carefully to avoid a ticket. The ski hut, an obvious landmark, is the main trailhead for the system. Sheep Creek Road has a large turnout at the west side of campus, though you have to cross the road to get to the well-marked trailhead. Get to Smith Lake (winter only) by following the unpaved path that parallels Sheep Creek Road to a trail that leads northeast to the lake. The trail is marked with unsigned posts about an eighth of a mile (0.2 km) northwest of the turnout. No parking is allowed along Sheep Creek Road where the trail meets the road.

A skate skier enjoying some of the best groomed trails.

On the north side of the trail system, parking is allowed at the Large Animal Research Station (LARS) on Yankovich Road. You will have to cross the road to reach the UAF trails but not the Skarland Trail, which can be found by following the fence east and then north. Another parking area is at Ballaine Lake, on the east side of the system, just off Farmers Loop Road.

To reach the Pearl Creek Nordic Park, take Farmers Loop Road northeast from University Avenue. Turn left onto Auburn Drive and drive to Pearl Creek Elementary School. The school will be on your left after about a half mile (0.8 km). Park in the school's parking lot. When school is in session do not park along the road to the school or in the round cul-de-sac, where buses turn around. The trails start on the far side of the soccer field and hockey rink.

3 GOLDSTREAM VALLEY TRAILS

R/T DISTANCE: Up to 11 miles (18 km) or more if linking trails

DURATION: 3 to 5 hours for the full distance

HIGH POINT: 700 feet (213 km)

TOTAL ELEVATION CHANGE: Less than 200 feet (61 m)

DIFFICULTY: Easy

ROUTE TYPE: Established trails (motorized allowed)

BEST SEASON: November to March

USGS MAPS: Fairbanks D-2

LAND MANAGER: Alaska Department of Natural Resources (Fairbanks),
907-451-2705

Goldstream Valley winter trails are a great option if you want to get away from the finely manicured trails of UAF and Birch Hill (Trips 2 and 4). The Goldstream trails are multiuse, so walkers, snowmachines, bikers, and dogs are allowed, as well as classical skiers. Some sections are long and wide enough to allow skate skiing. Most people conjure up images of muskegs and stunted black spruce when they think of Goldstream Valley. For the most part this is accurate. The vegetation reflects that this valley is typically colder than downtown Fairbanks. However, the valley does have nice stands of birch and white spruce.

Ballaine Road splits the valley, creating two parts: east Goldstream and west Goldstream. From the Ballaine Road parking area, the main trail of east Goldstream parallels Goldstream Creek on its south side. This trail cuts through mixed stands of spruce and birch and is wide enough to skate ski in many places. The farther you go, the narrower and less used the trail becomes. The trail does not cross any roads or power lines until you get all the way out to the town of Fox—an 11-mile (18-km) round trip. The trail eventually comes out to Goldstream Road near where that road and the Old Steese Highway come together. Another well-used trail parallels Goldstream Creek on the north side and connects to the southern trail at both

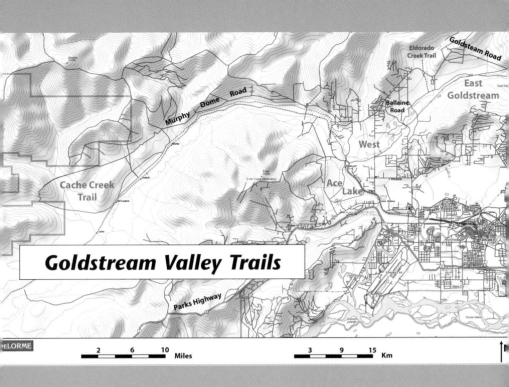

Goldstream Valley Trails

ends of the valley, making for a nice, long loop. However, the north trail often has sections of overflow, especially during spring. The Eldorado Creek Trail, another major trail, intersects the northern trail at about its midway point and heads north. It crosses Goldstream Road and follows El Dorado Creek up to the Trans-Alaska Pipeline right-of-way. These trails are popular with snowmachiners and mushers, so keep watch. There are many side and loop trails stemming off the main trails that are fun to explore, but be careful, as you can easily get lost.

The trails of west Goldstream can be reached a couple of different ways. You can cross Ballaine Road from the parking area and head down the steep embankment to the bike path. Or you can follow the rough trail that forms each winter on the northeast side of Ballaine Road to a crossing area less than a half mile to the north. This trail crosses Goldstream Creek, so look out for overflow. Formerly, the trails on the west side formed a large, 8-mile (13-km) loop, but recent development has disrupted connectivity. The trailhead by Ivory Jack's has been completely lost to development as well. Smaller (about 1–3 mile [1.6–4.8 km]) loops can still be made within this area depending on where snowmachines have made trails. A trail on the south side of this area runs just over 3 miles (4.8 km) to connect with the all-season trail paralleling Sheep Creek Road (see below). You can also access West Goldstream from its northwest section. About a quarter mile (0.4 km) west of Ivory Jack's, turn south on O'Brien Street and follow it about three-quarters of a mile (1.2 km) to its end. You can regain West Goldstream trail system here. Head to the southwest, toward the power line. The trail trends southward and runs into Sheep Creek Road just east of Ann's Greenhouses where you can turn around, cross the street, and heads toward Ace Lake (see below), or follow the all-season trail that parallels Sheep Creek until reaching the university. You can turn left (east) after about an eighth of a mile (0.2 km) on the all-season trail to connect back to Ballaine Road (see above) as well.

To get to the southwestern part of Goldstream Valley, use one of two trails near Ann's Greenhouses. One parallels the railroad tracks (southeast of Ann's Greenhouses) and another follows a power line from Ester Dome Road. Both trails connect to a series of trails that run all the way to Ace Lake. They are best suited for classical skiing and walking, as most are just one snowmachine track wide. The trails get tight in places with overhanging bushes, and it can be difficult to find your bearings. In certain areas, the number of trails and lack of distinguishing features can feel a bit like being in a maze. Bring a compass and know how to use it. Watch out for snowmachines and mushers. Also, please respect the numerous private properties scattered around this area.

There is also an unpaved path that parallels Sheep Creek Road from the UAF trails turnout to the railroad crossing about 2.9 miles (4.7 km) north of there. The path crosses many driveways and roads but is suitable for walking, running, biking, classical skiing, and often skate skiing. Dogs are also welcome. This path is really the only trail in the Goldstream system that is suitable for year-round use and makes for a good 6-mile (9.7-km) round trip.

The valley tightens as Goldstream Creek flows to the northwest and gets sandwiched between Ester and Murphy domes. Goldstream Creek, the Alaska Railroad, and various trails all make their way through this corridor before reaching the expansive Minto Flats. About halfway to the flats, some 18 miles (29 km) or so, Standard Creek Road bisects the valley as it comes down off the Old Nenana Highway. The Standard Creek area has logging trails and roads that are fit for mountain biking, but most of these trails are best suited for classical skiing. Another option is to park at Cache Creek (milepost 8.5, Murphy Dome Road) and drop down into the valley from there. Cache Creek Trail parallels the railroad and, by connecting with other trails, loops of varying length (up to 8 miles [13 km]) can be skied. Skiing from the start of the Cache Creek Trail to the end of Cache Creek Road can make an 8- to 10-mile (13- to 16-km) trip. You will need to shuttle a car to the end of Cache Creek Road, and the length of the ski will depend on how far the road has been plowed.

BE AWARE: Please respect the numerous pieces of private property scattered about. Further development may change the routes of these trails significantly. Most of these trails are created and maintained by snowmachiners and dog mushers, so expect to see some along the trail. Try to get off the trail to allow them by, especially if you

The East Goldstream Trail with Ester Dome in the background.

are out with your dog. Winter trail conditions are highly variable. These trails are generally too wet to use during the summer. Numerous spur trails head off all over the valley. Have fun exploring them, but be prepared to end up somewhere besides where you thought you were going. Trail routes will vary year to year depending on which trails the snowmachiners decide to use.

MORE ADVENTUROUS? The UAF Trail System (Trip 2) and Birch Hill (Trip 4) offer fantastic, well-groomed ski trails. Outside of town there are maintained ski trails at Two Rivers and Salcha elementary schools. All of these maintained trails have lit sections. If you are looking for adventure, try the White Mountains (Trip 34) or Angel Creek valley (Trip 22). The trails past Standard Creek Road lead all the way to Manley Hot Springs, Tolovana Hot Springs (Trip 37), Livengood, or Nenana—but only very hardy and experienced adventurers should attempt these long, remote winter trails.

DIRECTIONS: There are several places to access Goldstream Valley trails. One of the main spots is on Ballaine Road. Coming from University Avenue, follow Farmers Loop Road, then turn left (north) onto Ballaine. Follow it for about 2.5 miles (4 km), up and over the hill. As you are coming down, Goldstream Valley will open up in front of you, and there will be a large turnout on your right (east). The main trail starts on the north end of the turnout and then heads northeast. To gain the West Valley trails, carefully cross the road and drop down the steep embankment.

Another access point is the turnout on Sheep Creek Road for the University of Alaska Fairbanks trails (Trip 2). After parking, cross the street and follow the unpaved path northwest as it parallels Sheep Creek Road. The path ends at the railroad tracks (2.9 miles [4.7 km] north of the UAF turnout) just before Ann's Greenhouses. Another trail follows the railroad tracks south and gives you access to the southwestern part of the area, as does a trail along a power line off Ester Dome Road. To get to that trail, turn left onto Ester Dome Road about 3.1 miles (5 km) north of the UAF turnout on Sheep Creek Road. The power line crosses Ester Dome Road at its intersection with Schloesser Drive, almost a half mile (0.8 km) from Sheep Creek Road.

To get to the northwestern section of Goldstream Valley, use the small turnout off Goldstream Road, just to the east of Murphy Dome Road. The trail is south of the turnout and crosses Sheep Creek Road just south of Murphy Dome Road. To get farther down the valley, park at Cache Creek (milepost 8.5, Murphy Dome Road) and drop down into the valley from there.

4 **BIRCH HILL**

R/T DISTANCE: Up to 5 miles (8 km) or more by linking trails

DURATION: Up to you

HIGH POINT: 1,050 feet (320 m)

TOTAL ELEVATION CHANGE: Generally less than 500 feet (152 m); depends on route

DIFFICULTY: Moderate to expert (ski); easy to difficult (bike); easy to moderate (hike)

ROUTE TYPE: Established trail (nonmotorized)

BEST SEASON: All year; only skiing allowed Oct. 15–April 15

USGS MAPS: No USGS maps needed. Trail map provided, also maps posted at recreation area or available as a download from the Nordic Ski Club of Fairbanks website (see Appendix B).

LAND MANAGERS: Fairbanks North Star Borough, 907-459-1070; Nordic Ski Club of Fairbanks, 907-474-4242

Birch Hill, on the northeastern edge of Fairbanks, is easy to see from most of town. Its name comes from the beautiful, tall birch groves that adorn the park. Birch Hill Recreation Area is situated on Birch Hill and is the premier place to cross-country ski, possibly in the entire state. The trails are officially called the Jim Whisenhant Cross Country Ski Trails. The trail system is kept in great shape, and the snow comes early and stays late. The trail system and conditions are so good that serious skiers often come up from the Lower 48 to get a jump on the season. Races are frequently held here. While it is known as a great ski area, the recreation area is also fabulous during the summer for mountain biking, running, walking the dogs, or taking the kids for a stroll. The area is very relaxed during the summer season.

There are a few trails just for classical skiing on the east side of the recreation area (Classical Bear, Aurora Run, and North Star), but most trails have tracks for classical skiers on the side of the wide, groomed trails where skate skiers go zooming by. Few

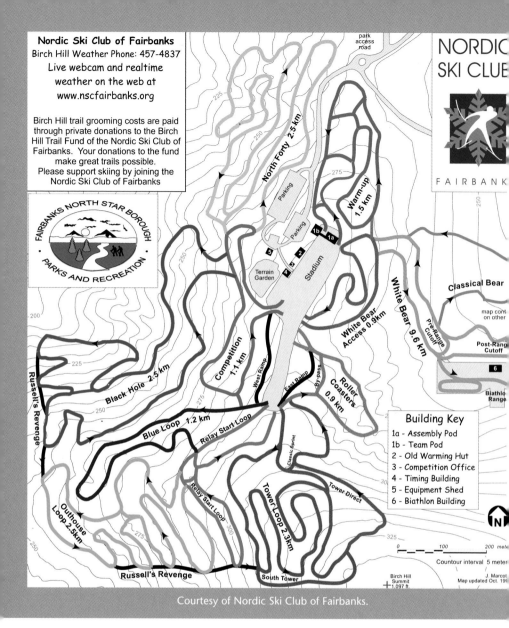

of the trails are designed for novices. These are centered on the stadium, the large open area just beyond the warm-up buildings. Most of the trails at the recreation area are much more challenging.

Birch Hill draws serious, skilled skate skiers. Many trails offer steep climbs, thrilling descents, and hair-raising curves. There are long trails, such as the 6-mile (9.6-km) White Bear, and short trails, such as Roller Coasters at about a half mile (0.8 km). The trails interconnect at numerous locations, so a trip around one trail can easily be added onto another and another trail. The length of your trip really depends on your skill, available time, and energy. All the trail connections can be confusing, so pay attention to where you are going.

Skier heads out of the stadium area.

BE AWARE: During winter, the trails of Birch Hill Recreation Area are solely for cross-country skiers. Dog walkers, bikers, snowshoers, walkers, runners, sledders, horse riders, snowmachiners, and snowboarders are not allowed. A large sign at the entrance lists these and other rules. Users and caretakers of the Birch Hill ski trails are fervent about skiing and their trails—be prepared to hear about it if you do not follow all the rules. Temperatures are generally a bit warmer on the hill during the winter. Avoid using the trails when they are wet, especially during the shoulder seasons. White Bear Trail stays wet the longest. Birch Hill hosts many events, so be sure to call the borough to find out if there is a race or camp or some other activity. In winter, also check with the ski club.

MORE ADVENTUROUS? You can connect trail after trail until you run out of steam, but the Birch Hill Recreation Area is not connected to other trail systems and is surrounded by housing developments and the military base. For other groomed trails try the UAF trails (Trip 2) or, outside of town, the Two Rivers and Salcha elementary school trails. All have some lit sections. For a more remote experience, look into exploring the White Mountains (Trip 34).

DIRECTIONS: Take the Steese Highway (Alaska 2) north about 2–3 miles (3.2–4.8 km). At its intersection with Farmers Loop Road, turn right at the traffic light. (If you go too far on the Steese Highway you will see an exit for Chena Hot Springs Road.) After the right, take an immediate left onto Birch Hill Road. It will parallel the Steese for about a mile (1.6 km) then veers off to the right (southeast). At the top of the hill, just over the crest, the road comes to a "T" intersection. Turn right, go around the wooded roundabout, and then go through the gate into the recreation area. The parking area is another quarter mile ahead (0.4 km).

White Bear Access Trail in the fall.

5 ESTER DOME

R/T DISTANCE: 0.25–10 miles (0.4–16 km) and longer loops can be strung
together

DURATION: 1 to 5 hours

HIGH POINT: 2,364 feet (720 m)

TOTAL ELEVATION CHANGE: Generally less than 2,000 feet (609 m); depends
on route

DIFFICULTY: Easy to moderate, depending on route choice

ROUTE TYPE: Established trail or route depending on your plans (motorized
allowed)

BEST SEASON: All year

USGS MAPS: Fairbanks D-2, D-3

LAND MANAGER: Alaska Department of Natural Resources (Fairbanks),
907-451-2705

Ester Dome is the landmark that anchors Fairbanks' west side, just as Birch Hill (Trip 4) anchors its eastern flank. Like Murphy Dome (Trip 6) to the northwest, Ester Dome offers an easy and quick way to get outside for a walk, hike, bike, run, snowshoe, or ski. The summit is lower than Murphy Dome and is not above tree line, though a few rocky outcrops offer nice views.

Runners in the Equinox Marathon actually have to climb this dome as part of their 26-mile (42-km) journey. The section that climbs the dome leaves Ester Dome Road at milepost 1.2. A sign marks the trail entrance. The trail there goes through nicely forested terrain, though it is relatively steep, crosses many roots, and can be muddy early in the season or after a rain. The trail rejoins Ester Dome Road near its intersection with Henderson Road. Runners follow the road, then a trail, to the top of the dome, which is covered with communication towers. Beyond the towers, the marathon course heads west, following a four-wheel-drive trail partway down the other side of the dome.

18

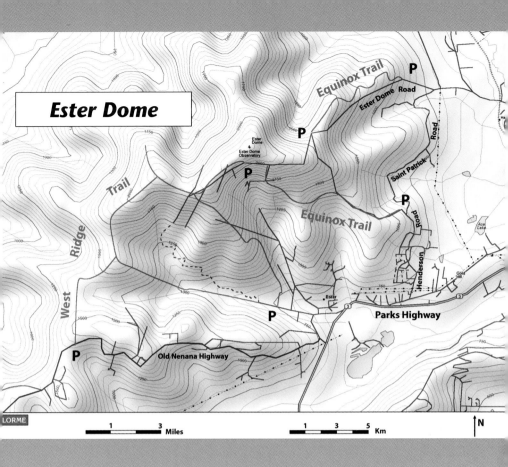

Ester Dome

Equinox Trail

Ester Dome Road

Road

P

P

Saint Patrick

Ester
Dome

Ester Dome
Observatory

P

P

Equinox Trail

Henderson
Road

Trail

Ace
Lake

Ridge

Ester

Gold
Hill

West

P

Parks Highway

P

Old Nenana Highway

LORME

| 1 | 3 | Miles |

| 1 | 3 | 5 | Km |

↑N

At a signed but otherwise indistinctive spot on the trail, runners must turn around, retrace their steps back over the top of the dome, and back down the road to a flat spot known as Ullrhaven (the site of a former ski lodge). That section of the course, the only part that is repeated, is known as the Out-and-Back. From Ullrhaven, runners head down the Alder Chute. This very steep and rocky trail follows a power line for about an eighth of a mile (0.2 km). The trail then takes a sharp left (heading east) off the steep power line and levels out. After the Alder Chute the trail is rather pleasant and makes for a nice, long walk down to the middle of Henderson Road near an old mine site. From there, the Equinox "trail" is actually a route that follows roads, power line right-of-ways, and trails back its starting point at UAF.

From the top of Ester Dome, there are many options to choose from. Nugget Creek Trail heads off to the north and then down to Goldstream Creek and Murphy Dome Road. The main trail, which is a rough four-wheel-drive road, continues along to the southwest along the top of the ridge. After about a mile (1.6 km), the trail splits, with one route heading west and the other southeast. Both trails are in fairly good shape, though the southeastern one is getting eroded in places. The trail that

Murphy Dome viewed from the summit.

heads southeast will bring you down the dome to a gravel road. Turn left (southeast) on the road to get to Ester. The other trail climbs a small knob. There a small winter trail heads north, but the main trail veers to the southwest. It takes you down, steeply at times, for about another mile (1.6 km).

Again, you must choose. You can either head west and make your way along a series of trails to the Old Nenana Highway or head east down a steep hill and follow the trail paralleling Ester Creek back to the Old Nenana Highway. From here, take a left (northeast) to reach Ester and the Parks Highway. Several spur trails branch off from the main trails; most head south toward Ester. All these trails are steep and some have other spur trails. It is easy to get lost in this area if you get off the main trails.

BE AWARE: Like many domes in the Interior, Ester Dome has communication facilities spread over its summit. Ester Dome probably has more towers and facilities than any other dome in the Interior, owing to its proximity to Fairbanks. Do not disturb these privately owned facilities. Motorized vehicles are allowed on the trails. Be careful in the rocky outcrop areas, as they are often party spots. Broken glass can cover the ground like carpet.

MORE ADVENTUROUS? Trails lead off of Ester Dome in many directions. The trail system is extensive; so if you are skilled at route finding, see where your feet will lead you.

DIRECTIONS: Take Sheep Creek Road, on the west side of Fairbanks, northwest and away from the University of Alaska Fairbanks. After about 3 miles (4.8 km), take a left onto Ester Dome Road, just past Ann's Greenhouses. At milepost 1.2, Ester Dome Road, the Equinox Marathon Trail breaks into the woods from the road. The summit is at milepost 4 and has several places to park. If you plan to start at the bottom, park at the paved parking lot on the north side of Sheep Creek Road between Ann's Greenhouses and Ester Dome Road.

6 *MURPHY DOME*

R/T DISTANCE: Up to 12 miles (19.4 km)

DURATION: Up to you, but 4 to 8 hours for the full distance

HIGH POINT: 2,930 feet (892 m)

TOTAL ELEVATION CHANGE: Up to 4,800 feet (1,462 m)

DIFFICULTY: Easy (if you stay high) to moderate (if you go all the way)

ROUTE TYPE: ATV trail or route depending on your plans (motorized allowed)

BEST SEASON: All year

USGS MAPS: Fairbanks D-3

LAND MANAGER: Alaska Department of Natural Resources (Fairbanks),
907-451-2705

When Fairbanksans need to get into the wilds but do not have much time, they head to Murphy Dome. At 15 miles (24 km) out of town, the dome is far enough out that you feel like you are getting away, but it is close enough that you can easily be home for dinner. It is a great place to take a leisurely stroll in the tundra, pick berries, or have a picnic. The dome is also a good place for a mountain bike ride. On a clear day, Murphy Dome offers some great views of Denali, and in the fall the colors of the area are vibrant.

Most visitors park up at the lot about a quarter mile (0.4 km) to the west of the "golf ball," a relic from the Cold War, though it is still in use. ATV trails turns west from the parking area near the top of the dome, cutting through the alder and willow bushes. The trails can be walked, biked, skied, or snowshoed depending on conditions. It is also popular with motorized users, including people in cars and trucks, so watch and listen carefully, especially when speeding downhill. The dome is a favorite berry picking spot, so many social trails take off from the ATV trail and the top of the dome. Because it is a favorite—and not a secret—picking can be hit or miss.

Take the right (northern) ATV trail to the west; it will gently descend the northwest slope of the dome, winding its way through the tundra. About a third of mile (0.5 km) down the road is a rock outcrop that is a nice destination for picnics or

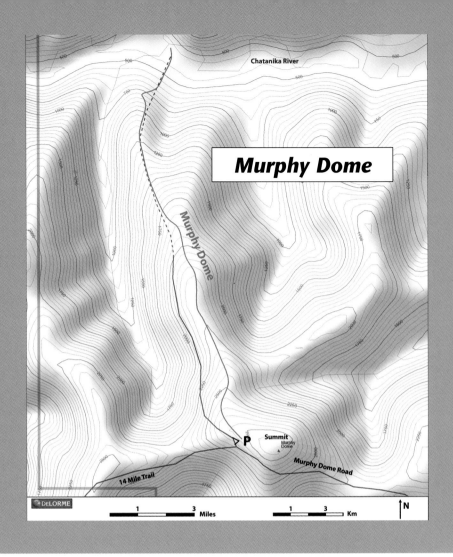

for beginners to test out some rock climbing skills. Always use a spotter! The road continues to descend and reaches another rock outcrop. The farther you descend the more trees start reappearing. The trail goes on for miles. The trail gets steeper at sections but the descent makes the going easy. Just keep in mind it will be completely uphill on the return journey. The trail gets wet as you approach Chatanika River some 6 miles (9.7 km) from the summit where you started.

BE AWARE: Stay away from the communication facilities on top of Murphy Dome, as they are run by the military. Motorized vehicles are allowed in the area. Murphy Dome is one of the closest spots for Fairbanksans to "get out," so expect to see other enthusiasts out there. Being significantly higher than town, snow can be much deeper and last longer. Strong winds are also common, even when they might not be bad in town.

MORE ADVENTUROUS? Trails lead off of Murphy Dome in many directions, heading to far-flung destinations. The 14-Mile Trail (dirt road), named after its distance from the start of the Murphy Dome Road, makes for a good mountain bike ride or ski. The berry picking is great out this way. The trail leads all the way down to Chatanika River (Trip 25). The trail is very rough and overgrown in places but can be driven by four-wheel-drive

Fall colors and views of Denali.

vehicles. Other trails head off the top of the dome down to the Chatanika as well; just remember it's all uphill on the way back.

Another popular option is to bike Old Murphy Dome Road out to Elliott Highway. Old Murphy Dome Road can be reached via Spinach Creek Road or near milepost 11, Murphy Dome Road. In winter, take Old Murphy Dome Road from the Elliott for 7 miles (11.3 km) past Resolution Road, where plowing usually stops. A trail leads to a 2,126-foot (647-m) high summit, just south of the road, for views of Goldstream Valley (Trip 3) and O'Connor Creek Valley. It is about a 5.5-mile (8.9-km) round trip.

DIRECTIONS: Take Sheep Creek Road, on the west side of Fairbanks, northwest and away from the University of Alaska Fairbanks. After about 4.5 miles (7.3 km), take a left onto Murphy Dome Road. The pavement will end around milepost 8. There are some parking spots at milepost 12 for those who would like to run, walk, or bike to the summit—and then have a fun descent down the big hill. Milepost 14 offers spots to pull off and berry pick, walk through the tundra, or have a picnic. Although somewhat overgrown, this is also the turnoff for the 14-Mile Trail, which is on your left (south). The summit is just before milepost 15. Park straight ahead after the gate. Do not approach the military facilities with the building that looks like a giant golf ball to your right (east).

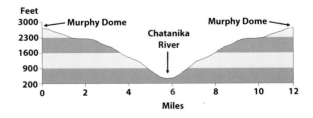

23

7 *LOWER CHENA RIVER*

ONE-WAY DISTANCE: Up to 9 miles (14.5 km)

DURATION: 2 to 5 hours for entire length

HIGH POINT: 430 feet (131 m)

TOTAL ELEVATION CHANGE: Less than 50 feet (15 m)

DIFFICULTY: Easy

ROUTE TYPE: Float (class I), suitable for canoes, kayaks, and rafts (motorized allowed)

BEST SEASON: June to September

USGS MAPS: Fairbanks D-2

LAND MANAGER: Alaska Department of Natural Resources (Fairbanks), 907-451-2705

The Chena River is the heart of Fairbanks. The community that was to become Fairbanks was established in 1901 when the *Lavelle Young*, a sternwheeler, went up the wrong river and got stuck. The supplies, originally bound for Tanacross, were offloaded and used to set up a trading post. A year later, gold was struck nearby, and the rest is history.

Today, the Chena runs through the middle of town and is one of the most used waterways in the state. It is great for an after-work paddle, relaxing family float, or practice for novice paddlers. With so many access points, you can be on the river for as little as five minutes or stretch it out for most of the day. Several restaurants, bars, and parks have boat launches or docks, so you can hop from one to the next. There are no rapids, and natural hazards are minimal. However, keep an eye and ear open for fast-moving motorized watercraft.

Graehl Park, on the east side of town, is a popular place to launch, as it is one of the farthest upstream access points in town. From Graehl it is about 3 river miles (4.8 km) downstream to the boat launch at Pioneer Park (river left, south bank). This stretch takes you under two road and two pedestrian bridges. With some paddling

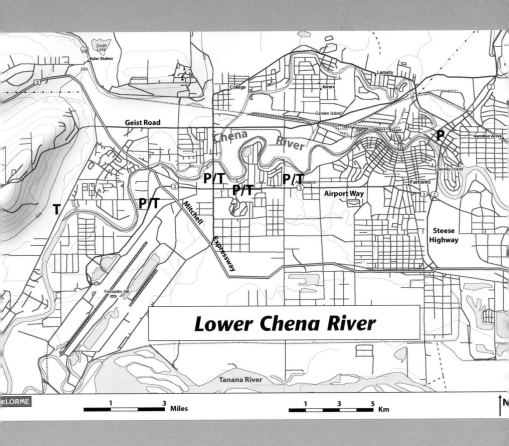

Lower Chena River

and no wind, this stretch can be done in less than forty minutes. Floating it with a headwind can take two hours.

From Pioneer Park you pass under Peger Road. Just under 2 miles (3.2 km) farther downstream is the boat launch for the Boatel Sleazy Waterfront Bar (river left, south bank), a bar. The float to the Boatel takes twenty-five minutes to over an hour from Pioneer Park.

Next up, about a quarter mile (0.4 km) downstream (another five to twenty minutes), is the Chena River State Recreation Site (river left, south bank). From there, the river passes under University Avenue, and the Bureau of Land Management offices are just around the corner (river left, east bank), another three to ten minutes downstream. From there, Chena's Fine Dining and Deck (river left, east bank), just about a mile (1.6 km) downstream (ten to forty minutes), has a dock. Another mile (1.6 km; ten to forty minutes) takes you to the dock of the Fairbanks Princess Riverside Lodge (river left, east bank). Within sight of the Princess is Pike's Landing restaurant (river left, east bank), which has its own boat launch, about three to ten minutes downstream. The Pumphouse bar and restaurant (river right, west bank), about 1.5

Paddling by downtown Fairbanks.

miles (2.4 km) past Pike's (twenty to seventy-five minutes), is the last public area to take out before the Chena reaches the Tanana River.

BE AWARE: Float times will vary greatly depending on river conditions, boat type, hazards, skill levels, motivation, and wind direction and speed. Chena River is probably the most popular river in the Interior, so expect company. The river often has fast motorboat traffic, so it is best to watch and listen for them. Keep to the side and stay out of the deepest river channel to allow them to pass. Canoeists may have to turn their bow into the wake to avoid swamping as larger boats go by. During winter, skiers are advised to avoid the river in town. A local power plant discharges warm water into the river, thinning and melting the ice.

MORE ADVENTUROUS? Just stay in your boat. The Chena dumps into the Tanana River, about 4 miles (6.4 km) downstream of the Pumphouse. It is another mile (1.6 km) to a parking area on Chena Pump Road, which will be on your right (northwest). The confluence of the two rivers can be a little squirrelly, but otherwise it is pretty mellow. If that still is not enough, you can paddle down the Tanana another 50 miles (80 km) to Nenana (Trip 8) or even farther to Manley Hot Springs.

DIRECTIONS: There are numerous access points along the lower Chena River in Fairbanks. Graehl Park can be found by turning onto Third Avenue between Steese

Expressway and Old Steese Highway. From Third Street turn onto Forty Mile Avenue: a left if coming from the Steese, or a right from the Old Steese. Follow Forty Mile three blocks, until you reach the park.

The next popular access point downstream is Pioneer Park. The dock is on the east side of Peger Road between Airport Way and Johansen Expressway.

The Boatel's boat launch can be reached by turning onto Washington Drive, off of Airport Way, then right onto Geraghty Avenue. The Boatel and its launch will be on your left.

Between Airport Way and the University Avenue bridge are the Chena River State Recreation Site (east side) and the Bureau of Land Management (BLM) offices (west side). BLM does not have a true launch, just a grassy slope sliding into the river, which requires a 40-yard (meter) walk.

Find the Pike's Landing launch by taking Airport Way west, toward the airport, for a half mile (0.8 km) past the Parks Highway overpass. Turn right on Hoselton Road. The launch is on the north side of Pike's. Keep following Hoselton for another third of a mile (0.5 km) to get to the Princess, which is on Pike's Landing Road (of course).

Find the Pumphouse launch by heading 1.25 miles (2 km) south down Chena Pump Road from the Parks Highway. The restaurant will be on your left, and the launch is on the south (far) side of the building.

For those who want to try a bit of the Tanana, head down Chena Pump Road for 4.5 miles (7.3 km) and turn left into the parking area.

8 *MIDDLE TANANA RIVER*

ONE-WAY DISTANCE: About 50 miles (80 km)

DURATION: 2 to 4 days

HIGH POINT: 420 feet (128 m)

TOTAL ELEVATION CHANGE: 70 feet (21 m)

DIFFICULTY: Moderate (float); difficult to expert (ski)

ROUTE TYPE: Float (class I), suitable for canoes, kayaks, and rafts: snowmachine trail (winter; motorized)

BEST SEASON: June to September (float); December to early April (ski)

USGS MAPS: Fairbanks D-2, D-3, C-3 to C-5

LAND MANAGER: Alaska Department of Natural Resources (Fairbanks), 907-451-2705

The Tanana River is one of the largest rivers in Alaska, stretching about 300 miles (484 km) from its origin near Northway until it dumps into the Yukon River at the village of Tanana. The river's silty waters cut through classic interior boreal forest and parallel Nenana Ridge near Fairbanks. The river, light tan in color from all the silt that it carries, is not technically challenging for paddlers, but its waters are fast-moving and cold. Strong winds can also sweep the river. Only paddlers with good backcountry skills should attempt this trip. The float from Fairbanks to Nenana is usually done as a relaxing weekend trip, but it can be done in one long day by motivated paddlers. There are plenty of good camping sites, as the river usually has abundant gravel bars. In winter, the river freezes solid. Heavy use by snowmachines produces a trail all the way to Nenana that can be traveled by classical or skate skiing. Top skate skiers can cover the entire distance in a day.

The river can be accessed in a few places, but the typical start is at the parking area on Chena Pump Road. The current runs about 3–5 mph (5–8 km/h) so town quickly fades behind you. There are not many landmarks. Try to keep track of the bluffs you go by—there are just a few. The first bluff is right at the start and is lined

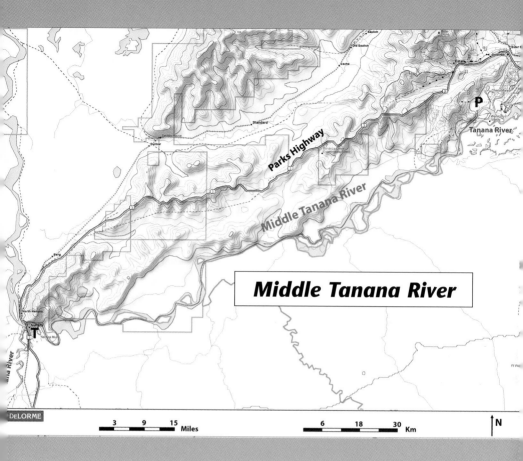

Middle Tanana River

| 3 | 9 | 15 Miles |
| 6 | 18 | 30 Km |

N

DeLORME

with houses. The houses quickly thin out, but a few along the way can be spotted from time to time. About 5 miles (8 km) downstream, a number of buildings are at Rosie Creek because the area has road access to the river.

The next 15 miles (24 km) are more remote and farther from the hills, often making it difficult to assess your position. The river is braided and has changed course in many places from where they are mapped on the USGS topographic maps. In general—but not always—large right-hand (northern) channels will be shortcuts. At about mile 20 (km 32), the river will come close to the second bluff and stay close for a mile (1.6 km) or so. Shortly after, Bonanza Creek will enter from the north. This area has road access as well and is home to forest research projects—please do not disturb them. The area is flat and covers about 2 river miles (3.2 km), where it again comes close to the hills. After a few more miles the river turns sharply to the south for a couple of miles.

You will be in the flats until about mile 40 (km 64.5), when you come close to another bluff. The river swings away from the bluff before coming back to its west end. The smooth tan silty wall of this end of the bluff is distinctive and sits opposite

Skijoring on the frozen river.

an old cabin. From there, you will start seeing signs of Nenana, such as radio towers and the railroad bridge. But town is still a few miles off, so do not get fooled!

BE AWARE: Strong, motivated paddlers in canoes or kayaks can complete this as a day trip in under ten hours—given favorable water and weather conditions—but twelve to fourteen hours is more common. Float times will vary greatly depending on river conditions, boat type, hazards, skill levels, motivation, and wind direction and speed. All boaters should have enough gear and food for two days longer than the anticipated trip duration: this includes paddlers intending to complete the trip in one long day. The Tanana River and its valley are wide; strong headwinds can arise quickly and last for days, greatly slowing progress. Also, the river often has fast-moving motorboats cruising up and down it, so it is best to keep an eye and ear open for them. Keep to the side to allow them to pass.

In winter, under ideal conditions, expert skate skiers can complete the trip in as little as four hours and can go either from Fairbanks to Nenana or Nenana to Fairbanks. Be sure to have a plan if something goes amiss. Snowmachines in winter are much more common than boats in the summer. Skiers should also be on the lookout for dog teams and skijorers.

MORE ADVENTUROUS? Just stay in your boat. You can float all the way to Manley Hot Springs, if you have the time to cover the nearly 100 additional miles (160 km). If you are looking for more challenging water, try the Nenana (Trip 13). Skiers looking for more of a challenge should try the White Mountains (Trip 34).

Cruising down the Tanana River.

DIRECTIONS: From the Parks Highway, head southwest on Chena Pump Road for 4.5 miles (7.3 km). Turn left into the parking area before the big hill. This is the put-in for boaters, and it can be the start or finish for skiers.

The other terminus is at Nenana. Head south out of Fairbanks on the Parks Highway toward Anchorage. Turn left at milepost 304.5 onto A Street, which will take you into the heart of Nenana. Turn right on Front Street after about a quarter mile (0.4 km). Turn left after about a quarter mile (0.4 km) and cross two sets of railroad tracks. These are active tracks so check both ways—there are no gates. Turn right and park in the parking area about 100 yards (meters) down.

9 *CHENA LAKE*

Moose Creek Dam Bikeway

R/T DISTANCE: 10.6 miles (17 km)

DURATION: 1 to 5 hours

HIGH POINT: 500 feet (152 m)

TOTAL ELEVATION CHANGE: Less than 20 feet (6 m)

DIFFICULTY: Easy

ROUTE TYPE: Paved trail (nonmotorized in summer)

Lake Park Bike Trail

R/T DISTANCE: 5.5 miles (9 km)

DURATION: 1 to 3 hours

HIGH POINT: 500 feet (152 m)

TOTAL ELEVATION CHANGE: Less than 20 feet (6 m)

DIFFICULTY: Easy

ROUTE TYPE: Dirt road (motorized allowed)

River Park Nature and Ski Trails

R/T DISTANCE: 1.5–4.2 miles (2.4–7 km)

DURATION: 1 to 3 hours

HIGH POINT: 500 feet (152 m)

TOTAL ELEVATION CHANGE: Less than 20 feet (6 m)

DIFFICULTY: Easy

ROUTE TYPE: Established trail (nonmotorized)

BEST SEASON: All year

USGS MAPS: Fairbanks D-1

LAND MANAGER: Fairbanks North Star Borough, 907-488-1655

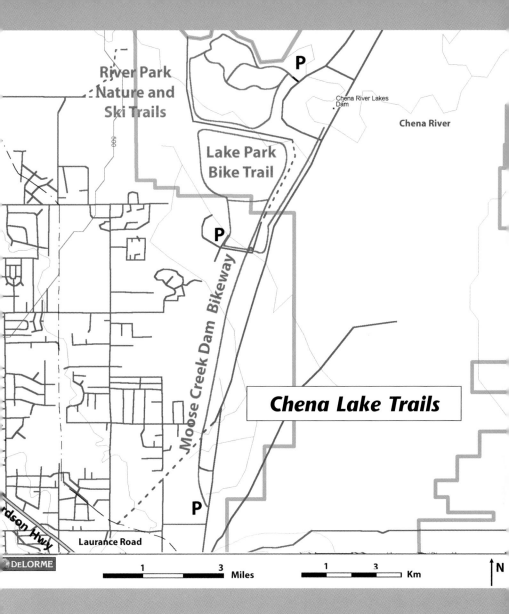

River Park Nature and Ski Trails

P

Chena River Lakes Dam

Chena River

Lake Park Bike Trail

P

Moose Creek Dam Bikeway

Chena Lake Trails

P

Laurance Road

rdson Hwy

DeLORME

1   3
Miles

1   3
Km

↑N

In 1967, almost all of Fairbanks suffered severe flooding from the Chena River. In response, the U.S. Army Corps of Engineers created the Chena Flood Control Project. Construction started in 1973 and was completed by 1979. The project can divert floodwaters of the Chena River south safely around Fairbanks and into the larger Tanana River. Fill was taken from the downstream side of the dam and dike to aid in their construction, creating Chena Lake (although there is only one lake, the area is sometimes referred to as Chena Lakes). A recreation area was created around the lake, river, and flood control project. The 2,000-acre (810-hectare) recreation area, which is divided into the Lake Park and the River Park, is home to moose, black bears, beaver, goshawks, and other wildlife.

In winter, trails up to 12 miles (19.4 km) long are groomed for skiers, skijorers, and mushers. Both the River and Lake Parks can be snowshoed in the winter, on and off trail. (Many of the winter trails in the recreation area are multiuse, so they are open to motorized use.)

Moose Creek Dam Bikeway

The Moose Creek Dam Bikeway connects the two parks of the recreation area. This paved trail is great for cruising, whether you are whizzing by on your road bike or pushing the stroller. Also extremely flat, this trail runs parallel to the flood control dam through birch, spruce, and tamarack stands. It crosses a few recreation area roads and runs quite near Laurance Road at the far end of the bikeway. It ends at a visitors' kiosk near the dam, which is also a salmon-viewing area.

Lake Park Bike Trail

The Lake Park is very popular for its swimming beach, picnic areas, campgrounds, and playground, but it is also a great spot to fish or take the canoe out for a leisurely paddle. The Lake Park also has a bicycle trail. It is an old dirt road that heads north from the first parking area. It starts by paralleling the lake shore and then breaks off into the woods. It is a gentle ride through mostly poplar trees. The flat trail makes a loop, coming back to the parking area after about 5.5 miles (8.9 km). Many other old dirt roads and social trails break off from the bike trail and can be fun to explore. However, some lead through wet, boggy areas. All of these areas can be skied in winter and long sections are groomed.

River Park Nature and Ski Trails

Access to the Chena River (see Trips 7 and 15) can be had at the River Park section of the recreation area. The River Park features three loop trails, all starting and ending at the same point, with virtually no change in elevation. The trails wander through towering birch groves, but there are also stands of spruce and tamarack. Oxbow lakes, evidence of the wandering nature of the Chena River, can also be seen. Two of the trails are called ski loops, probably because they are a bit wetter in the summer, but they can be easily hiked. All three trails are great for walking, trail runs, biking, and skiing. The shortest of the three is the Black Loop Ski Trail, which is about 1.5 miles (2.4 km) long. The Nature Trail (also known as the Yellow Loop Ski) has placards with information about the plants and wildlife found in the recreation area and is about 2.7 miles (4.4 km) long. Running along the perimeter of the River Park is the

4.2-mile (7-km) Green Loop Ski Trail. This trail is groomed and can be skate skied. Skijoring is discouraged in this section of the park.

ALL ROUTES BE AWARE: There is a summer seasonal fee to gain entrance to the recreation area. Bow hunting is permitted for a short time in fall, and off-road vehicles are permitted in some areas during certain times of the year.

MORE ADVENTUROUS? The dam and the lands to the east side of them are open to nonmotorized travel. Go explore around the floodplain—just not while it is flooding!

DIRECTIONS: From Fairbanks, take the Richardson Highway (Alaska 2) southeast toward North Pole. About a mile past North Pole you will see signs

Ski trail in the River Park.

for Chena Lake Recreation Area. Take the Dawson Road/Buzby Road exit on the right. At the end of the off ramp, turn left onto Dawson, go 100 yards (91.5 m) and turn right onto Mistletoe Drive. Go one mile (1.6 km), then turn left onto Laurance Road.

There is parking available about a half mile (0.8 km) down Laurance Road on the left. This is the start of the Moose Creek Dam Bikeway. There is a seasonal fee station operated by the Fairbanks North Star Borough 2.5 miles (4 km) farther down Laurance. Take a left after 3.5 miles (5.6 km) to enter the Lake Park of the recreation area, where campgrounds, a swimming beach, a playground, and the start of the Lake Park Bike Trail are found. The bike trail begins at the first parking lot about a quarter mile (0.4 km) from Laurance Road.

Continue down Laurance Road 4.8 miles (7.7 km) before turning left to reach the River Park Nature Trail, campgrounds, and boat launch. The boat launch is at the end of this road, while the parking lot for the nature and ski trails is on the left, about a half mile (0.8 km) from Laurance Road. The Moose Creek Dam Bikeway and Laurance Road end at the Chena River. A visitors' kiosk is here, as well as the flood control dam.

When you go back toward Fairbanks, just take a left from Laurance Road onto the Richardson Highway.

10 CHENA AND PILEDRIVER SLOUGHS

Chena Slough

R/T DISTANCE: Up to 5 miles (8 km) but many other options

DURATION: 1 to 4 hours

HIGH POINT: 470 feet (143 m)

TOTAL ELEVATION CHANGE: Less than 20 feet (6 m)

DIFFICULTY: Easy

ROUTE TYPE: Float (class I), suitable for canoes or kayaks (nonmotorized)

Piledriver Slough

ONE-WAY DISTANCE: Up to 12 miles (19.4 km) but many options

DURATION: Up to 12 hours, but much shorter trips possible

HIGH POINT: 540 feet (165 m)

TOTAL ELEVATION CHANGE: Less than 30 feet (9 m)

DIFFICULTY: Easy

ROUTE TYPE: Float (class I), suitable for canoes or kayaks (motorized allowed)

BEST SEASON: May to September

USGS MAPS: Fairbanks D-1 (Chena Slough), C-1 (Piledriver)

LAND MANAGERS: Alaska Department of Natural Resources (Fairbanks), 907-451-2705; Fairbanks North Star Borough, 907-488-1655; Eielson Air Force Base, Natural Resource Office, 907-377-5782

Chena Slough

Chena Slough is a slow-moving, shallow, and clear waterway that runs north of the town of North Pole and south of the main Chena River. It works well for an after-work paddle or a place to learn (or teach) some strokes. Although the slough's banks are dotted with houses and it abuts Badger Road in many places, it is a surprisingly

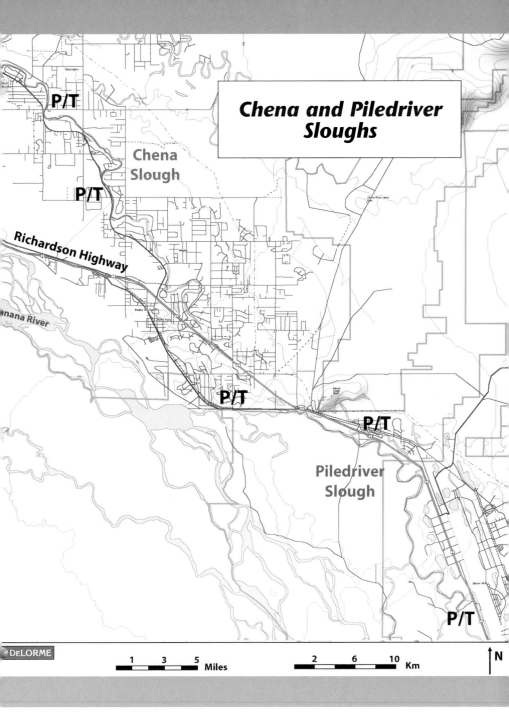

Chena and Piledriver Sloughs

Chena Slough

P/T

P/T

Richardson Highway

Tanana River

P/T

P/T

Piledriver Slough

P/T

DeLORME

| 1 | 3 | 5 |
Miles

| 2 | 6 | 10 |
Km

↑ N

good place to watch birds or catch fish. Towering white spruce trees line many stretches and almost make you feel like you have escaped town. Most people paddle up or down the slough and then back to where they put in, though one-way floats are easy to manage. The slough has a slight current to it, which you have to fight when heading upstream. I would recommend heading upstream first, while you have energy, so you can just float back to the start if you're tired.

It is about 2 river miles (3.2 km) from the Persinger Drive put-in to Peede Road, making for a 4-mile (6.5-km) round trip. From Peede Road to Nordale Road and back is about 2 miles (3.2 km). It is about another 2.5 river miles (4 km) from Nordale Road to Repp Road, making for a 5-mile (8-km) round trip. You can paddle upstream from Repp Road for about a mile (1.6 km), depending on water levels, before it gets too shallow. There are many places to launch along the slough, so longer floats can be strung together if you are willing to portage over some bridges. There are guardrails and traffic, so I would recommend against it.

Piledriver Slough

If Chena Slough is just too suburban for you, try driving down the highway a bit farther to Piledriver Slough. Though you can still make out highway noise, the setting is much more natural. Piledriver Slough is a spruce-lined channel of the Tanana River that parallels the Richardson Highway. There are a number of put-in and take-out locations, which makes this a nice place to go for a short float or to practice strokes. Due to the slow current, people often canoe up the slough and drift or paddle back down to where they started. It is also possible to put in at one location and paddle down as much as 12 miles (19.4) to a different take-out. The water is slow-moving, so anticipate the trip taking longer than you might think.

ALL ROUTES BE AWARE: There is a slight current in both sloughs, so heading upstream will likely take you two to three times longer than heading downstream. Where possible, head upstream first so you know you can make it back to the start with no problem. The water can be very shallow in places in the Chena Slough. Culverts, rather than bridges, are used at the road crossings. Most of these crossings have guardrails and traffic, so portaging is not fun. There can be many fishermen along Chena Slough; try to stay out of their way. Chena Slough is a pretty urban trip; please respect the private property that lines most of the slough. For Piledriver Slough, be sure to note very carefully where your take-out spot is going to be—many of the access points look similar. Permits are required for hunting and fishing on Eielson Air Force Base. Call the Base Natural Resource Office (907-377-5782) for details.

MORE ADVENTUROUS? Head out to Chena Lake Recreation Area (Trip 9). From there put your canoe in the Chena River and float down to Nordale Road, which can be done in day. If you float past Nordale, you will eventually get to Fairbanks, and you can keep right on going (Trip 7). You can also put in to the Chena Slough at Persinger Drive and reach the Chena River in under a half mile (0.8 km). From there you can continue into Fairbanks, which should only take a few hours. Those looking for a multiday trip can launch from Dyke Road on Piledriver Slough and paddle the Tanana River to Fairbanks or all the way to Nenana (Trip 8).

DIRECTIONS: To reach Chena Slough from Fairbanks, take the Richardson Highway (Alaska 2) southeast toward North Pole. About 3.5 miles (5.6 km) past the junction of the Richardson and the Mitchell Expressway (Alaska 3) take the Badger Road

The quiet waters of the Chena Slough.

exit. Stay on Badger for 3 miles (4.8 km), then turn left onto Old Badger Road. After about three-quarters of a mile (1.2 km), turn left again onto Persinger Drive. Drive about 100 yards (meters), then park on your left after you cross the slough.

Another spot to put in is at Peede Road. Do not turn onto Old Badger Road. Stay on Badger Road for 5.5 miles (9 km) before turning left onto Peede Road. There is a small park with a parking area on the left after about 50 yards (meters). One more option is to put in at Repp Road, a left turn about 7.2 miles (11.6 km) down Badger Road. Parking is on the right.

For Piledriver Slough: Take the Richardson Highway southeast out of Fairbanks. About a mile (1.6 km) past North Pole you will see signs for a left-hand exit onto Laurance Road for the Chena Lake Recreation Area. To reach the farthest downstream take-out of the slough, turn right onto Laurance Road here. Turn left onto Dyke Road after about a quarter mile (0.4 km). In about three-quarters of a mile (1.2 km) the road reaches the dike. The slough is on the other side, up and over a steep embankment of the dike. The slough returns to the Tanana River less than a mile (1.6 km) downstream (west) of here.

Reach the launch sites for the slough by going farther down the Richardson Highway. Reach one site by turning right onto a dirt road off the Richardson at milepost 345.2. Follow the dirt road for about 1.5 miles (2.4 km) until you see the slough on your left. There is only a very small spot to park here. You may find more parking at another launch site about a half mile (0.8 km) up this road. You can also turn right off the Richardson at milepost 343.8 onto Eielson Farm Road. There is parking on either side about a quarter mile (0.4 km) down the road.

For the furthest upstream put-in, turn right off the Richardson Highway at milepost 338.7. Follow the road about a half mile (0.8 km) to where it ends at a small turnaround. There is a 25-yard (meter) trail heading east down to the slough.

11 *ISBERG*

R/T DISTANCE: Up to 5.5 miles (9 km)

DURATION: 1 to 3 hours

HIGH POINT: 850 feet (259 m)

TOTAL ELEVATION CHANGE: Less than 500 feet (152 m)

DIFFICULTY: Easy

ROUTE TYPE: Established trails (motorized allowed)

BEST SEASON: November to March

USGS MAPS: Fairbanks D-3

LAND MANAGER: Alaska Department of Natural Resources (Fairbanks), 907-451-2705

Although the trails have been around for a while, Isberg Recreation Area was officially designated in 2006. The area covers about 400 acres (162 hectares) on the backside of Chena Ridge wedged between the Parks Highway, Isberg Road, and Cripple Creek Road. Its trails are good for classical skiing, skijoring, and walking, but they are multiuse so watch out for snowmachiners and dog teams. Much of the area is open enough for off-trail snowshoeing. Most of the area consists of black spruce forest on gentle slopes, but there are some nice birch and white spruce trees and several steep hills.

The trailhead at Oboe Court is at the southwestern corner of the recreation area. You can either head north-northeast down a relatively narrow trail through the spruce or follow the power line due east. These trails form two sides of a triangle, to which most of the trails connect. The trail through the spruce runs about a mile (1.6 km), heading gently downhill. Three-quarters of the way along that trail, a smaller trail heads off to the east and connects to a north-south power line. After a mile (1.6 km) the trail reaches a four-way intersection, where the north-south power line intersects the trail at a 90-degree angle. The trail to the left and the one that goes straight meet up again about a half mile (0.8 km) down the trail. Going straight keeps you farther away from Cripple Creek Road.

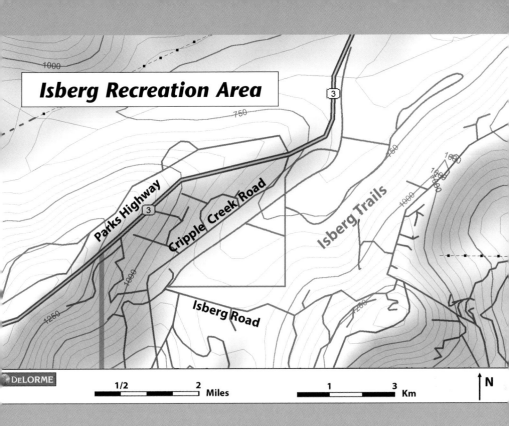

Isberg Recreation Area

Parks Highway

Cripple Creek Road

Isberg Trails

Isberg Road

DeLORME

1/2   2 Miles

1   3 Km

N

You have three options where these two trails meet up again. One is to return to the four-way intersection on the trail you did not take. Another is to follow the trail that continues to the northeast and parallels the Parks Highway, until it ends at milepost 350. The third option is to take the trail to the southeast that runs into the Lower Chena Ditch Trail (see below).

Taking a right at the four-way intersection will put you on the power line heading south. The Lower Chena Ditch Trail breaks off the power line, heading southeast, after about 75 yards (meters). The trail climbs steeply up the backside of Chena Ridge for about a quarter mile (0.4 km). It then heads downhill for about a mile (1.6 km) before reaching the intersection with that short southeast-trending trail mentioned above. You can loop back on that trail or continue on for another quarter mile (0.4 km) where there is another intersection. This intersection is the start and end of a mile (1.6 km) loop, so in order to return you must retrace your path back to the power line. Once on the power line heading south there will be a steep hill. At the top of the hill, the power line makes a 90-degree turn to the west. This will lead you back to the trailhead at Oboe Court. There are numerous other trails, such as the one heading east instead of heading west back to the trailhead or ones heading to Ester, that can be fun to explore and extend your outing.

Bluebird day in Isberg Recreation Area.

BE AWARE: Parcels of private property surround the recreation area; please respect their privacy. Most of these trails are made by snowmachiners, so expect to see some along the trail. These trails are also popular with dog mushers, so keep an eye out for them as well. Some of these trails are too wet to use during the summer season.

MORE ADVENTUROUS? The Goldstream Valley trails (Trip 3) offer similar-style trails, though less hilly. The UAF Trail System (Trip 2) and Birch Hill (Trip 4) offer fantastic ski trails that are well groomed, though dogs are not allowed at Birch Hill and on the groomed trails at UAF. If you are looking for a more wild adventure, try the White Mountains (Trip 34) or Angel Creek Trail (Trip 22).

DIRECTIONS: Take the Parks Highway (Alaska 3) south out of Fairbanks toward Anchorage. At milepost 349, a couple miles past Ester, turn left onto Cripple Creek Road. Follow Cripple Creek for 1.5 miles (2.4 km) and then turn left onto Isberg Road. After about 100 yards (meters) turn left onto Oboe Court. Park on the right side of the road. With the official establishment of the recreation area in 2006, new parking areas have been proposed. Look for them coming soon on Cripple Creek and Isberg roads.

12 *MOUNT HEALY VIA BISON GULCH*

R/T DISTANCE: 11 miles (17.7 km)

DURATION: 4 to 9 hours

HIGH POINT: 5,600 feet (1,705 m)

TOTAL ELEVATION CHANGE: 11,800 feet (3,594 m)

DIFFICULTY: Difficult

ROUTE TYPE: Mostly established trail (route to summit; nonmotorized)

BEST SEASON: May to September

USGS MAPS: Healy D-4, D-5; or Trails Illustrated Denali

LAND MANAGER: Alaska Department of Natural Resources (Fairbanks),
907-451-2705

While the summit of Mount Healy lies within the boundary of Denali National Park, the Bison Gulch trailhead is on state land. The trail at Bison Gulch offers Interior residents the closest and most direct route to the alpine and a serious mountain climb. The trail is steep and unrelenting, but if you have been longing for a no-nonsense hike this is it.

Starting across the highway from the parking area, the trail immediately diverges into several routes. Aside from the one that leads directly down to the creek, they all quickly meet again. The path to the right looks intimidating because it is steep and composed of loose, sharp rock. However, the other paths face the same challenge just a few feet beyond sight. This right-hand trail is a good way to start; it gives you an idea of what the rest of the day will be like. This initial pitch is steep but short-lived. It brings you to a vegetated bench that can be a little wet. Dwarf birch, willows, and blueberry bushes clog the trail, but the way is obvious—keep heading up.

The trail is steep and rocky with a few plateaus that make nice resting places. At the first big rocky outcropping, the last of the shrubs disappear. This is a good place to rest or even stop for those not wanting to attempt the summit. At times Dall

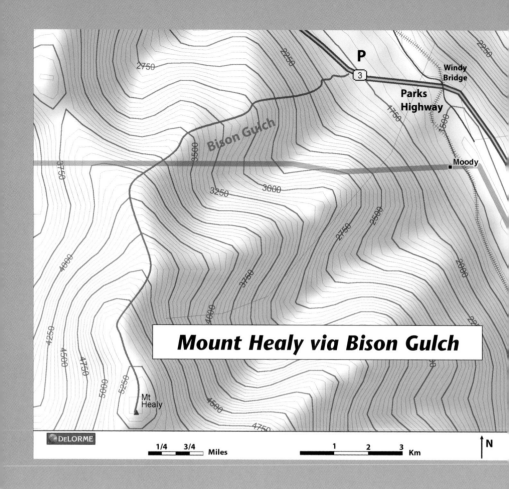

sheep can be seen on the mountain's slopes. More frequently they can be spotted on the slopes across the highway to the east from here. The trail's gradient lessens a bit after the outcropping but still climbs consistently up to a short bench.

From this bench the going gets steeper, and the trail is harder to follow. Route-finding ability is required even in good weather conditions. After a steep pitch, you will reach a ridge that runs north-south. Take this ridge to the south (left). The terrain is much more rugged. The rocks are sharp and chew up laces, gaiters, and gloves. Pick your way over numerous rocky outcrops to figure out which is the true summit of Mount Healy.

BE AWARE: Traffic comes hurtling down the Parks Highway. Be very careful crossing the highway, especially if you have dogs or children. The trail is steep and there are plenty of areas of loose talus. The trail gets harder to follow the higher you go. There are portions of the trail that are highly exposed (e.g., follow knife-ridges).

Inclement weather can descend upon you rapidly, so be prepared for all sorts of weather conditions, including gale-force winds.

MORE ADVENTUROUS? Strong hikers can continue southward past the summit and join up with the Mount Healy Overlook Trail that originates near the Denali National Park and Preserve backcounty office, west of the railroad tracks. This requires some route-finding ability and a way to get back to Bison Gulch—not to mention plenty of energy. If even that does not sound like enough, highly experienced uber-athletes can head west past the summit for more than a dozen miles (19.4 km) of up and down ridge walking to reach the Savage River parking

The view east from the slopes of Mount Healy.

area, 14 miles (22.6 km) in on the Denali Park Road. There are an infinite number of hikes in Denali. See Appendix B for some suggested guidebooks for this beautiful part of the Interior.

DIRECTIONS: Take the Parks Highway (Alaska 3) south out of Fairbanks toward Anchorage. The parking area is at milepost 243.5, which is south of the town of Healy. The parking area is a bit hidden, so watch carefully for it. Shortly after topping a hill you will descend, and the road will curve left. Right at that curve the parking area is on the left (east) side of the road. The parking area is paved and can fit ten cars or so. The trailhead is just across the highway at the right (north) end of the guardrail.

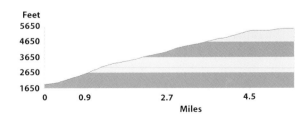

13 NENANA RIVER

ONE-WAY DISTANCE: 18, 22, or 40 miles (29, 35.5, or 64.5 km), with longer trips possible

DURATION: 3 hours to 3 days

HIGH POINT: 2,400 feet (722 m)

TOTAL ELEVATION CHANGE: Up to 600 feet (183 m)

DIFFICULTY: Easy to moderate

ROUTE TYPE: Float (class I–II, possible class III section); suitable for canoes, rafts, and river kayaks (motorized allowed)

BEST SEASON: June to September

USGS MAPS: Healy B-3, B-4, C-4 (upper stretch); Healy D-4, D-5; Fairbanks A-5, B-5, C-5

LAND MANAGER: Alaska Department of Natural Resources (Fairbanks), 907-451-2705

The Nenana River drains the snow-draped southern slopes of the central Alaska Range. Rather than heading east to join the Susitna River, it turns west and runs into the northern flanks of the Talkeetna Mountains. Having yet another chance to head south, the Nenana shies away from the Chulitna River valley. It turns northwest around the Reindeer Hills and makes a dramatic cut back through the Alaska Range. The river offers excellent wilderness float trips and some of the state's top road-accessible white water. The most difficult and popular white water is in the canyons downriver of Denali National Park and Preserve entrance. These rapids are class IV and should be run only by experts or with commercial outfitters. Everyone running the white water section should use a dry suit and wear a helmet. Above and below the canyon, class I and II waters prevail and are the focus of this trip.

Starting where the Nenana River last meets the Denali Highway is a great choice because the area is rugged and wild. Spruce trees line the banks with the Alaska Range as the backdrop. The river can be shallow, a bit narrow, and prone to small sweepers

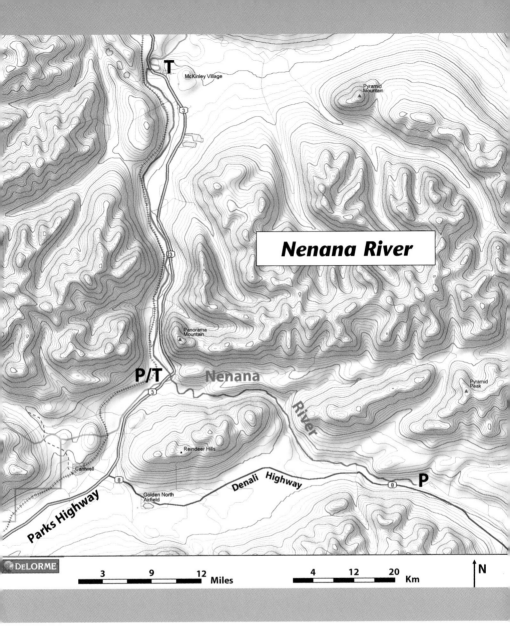

Nenana River

| 3 | 9 | 12 |
Miles

| 4 | 12 | 20 |
Km

N

in this upper reach. There are some tight turns and smallish runs to keep paddlers on their toes, but the river mellows downstream. The river flows westward, giving paddlers the impression that they will parallel the Denali Highway. However, after about 6 miles (9.7 km) the river veers northwest and flows north of the Reindeer Hills. Suddenly, mountains are all around. There are good camping sites all along the river from the put-in until here.

North of the Reindeer Hills, the river turns westward again. Here you are sandwiched between the jagged peak of Panorama Mountain to the north and the

Paddling the upper section of the Nenana River.

Reindeer Hills to the south. The river slowly gets larger and slower in this reach and meanders a bit before reaching Windy bridge, some 18 miles (29 km) from the start. This upper section can be done as a day trip or broken into short sections for an overnight trip. The float takes three to six hours.

From Windy bridge to McKinley Village, a tourist enclave south of the park entrance, is another 22 miles (35.5 km) of mostly class I and II water. At certain water conditions, there is a class III section, which should be run only by experienced paddlers with white water skills and rescue equipment. The river is bigger below Windy bridge and takes you north. Logjams are more prevalent and there are some sharp turns. One of these turns, a couple miles north of the bridge, bounces off the roadway riprap at milepost 219 and through a narrow rock outcrop. Shortly after, the river funnels through another tight spot, creating larger waves and hydraulics. At high-water levels, the run is class III and can be quite difficult for canoes. These rapids should be scouted first, which can be easily done from the road. During low-water levels, you might scratch your head and wonder what I was talking about.

The river veers away from the road about halfway to McKinley Village, providing the most solitude for this portion of the river. This 22-mile (35.5-km) stretch of river can be done as a long day trip or broken into two shorter sections for an overnighter. It has several good camping spots. This section can also be added to the upper section for a 40-mile (64.5-km) trip. Float time for the lower section is similar to the upper section.

BE AWARE: The Nenana River has class IV white water and is very dangerous in the gorge. Only highly experienced paddlers with dry suits and helmets should attempt this section of the river. All others need to pull out at McKinley Village. Even the upper stretches should be paddled with caution, because the Nenana's waters are swift, strong, and very cold. Commercial operators run many rafts through the gorge during the height of tourist season.

Motorized watercraft are allowed on the river, and are common near the Windy bridge. Most common are large motorized boats that carry tourists about 10 miles (16 km) upriver from the bridge. If possible, check at the bridge to get their schedule. The boats move fast and have large wakes.

A couple of miles below the bridge, the river comes back to the Parks Highway heading northeast. The roadside is protected by rock riprap and the river is deflected to the northwest and through a narrow gorge. This section is especially difficult class III at high-water levels. Scout this section (milepost 219 Parks Highway) before attempting it, especially those attempting it in canoes. Under good conditions, experienced paddlers want to run and re-run this section.

MORE ADVENTUROUS? If you have the gear and experience, try the Nenana Gorge, with its class IV white water. Ask one of the rafting companies where to put in. For a longer and more remote trip (without the technical white water), start on the river just south of Healy (milepost 248.8) and float to the town of Nenana some 55 miles (88 km) to the north. This section of the river is rated class II and is often braided. There is also a river access point about halfway between Healy and Nenana at the Rex bridge (milepost 275.8). Access is also possible at the Anderson River Park in the town of Anderson (turn at milepost 283.5). Advanced river and backcountry skills are required for these sections. At Nenana, the Nenana and Tanana rivers meet and boaters can float all the way to Manley Hot Springs.

DIRECTIONS: Take the Parks Highway (Alaska 3) south out of Fairbanks toward Anchorage. McKinley Village (take-out for the lower section) is at milepost 231.1. The Windy bridge over Nenana River (access point for both sections) is at milepost 215.8, 6 miles (9.7 km) north of Cantwell.

To get to the put-in for the upper section, turn left onto Denali Highway (Alaska 8) in Cantwell. Follow the highway for 16 miles (26 km), where there is a sign that marks river access, and the river is visible. A couple of unimproved access points are in this area within a mile (1.6 km) in either direction. Farther upstream, the river veers away from the road and never gets close again.

14 *KESUGI RIDGE*

ONE-WAY DISTANCE: 17, 27, or 33 miles (27.4, 43.6, or 52.2 km)

DURATION: 2 to 4 days

HIGH POINT: 3,600 feet (1,095 m)

TOTAL ELEVATION CHANGE: 6,400 or 9,500 or 10,800 feet (1,950 or 2,895 or 3,290 m)

DIFFICULTY: Moderate to difficult

ROUTE TYPE: Established trail (nonmotorized)

BEST SEASON: May to September

USGS MAPS: Talkeetna Mts. C-6, D-6; Talkeetna C-1, D-2; or Trails Illustrated Denali

LAND MANAGER: Alaska Department of Natural Resources (Fairbanks), 907-451-2705

Kesugi Ridge, halfway between Fairbanks and Anchorage, is a popular back-packing trip for Interior and Southcentral residents. Though the trail is just outside my definition of the Interior, its popularity with Interior residents justifies its inclusion. The trail is within Denali State Park, which is adjacent to the southeast corner of Denali National Park and Preserve. The majority of the hike is in alpine country and offers unsurpassed views of Denali (Mount McKinley) and the Alaska Range. The trail has some steep pitches, but long stretches are in relatively flat and rolling terrain.

A short but relatively steep hike from the Little Coal Creek trailhead brings you to a bench above tree line. This bench is on Kesugi Ridge and can offer incredible views of Denali and its surrounding peaks. Denali, the highest peak in North America, is shrouded by clouds most of the summer, but do not let this dissuade you from this hike. The trek is well worth the effort even if the mountain is obscured the entire time.

The hike is generally considered a through hike (i.e., you do not end up where you started); however, pleasant day hikes can be made from any of the four trailheads.

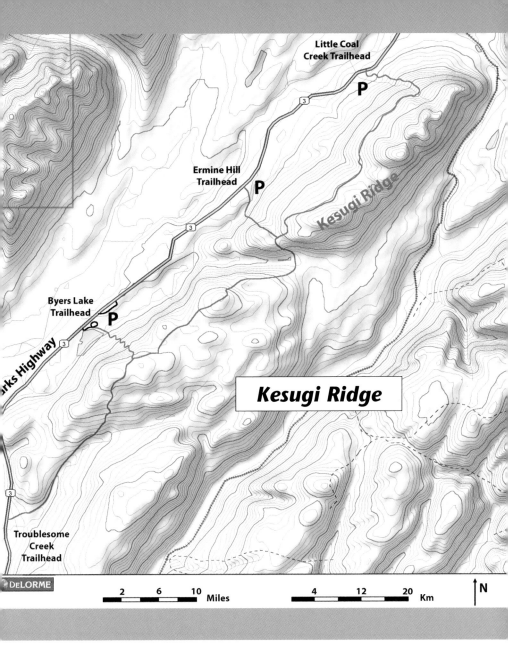

The Byers Lake campground area offers the most day hiking opportunities. The area also offers canoe and public-use cabin rentals, and chances to see spawning salmon. From north to south, the trailhead names are Little Coal Creek, Ermine Hill, Byers Lake, and Troublesome Creek. The Byers Lake campground is well marked. The other trailheads are marked with small, brown road signs that can be difficult to spot. There is no best location to start, so I will describe the trip as originating from the northernmost trailhead, Little Coal Creek.

The trail begins in a mixed forest of spruce and aspen. Although it rolls up and down, you are definitely heading uphill. After the first little section, the trail starts climbing more obviously. The hiking is pleasant with the sounds of a stream tumbling by and open meadows where you may catch a glimpse of a moose. The trail urges you on for the trees get shorter and thin out the farther you go, giving way to alpine vistas. Huffing and puffing, you make your way above tree line into the shrubby alders. Though the tall alders obscure the view, what you can see leaves no doubt that rewards are just ahead. For late starters or slow hikers there are great spots to camp just above shrub line. For most people, the hike takes about an hour and a half to get above tree line. Here the massive Eldridge Glacier and Chulitna River come into view, creating wonderful vistas. Though probably a bit winded by now, you will notice the gradient start to flatten. Up just a bit farther is your first decision point.

The trail splits here with seemingly equal use on both branches. The social trail continuing straight uphill leads to the summit of Kesugi Peak. This nontechnical climb is a great side trip for those with lots of energy. (See "More Adventurous?" below.) The main Kesugi Ridge trail veers sharply to the right (south) and crosses a small boulder field that conceals Little Coal Creek. When you climb out of that ravine, you are now undoubtedly in alpine country. The trail flattens out for a half mile (0.8 km) or so and can be wet from late-melting snowfields. Another short climb out of this bowl and the really spectacular views unfold.

From here you have unobstructed views of Eldridge Glacier and all the towering peaks that help create it: Denali, Huntington, Foraker. This jaw-dropping vista is impossible to sufficiently describe and is a view seldom matched by mortals who are not among the elite mountaineers in the world. Great camping sites abound in this area, but try to hide your camping area from the trail. Water from small lakes is plentiful.

The next several miles of trail—relatively flat with some ups and downs—fly by as you take in the view. The trail veers southeast and over a knob, revealing the Susitna

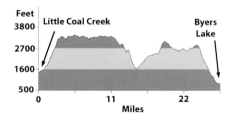

River on the east side of the ridge. The trail is rocky but easy to follow. Adventurers who like bouldering should take time to enjoy the several-acre playground near mile 10 (km 16). There are dozens of great granite boulders to test yourself (make sure to use a spotter). Or you can just lean up against one to take a well-deserved rest.

The trail winds around the boulder field and begins a long, slow climb up to a high point. This is probably the easiest place where you can lose the trail, so pay attention. The high point is a rocky promontory. From there you can see a large rock outcrop (a popular camping spot) to the southeast, a small lake in a saddle several hundred feet below to the south, and the highway to the west and southwest. A social trail heads down this steep embankment to the south and seems to be the logical choice to get to the Ermine Hill trailhead. However, it quickly braids and then dies out, forcing you to come back up the hill. Instead, follow the trail that leads you along the north side of the rock outcrop. For those going to the Ermine Hill trailhead, it feels like you are heading too far east because the trailhead lies west, but this is the correct path. The trail heads down a really steep slope with very loose gravel. Use extreme caution. The pitch is relatively short and at the bottom you cross a section of boardwalk to an open field above the small lake you saw from the rock outcrop.

The trail splits here. The trail to the left and uphill (see below) is the route to Byers Lake and beyond. The trail to the right (heading east) goes to the Ermine Hill trailhead. It follows the south side of the lake. This trail eventually splits into two trails. One is steep and the other is extremely steep with lots of roots. The extremely steep trail is slightly shorter but if you have weak knees or poor balance, take the less steep (main) trail as it has switchbacks. After finally descending off the ridge, you have another 1.5 miles (2.4 km) to go, which are uphill, to reach the Ermine Hill trailhead. This route is 17 miles (27.4 km) from the Little Coal Creek trailhead.

Many people choose to bypass the Ermine Hill trail and continue on to Byers Lake. To take this route, head uphill at the small lake. This is another place where people often lose the trail. Several social trails head straight up the steep hill over loose, granular rock. While the trail does head uphill, it is not that steep. Follow it over a rise. It runs between folds of salt-and-pepper granite outcrops. Little vegetation grows here. On the far side of the granite outcrops woody vegetation returns, and the trail drops precipitously into a valley. Returning into the trees feels like being on another planet after so much time up in the alpine. The ground is really wet in the valley, but boardwalk installed during 2001 and 2002 has made this section of trail more enjoyable.

The time below tree line is short. Before long you begin a long, steady hike up the southern half of Kesugi Ridge. The views along the southern half of the ridge are not as spectacular as elsewhere along the trail, but that may be because you will be spending most of your time head down hunting for abundant blueberries when

Hikers passing Eldridge Glacier.

they are in season. Along this part of the trail blueberries grow on high bushes and are easy to grab without breaking stride. Plump and juicy, these treats may slow you down. However, avoid camping in these berry-rich areas as bears enjoy them too! You will pass a long, skinny lake to the south that is quite scenic.

The rocky trail continues to climb to a high point at 2,970 feet (905 m). It is called VABM Golog on USGS maps. This makes an excellent spot to take a break. There are another 4 miles (6.4 km) of ups and downs, though modest in stature, to a creek. The trail drops down to cross the creek, leading many trekkers to think they are on their way down. But the trail climbs out of the ravine and continues for another 1.5 miles (2.4 km) before reaching the final intersection. From this intersection, the trail to the Troublesome Creek trailhead is 6 miles (9.7 km) longer than the trail to the Byers Lake trailhead. From Little Coal Creek to Byers Lake is 27 miles (43.6 km), while from Little Coal Creek to Troublesome Creek is 33 miles (52.2 km). The trail to Troublesome Creek has a tendency to be wet and does not offer any more fantastic views of the Alaska Range. This section is also closed from mid-July to August due to bears feeding on spawning salmon.

For these reasons, most hikers opt to head west toward Byers Lake at this intersection. Like at Ermine Hill, this trail's descent is very steep, especially for weary legs. The drop is about 1,500 feet (457 m) in just over a mile (1.6 km). Do not drink from the creek at the bottom of the descent; it is known to carry giardia, an intestinal parasite. Upon completing the descent, hikers need to make their way around the north side of Byers Lake. Take a right where the trail intersects the trail that encircles the lake. After another 1.5 miles (2.4 km) through beautiful rolling terrain with large trees, the trail ends at the far end of the campground. Follow the campground road (left, south) another half mile (0.8 km) to the trailhead parking spot.

BE AWARE: Parking stickers or fees are required for parking at Byers Lake campground. Bears are frequently seen in the campground and the lower elevation forest because of the abundance of berries, salmon, and, unfortunately, human trash. Always keep an eye open and make plenty of noise. Above tree line, fog and fresh snow can make the trail difficult to follow. Be sure to bring a map and compass and know how to use them. Although you are generally high enough not to hear the Parks Highway, it is in sight for long stretches of the hike.

MORE ADVENTUROUS? There are two summits near the beginning of the trek, Kesugi and Indian peaks, though you will likely not find their names on a map. Indian is named after the VABM marker placed at its summit. Both summits can be reached without technical equipment and will add on a half day to the trip for hikers in excellent condition. The summits are around 4,600 feet (1,400 m). To reach Kesugi Peak, keep heading east along a social trail as the main trail curves to the south and crosses Little Coal Creek. Indian Peak can be reached by heading south-southeast from Kesugi Peak. If you just want to summit Indian Peak, cross Little Coal Creek and ascend Indian from the south face. If you really want more adventure, try doing the entire trail in a day. The experienced, light, and fast uber-athlete can complete the trail from Little Coal Creek to Byers Lake in a tough fourteen-hour day.

DIRECTIONS: Take the Parks Highway (Alaska 3) out of Fairbanks toward Anchorage. Pass the entrance to Denali National Park and Preserve (milepost 237) and the town of Cantwell (milepost 210). Ten miles (16 km) south of the Hurricane Gulch bridge, you will see a small, brown sign marking Little Coal Creek at milepost 163.8. Take the small dirt road to your left (southeast) to reach the parking lot and trailhead.

To reach the Ermine Hill trailhead (milepost 156.5), drive about 7 miles (11.3 km) farther south along the Parks Highway. The trailhead is a turnout just off the road on your left (southeast).

Byers Lake Campground (milepost 147) is about 9 miles (14.5 km) south of the Ermine Hill trailhead and is well marked. Overnight parking for hikers is in a small lot on the right before the actual campsites. The Byers Lake area offers day hiking, canoeing, berry picking, and salmon viewing. The least used trailhead is Troublesome Creek, about 10 miles (16 km) south of Byers Lake (milepost 137.3 Parks Highway).

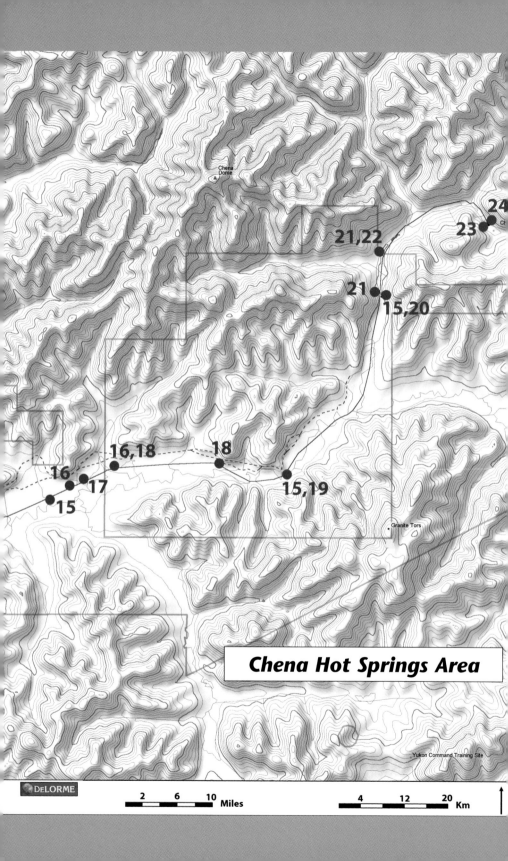

Chena Hot Springs Area

DeLORME

2   6   10 Miles

4   12   20 Km

Chena River State Recreation Area Region

The most popular recreational destination for Fairbanksans is the Chena River State Recreation Area. It is about an hour's drive east of Fairbanks. In addition to the recreation area, this region includes Chena Hot Springs Resort. Together they offer a wide variety of opportunities to enjoy the outdoors. This area is also home to the highest density of outdoor adventures described in this book. They include short but pleasant day hikes, floats down the Chena River, intense backpacking trips, rock climbing, and skiing. If that was not enough, each trip can easily culminate in a soothing soak in the hot springs. Chena Hot Springs Resort is at the terminus of the Chena Hot Springs Road at milepost 56.5.

15 *UPPER CHENA RIVER*

ONE-WAY DISTANCE: 1–35 miles (1.6–56.5 km; many put-in and take-out options)

DURATION: 1 hour to 1 week

HIGH POINT: 975 feet (297 m)

TOTAL ELEVATION CHANGE: Less than 550 feet (167 m)

DIFFICULTY: Moderate

ROUTE TYPE: Float (class I with sections of class II more common upriver); suitable for canoes, river kayaks, and rafts (motorized allowed)

BEST SEASON: June to September

USGS MAPS: Circle A-5; Big Delta D-5, D-6

LAND MANAGER: Alaska Department of Natural Resources (Fairbanks), 907-451-2705

Gold found in tributaries of the Tanana River sparked a rush in the Interior and lead to the founding of Fairbanks. The Chena River is probably the most used river in the Interior these days, but it is now used for recreation activities rather than shipping goods between the gold fields and the city. The upper Chena River has numerous access points within the Chena River Recreation Area, which makes it easy to find a float of just the right length. The upper Chena is also far enough out of Fairbanks that you get that natural aesthetic that the lower river lacks. The upper Chena winds its way through typical boreal forest, crossing and re-crossing under Chena Hot Springs Road. There are large white spruce lining the riverbank along many stretches.

The upper reaches of the river are more challenging than its lower reaches. Logjams, sweepers, overhanging vegetation, and swift currents are common. Downed trees can completely span the narrower channel, especially above the third bridge. The North Fork of the Chena meets with the East Fork just downstream from the third bridge. The river is much easier to navigate after the confluence. The float from the fourth bridge at the Angel Rocks trailhead (Trip 20, milepost 48.9) to the third

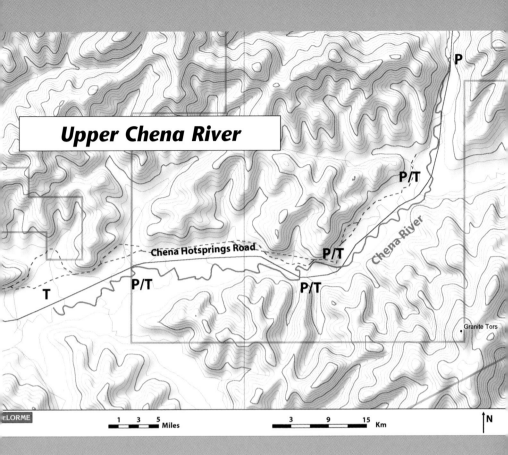

Upper Chena River

P/T

P/T

Chena Hotsprings Road

P/T

P/T

P/T

Chena River

T

Granite Tors

DELORME

1 3 5
Miles

3 9 15
Km

N

bridge (milepost 44) can take a couple of hours to cover the 7 miles (11 km), because you probably will need to get out and scout smaller, shallower areas.

The float from the third bridge to the second bridge (milepost 39.5) is popular because of its length (about 6 miles [9.7 km], which takes about one and a half to two and a half hours), and because it is as far up the river you can go without most of the really challenging stuff. The second bridge is at the Granite Tors campground and trailhead (Trip 19) parking lot. You can continue on another half-hour or so (about 2 miles [3.2 km]) to reach the first bridge at milepost 37.8. There are some big turns in this short section. The average gradient from the fourth to the first bridges is about 10 feet per mile (2 m per km).

The float from the first bridge down to the next major developed area (Rosehip Campground, milepost 27) can take three to five hours (about 18 miles [29 km]). However, there are several access points if you want to do a shorter section. Access roads are at mileposts 31.6, 28.6, and 28. Float time from the first bridge to the access road at milepost 31.6 is about two to three hours (about 10 miles [16 km]), another half-hour to hour to the road at milepost 28.6 (about 5 miles [8 km]), another

Canoeing the upper Chena on a hot summer day.

half-hour to the road at milepost 28 (about 2 miles [3.2 km]), and another half-hour to Rosehip Campground (about a mile [1.6 km]). Floats from mileposts 31.6 and 28.6 to Rosehip Campground are also very popular. The gradient of the river from the first bridge to Rosehip is about 5 feet per mile (1 m per km).

Float times vary greatly depending on river conditions, hazards, skill levels, and motivation. Some people will paddle hard the entire way and others will lounge around, taking breaks on nice beaches. The Chena is great for either or anything between.

BE AWARE: The Chena River is probably the most popular river in the Interior. Be on the lookout for other boats, including motorized ones. The Chena is considered a relatively easy float, but that reputation has lulled many paddlers into carelessness. The river has many logjams, sweepers, and overhanging bushes. This is especially true farther upriver, on sharp bends, and early in the year before people have cleared the channel. Capsizing is common above the third bridge and along the whole upper Chena River for inexperienced or inattentive paddlers. Always wear a life jacket, as the river water is cold and swift. The river is braided in some locations, so be careful to find the main channel.

Extra caution should be used during the shoulder seasons. Ice in the spring and high water from heavy rains or snowmelt will make the river more perilous. The river is usually fairly clear high up, so use turbidity to help determine high-water levels. Boaters are always encouraged to stop and scout the river. Parking at Granite Tors and Angel Rocks trailheads requires a fee.

MORE ADVENTUROUS? Just bring your gear and sense of adventure, and let the Chena take you. The middle Chena River is much less used than either the lower or upper parts of the river. Approximate float times from Rosehip Campground to Grange Hall Road, Nordale Road, and Fairbanks are two to four hours, twenty-five to fifty-five hours, and thirty-two to sixty hours, respectively. Pick up USGS maps Fairbanks D-1 and D-2. The river gradient is even less (about 3.5 feet per mile [0.6 m per km]) from Rosehip Campground to Fairbanks than on the upper river. Also useful is the "Chena River Trail Guide," a pamphlet by the Alaska Department of Natural Resources. It is available from DNR or the Alaska Public Lands Information Center (see Appendix B). If that is still not long enough, the lower Chena dumps into the Tanana River (Trip 8) for an even longer and wilder adventure.

DIRECTIONS: Take the Steese Highway (Alaska 2) north out of Fairbanks. The first exit ramp is for Chena Hot Springs Road. Take this exit, and follow the road to the east (right), looking for mileposts until you reach your chosen destination.

16 *COMPEAU AND COLORADO CREEK TRAILS*

ONE-WAY DISTANCE: 24.5 miles (40 km); add 2.5 miles (4 km) to complete round-trip loop

DURATION: 2 to 3 days, but day hikes or ski trips from either end

HIGH POINT: 2,600 feet (792 m)

TOTAL ELEVATION CHANGE: 6,300 feet (1,919 m)

DIFFICULTY: Moderate

ROUTE TYPE: ATV trail (motorized allowed)

BEST SEASON: All year

USGS MAPS: Big Delta D-6

LAND MANAGER: Alaska Department of Natural Resources (Fairbanks), 907-451-2705

One adventure, two very different trails. Though designated as separate trails, the Compeau and Colorado Creek trails connect and form almost a complete loop. Both trails start off Chena Hot Springs Road and are open to motorized vehicles. The trails are well marked (Compeau Trail with blue and black markers and Colorado Creek Trail with blue markers) and even have mileage signs. The Chena Hot Springs Winter Trail (orange markers) parallels Chena Hot Springs Road and intersects the Compeau and Colorado Creek trails perpendicularly near their trailheads. Pleasant day hikes can be made from either trailhead, but the trails are very different.

The Compeau Trail is a new addition to the recreation area, built in 2006. It was designed to be a sustainable ATV trail. It climbs to the ridgeline quickly and offers commanding views at times. The Colorado Creek Trail is an example of the damage that can be done from improper ATV use. The trail is braided in several places where new routes were pioneered to go around deeply rutted areas. The trail is relatively flat, as it stays on the valley floor, and can be very wet.

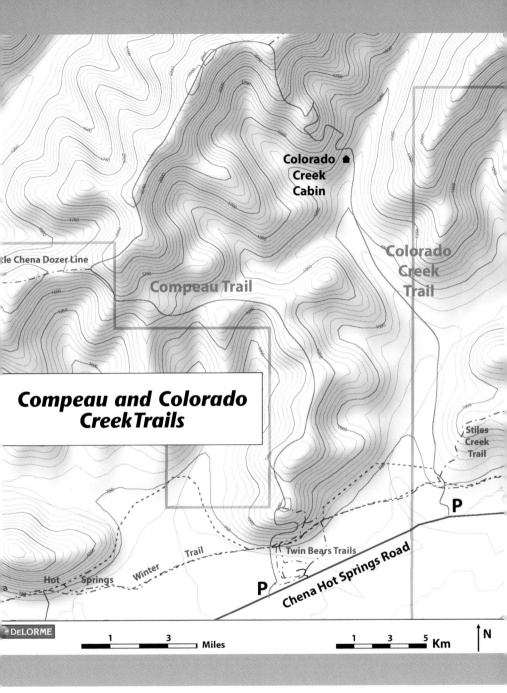

Compeau and Colorado Creek Trails

Colorado Creek Cabin

Colorado Creek Trail

le Chena Dozer Line

Compeau Trail

Stiles Creek Trail

P

Hot Springs

Winter Trail

Twin Bears Trails

P

Chena Hot Springs Road

DELORME

1 3 Miles

1 3 5 Km

N

The trailhead for the Compeau Trail is at the east end of the parking area and has blue and black trail markers. The beginning of the trail is lined with large poplars, birch, and white spruce. After a short way a multiuse trail enters from the right (east). It leads to Twin Bears Camp (Trip 17). Follow the trail left (north) for another half mile (0.8 km) where you will reach its intersection with Chena Hot Springs Winter Trail (orange markers), a multiuse trail that runs from Chena Hot Springs Resort to Fairbanks. Again, go straight to stay on the Compeau Trail. Smaller black spruce replace the larger trees in this section. Wetter areas have plastic matting to protect the trail. Shortly after the intersection, the trail begins a long, gentle climb up the south slope of Twin Bears Mountain (Trip 17). The gentle climb (grades of 10 percent or less) and switchbacks are designed to protect this trail from erosion, making it more sustainable.

Around 2.5 miles (4 km) in, you get views to the north. These can be your first good views in summertime because the hill has many trees. Shortly after the views, there is a junction. The trail to the right (south) connects with Twin Bears Mountain Trail (Trip 17) after about 100 yards (meters). Turn right and go another 100 yards (meters) to reach the 1,452-foot (442-m) summit of Twin Bears Mountain. This is a good day-trip destination. You can retrace your steps or follow the steeper Twin Bears Mountain Trail down to make a 5-mile (8-km) round-trip loop. For those returning on the Twin Bears trail, turn right (west) when you reach Chena Hot Springs Winter Trail (also known simply as the Winter Trail). The Compeau Trail will be just ahead.

For those continuing on, veer left (north) at the junction with the connector trail. The Compeau Trail heads downhill before reaching mile 3 (km 4.8). It heads generally northward for the next mile, offering more and more views. The Stiles Creek Trail (Trip 18) area and Granite Tors (Trip 19) can be seen to the east. The trail drops again and changes course after 4 miles (6.4 km), turning in a more westerly direction.

The trail continues over the rolling forested hills to the west for another 5 miles (8 km). At mile 10 (km 16), the trail intersects with a firebreak, known as the Little Chena Dozer Line. This line was put in during the extreme fire season of 2004. It starts from 6 miles (9.7 km) in on the wood-cutting road that goes past Two Rivers Elementary School (milepost 18, Chena Hot Springs Road) and runs to the Chena

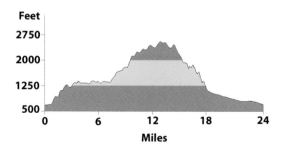

View to the west from Colorado Creek Trail.

Dome Trail (Trip 21) and goes beyond. The intersection is 8.5 miles (13.7 km) up the dozer line from Two Rivers. The dozer line is motorized for 13.5 miles (21.7 km). Follow the dozer line to the right (northeast) for 5 miles (8 km). This section reaches the highest point of the trail at 2,600 feet (792 m) and just barely puts you in alpine country. This part of the trail has wonderful views.

At mile 15 (km 24.2) the Compeau Trail leaves the dozer line, which continues northeast but is closed to motorized use. The Compeau Trail veers to the southeast and reaches the Colorado Creek Cabin after 3.5 miles (5.6 km) of gently but steadily descending trail. The cabin was nicely remodeled in 2006. It sleeps four and has a woodstove. It can be reserved through the Department of Natural Resources (see Appendix B). Follow the Compeau Trail back to the west to find dead wood for a fire.

From the cabin, the Colorado Creek Trail heads out to Chena Hot Springs Road. Follow the trail (blue markers) to the southeast for about a half mile (0.8 km), crossing a small creek, to reach the main trail. The main trail continues up the valley to the left (north), but the trailhead is to the right (south). To the south the trail runs through quintessential taiga; stunted black spruce dominate the lowland flats, but birch groves drape the rolling hills lining the valley. The trail very gently descends but is rutted and braided for almost its entire length. It is best used during winter, though it is

Compeau Trail in the low light of a mid winter day.

passable in the summer. The last mile (1.6 km) of the Colorado Creek Trail is usually very wet and deeply rutted. It shares its beginning with Stiles Creek Trail (Trip 18), which joins from the left (east).

The trail intersects the Winter Trail about a half mile (0.8 km) from the trailhead. In winter, you can turn right (west) and follow the Winter Trail back to the Compeau Trail (2.5 miles [4 km]) to complete the loop but it is very wet in the summer. Just stay on the Colorado Creek Trail if you have a shuttle vehicle at the trailhead or you would rather walk down Chena Hot Springs Road back to your vehicle. You can also hike to the cabin and back in a day using solely the Colorado Creek Trail, which is a 13-mile (21-km) round trip.

BE AWARE: Off-road vehicles are permitted on both trails throughout the year. Travel along the ridge on the Compeau Trail can be dangerous during high wind, fog, or whiteout conditions. Water sources along the ridge can be scarce, especially in late summer. These trails are often used as traplines; please do not disturb any traps and keep an eye on your dogs! Note: the beginning of the Colorado Creek Trail is being/has been rerouted.

MORE ADVENTUROUS? You have many options. At mile 10 (km 16) of the Compeau Trail you can head west along the Little Chena Dozer Line, going all the way back to a wood-cutting road that runs beyond Two Rivers Elementary School (milepost 18, Chena Hot Springs Road). At mile 15 (km 24.2) of the Compeau Trail you can follow the dozer line northeast to the Chena Dome Trail (Trip 21). Another alternative is to follow the Colorado Creek Trail past the cabin and up the valley. Experts can follow it up the valley and then find a route up to the Chena Dome Trail and connect with the Angel Creek Trail (Trip 22). Very fit and experienced mountain bikers may enjoy riding the Compeau Trail (please wait until drier conditions). Uberathletes may want to cover the 27-mile (44-km) loop in one very long day.

DIRECTIONS: Take the Steese Highway (Alaska 2) north out of Fairbanks. The first exit ramp is for Chena Hot Springs Road. Take this exit and follow the road east to milepost 29.6. The trailhead for the Compeau Trail is on the left (north) and is marked, but the sign is small. The Colorado Creek trailhead is 1.5 miles (2.4 km) farther east at milepost 31.5. The trailhead is also on the left (north) side and is well signed.

17 *TWIN BEARS TRAILS*

R/T DISTANCE: Up to 5 miles (8 km)

DURATION: Up to 4 hours

HIGH POINT: 1,452 feet (442 m)

TOTAL ELEVATION CHANGE: Up to 1,500 feet (457 m)

DIFFICULTY: Easy to moderate

ROUTE TYPE: Mix (some motorized, some nonmotorized)

BEST SEASON: October to March, but can be done the year round

USGS MAPS: Big Delta D-5, D-6

LAND MANAGERS: Alaska Department of Natural Resources (Fairbanks), 907-451-2705; Twin Bears Outdoor Education Association, 907-451-2753

Twin Bears Camp is nestled on the shores of Twin Bear Lake, just off the Chena Hot Springs Road at milepost 30. Surrounding the camp are a number of trails, all of which have a different feel. All the trails can be skied or snowshoed in winter, and a couple of the trails can be used year round.

The Twin Bears Mountain Trail takes hikers and snowshoers up a fairly steep trail that leads to the 1,452-foot (442-m) summit. The 5-mile (8-km) round trip makes for a nice day hike. Follow the Nature Trail to the Ski Loop, heading west away from camp. Both trails have signs. You can follow either the boardwalk or Ski Loop as they veer off to the north. After about a quarter mile (0.4 km), you will reach the Chena Hot Springs Winter Trail. The trail continues directly in front of the boardwalk trail. For those using the Ski Loop, you must turn right (east) on the Winter Trail for about 10 yards (meters) before turning left (north) to regain the trail. The trail goes through a mixed boreal forest before reaching a trail junction at about the halfway point (1.5 miles [2.4 km]) of the Ski Loop. The much smaller Ski Loop veers away from the main trail and heads east then turns south. It re-crosses the Winter Trail before completing its 3-mile (5-km) loop back to camp.

At that halfway junction, stay on the main trail to keeping heading toward the summit, which will begin to climb more steeply. The climb is steady but not overly

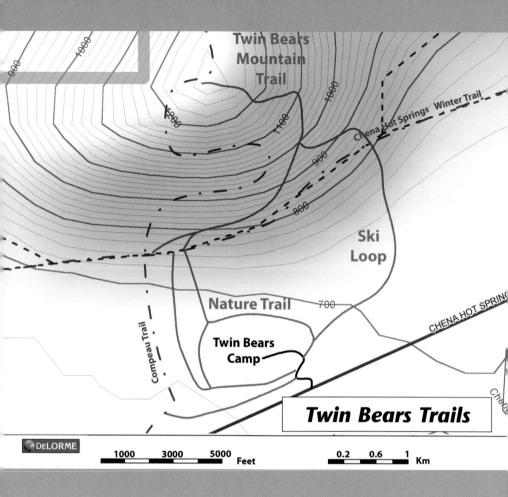

Twin Bears Trails

1000 3000 5000 Feet

0.2 0.6 1 Km

steep. About 50 yards (meters) before the summit a trail breaks away to the right (north). It is about 100 yards (meters) long and connects to the Compeau Trail (Trip 16). During summer, leaves will obscure the view to the south from the summit. You can continue along for another 50 yards (meters) to the north viewpoint, which has better views. You can retrace your steps to return or take the Compeau Trail back. To do that, turn left (west) on the Compeau Trail. The descent will be much gentler. Upon reaching the Winter Trail, turn left (east) until you reach the Twin Bears trails a couple yards (meters) ahead. In addition to the Twin Bears Mountain Trail and the Ski Loop, the camp also has a short nature trail encircling Twin Bears Lake and a multiuse trail running from near the camp entrance to the beginning of the Compeau Trail.

BE AWARE: Off-road vehicles are permitted on some of the trails throughout the year. Some of the trails can be very wet in the summer. Use of the camp facilities is by reservation only. The entrance gate may be locked, but you can park near it.

Please do not block the gate. If the gate is open, you may park at the camp.

MORE ADVENTUROUS? The Chena River State Recreation Area has lots of opportunities for you to choose from, for all different ability levels. From the top of Twin Bears Mountain you may continue farther using the Compeau Trail (Trip 16), which you can hike for miles and miles. (See hike description for directions to Compeau Trail from Twin Bears Mountain.)

DIRECTIONS: Take the Steese Highway (Alaska 2) north out of Fairbanks. The first exit ramp is Chena Hot Springs Road. Take this exit, and follow the road east to Twin Bears Camp at milepost 30. Turn left (north) on the dirt road to get to the camp and trails.

The Ski Loop trail.

You can also park at the Compeau Trail trailhead, just before Twin Bears Camp at milepost 29.6. It is also on the north side of the road. Follow the trail for an eighth of a mile (0.2 km) or less and turn right (east). This multiuse trail will lead you to the entrance of the Twin Bears Camp. Another option is to go farther on the Compeau Trail for a little over a half mile (0.8 km) until you reach the Chena Hot Springs Winter Trail. Turn right (east), and follow it to the Twin Bear trails, which will be less than a quarter mile (0.4 km) ahead.

18 STILES CREEK TRAIL

R/T DISTANCE: 16 miles (25.8 km) with shuttle or 20 miles (32.3 km)

DURATION: 5 to 10 hours or up to 2 days

HIGH POINT: 1,750 feet (533 m)

TOTAL ELEVATION CHANGE: 4,000 feet (1,218 m)

DIFFICULTY: Moderate

ROUTE TYPE: ATV trail (motorized allowed)

BEST SEASON: All year

USGS MAPS: Big Delta D-5, D-6

LAND MANAGER: Alaska Department of Natural Resources (Fairbanks), 907-451-2705

The Chena River State Recreation Area is one of the most popular spots in the region. Within the recreation area, floating the Chena River (Trip 15) and hiking the Angel Rocks (Trip 20) and Granite Tors (Trip 19) trails garner the most visitors. There are, however, lesser-known trails that are worth checking out. The Stiles Creek Trail is one. The trail starts at milepost 31.5 Chena Hot Springs Road. It is open to motorized vehicles and is the same as the Colorado Creek Trail (Trip 16) for the first mile (1.6 km). The trails are well marked (Stiles Creek Trail with red markers and Colorado Creek Trail with blue markers) and even have mileage signs. The Chena Hot Springs Winter Trail (orange markers) parallels Chena Hot Springs Road, and intersects the trail perpendicularly about three-quarters of a mile (1.2 km) in from the road. The first mile (1.6 km) is usually very wet and deeply rutted. At this point, the Stiles Creek Trail breaks away from the Colorado Creek Trail.

The Stiles Creek Trail veers quickly off to the right (east) and begins climbing a hill to reach the ridge. The hill is not overly steep, but it is fairly long. Following the red markers and wide trail, you will head through a dense birch forest. Labrador tea lines the sides of the trail. Eventually gaining the ridge, the trail flattens out and leads eastward. Though relatively flat, the trail keeps climbing and makes its way over

70

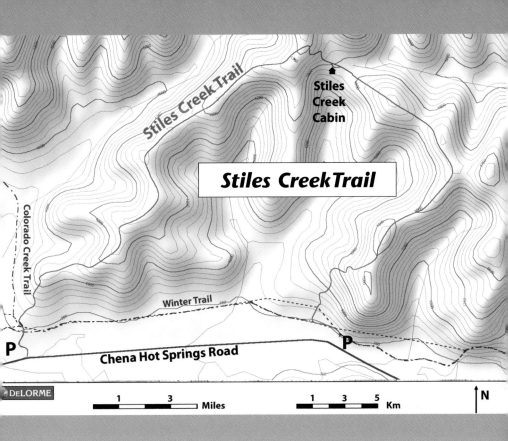

Stiles Creek Trail

Stiles
Creek
Cabin

Stiles Creek Trail

Colorado Creek Trail

Winter Trail

P

P

Chena Hot Springs Road

DeLORME

1   3   Miles

1   3   5   Km

N

rolling hills through a variety of forest types. These hills help shape the composition of the boreal forest and provide nice views of the Colorado Creek valley. Farther along, views of the southern portion of the Chena Dome Trail route are fantastic. After ascending another hill at mile 7.5 (km 12), be sure to follow the red trail markers, as numerous side trails appear. Most of these social trails all lead down off the hill to the same spot, the Stiles Creek Cabin at mile 7.75 (km 12.5).

The cabin is relatively new, and has nice views and a southern exposure. It sleeps up to six people and has a great loft and woodstove. Reservations can be made online through the Alaska State Parks web page, over the phone, or in person. Dead trees can be cut for firewood, but the popularity of this cabin may make that wood source scarce. Water can be found in the summer by following a small trail heading east at the mile 8 (km 13) marker. Use snow in the winter.

Past the cabin the trail continues through rolling hills of birch, spruce, aspen, and even the occasional tamarack. There are more great views over the next few miles, including the Stiles Creek valley to the northeast. Around mile 12 (km 19.3) the Stiles Creek Extension Trail (black and red markers) breaks away to the east and eventually meets Chena Hot Springs Road at milepost 41.6. The Stiles Creek Trail

continues southward. From the hill at mile 13 (km 21), you can look back and see most of the route you have taken. This is also where the trail begins its winding descent off the ridge. Reaching the flats, the trail once again gets wet and rutted. The trail again intersects Chena Hot Springs Winter Trail (orange markers) at mile 14.75 (km 23.8).

At this point, you can go right (west) and follow the Winter Trail to the west for 4 miles (6.4 km) until you reach the overlap of the Stiles and Colorado Creek trails again. From there veer left for another three-quarters of a mile (1.2 km) back

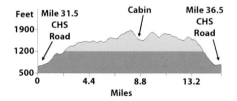

72

to the start. However, in summer this section of the Winter Trail is extremely wet and involves a stream crossing. Alternatively, you can turn left (east), follow the Winter Trail for 1.25 miles (2 km), and end up at the Shooting Range at milepost 36.5, Chena Hot Springs Road. The Winter Trail here is also very wet and rutted, making travel much harder in the summer. The Stiles Creek Trail can be traveled with a mountain bike. It is rooty in spots and there are several places where all but the most expert riders will have to get off and push.

BE AWARE: Off-road vehicles are permitted on the trail throughout the year. The trail is very wet and deeply rutted for the first and last miles. Water is sparse but can be found at mile 8 (km 12.9) by following a small side trail down steeply to the east. Note: the beginning of the Stiles Creek Trail has been rerouted.

MORE ADVENTUROUS? At mile 7.5 (km 12) of the Stiles Creek Trail, test your orienteering and bushwhacking skills to make your way along the high ridge over to the Chena Dome Trail (Trip 21). The Compeau and Colorado Creek trails (Trip 16) might also suit your fancy.

DIRECTIONS: Take the Steese Highway (Alaska 2) north out of Fairbanks. The first exit ramp is to Chena Hot Springs Road. Take this exit, and follow the road east to milepost 31.5. The trailhead for both the Stiles Creek and Colorado Creek (Trip 16) trails is on the left (north) side and is well marked. If you plan to do a shuttle, take your second vehicle 5 miles (8 km) farther east to milepost 36.5. Turn left where a sign marks the Shooting Range . The trailhead can be found about 150 yards (meters) to the northwest, around the small pond.

19 *GRANITE TORS*

Complete Loop

R/T DISTANCE: 15 miles (24.2 km)

DURATION: 6 to 12 hours or 2 to 3 days

HIGH POINT: 3,345 feet (1,019 m)

TOTAL ELEVATION CHANGE: 6,300 feet (1,919 m)

DIFFICULTY: Moderate; rock climbing routes for all levels

ROUTE TYPE: Established trail (nonmotorized)

Three-Mile Loop

R/T DISTANCE: 3 miles (4.8 km)

DURATION: 0.5 to 2 hours

HIGH POINT: 800 feet (244 m)

TOTAL ELEVATION CHANGE: Less than 100 feet (30 m)

DIFFICULTY: Easy

ROUTE TYPE: Established trail (nonmotorized)

BEST SEASON: May to September

USGS MAPS: Big Delta D-5

LAND MANAGER: Alaska Department of Natural Resources (Fairbanks), 907-451-2705

The Granite Tors Trail is one of the few well-known trails in the Interior and one of the most popular in the Chena Hot Springs area. This popularity originated with the rock climbing expeditions into the region dating back to 1969. As its name suggests, the trail boasts a series of granitic towers. These tors offer rock climbing routes for all abilities (5.5 to 5.11); however, just hiking by is enough for most trekkers. The formations are quite spectacular. Portions of both legs, parts of the upper trail, and nearby hills were burned in an intense

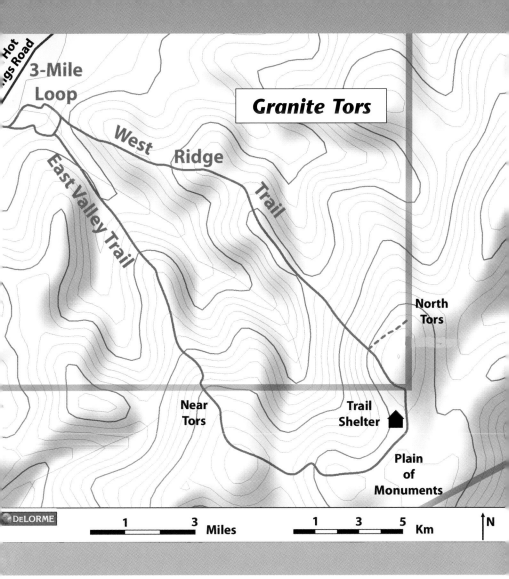

2004 forest fire. A 3-mile loop trail, following the complete loop, has been
rebuilt since the fire and provides an easy, relatively flat walk through muskeg,
the old burn, and tall riparian white spruce—but there are no tors.

From the parking lot, you must cross the bridge and Chena Hot Springs Road to
access either loop trail, which are on the south bank of the Chena River. The trail
heads east, following a levee for about 100 yards (meters) to a trail junction. The West
Ridge Trail heads north, following the Chena. The East Valley Trail keeps heading
east. These two trails are really two ends of the 3-mile (4.8-km) loop and complete
loop that encircles Rock Creek valley. Both the West Ridge and East Valley Trails
take you to the tors. The mile markers are in order following the West Ridge Trail,

75

Tors near the trail shelter.

which rises more gently. However, the East Valley Trail offers you quicker access to some of the tors and gets more traffic. I will describe the route following the West Ridge Trail and the mile markers, making a clockwise loop.

The trail winds its way through the forest lining the bank of the Chena River. Wetter parts of the trail have boardwalk. Shortly after crossing Rock Creek via a foot bridge, the trail veers away from the Chena. A mile (1.6 km) in, before the trail starts climbing, the 3-mile loop trail breaks away to the south (right) and is signed. It leads across the valley floor, connecting to the East Valley Trail. Turn west (right) to head back to the trailhead and complete the short loop on the trail consisting of mainly boardwalk. The distance was measured from the parking lot, so it may feel shorter than the advertised 3 miles (4.8 km).

For those wanting to go to the tors and/or do the complete loop, continue heading east at this junction. The trail will start to climb steadily, but it is not very steep. Once out of the boggy lowlands, the West Ridge Trail takes you through picturesque stands of birch and aspen. The trail climbs 1,000 feet (305 m) in about 2 miles (3.2 km) before reaching the ridgeline.

Though no longer as steep, the trail continues to climb and gets rockier. After topping out at 2,211 feet (673 m), the trail dips, heads over a small rise, and then drops again. Another steady climb awaits you. A third of the way up this 1.5-mile (2.4-km), 1,000-foot (305-m) ascent is a half mile (0.8 km) spur trail, at mile 5.5 (km 9), leading to the North Tors. These tors make a nice side trip or day hike destination but

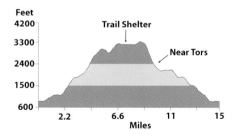

this route can be followed north for miles using rock cairns as markers. At the top of the ascent, the West Ridge Trail heads southward and a bit downhill into a forested saddle. The public-use trail shelter, at mile 7 (km 11.3), is at the far end of this stand of trees. The shelter can not be reserved. It is available on a first-come, first-served basis, so if you are planning to overnight be prepared to camp out.

The Near Tors are closest to the trailhead.

The shelter looks out on the Plain of Monuments. Some 80 million years ago, molten earth made its way toward the surface and then cooled. The granite tors, some towering 100 feet (30 m) over the tundra, were created as the surrounding soft earth eroded, leaving them exposed. There are numerous formations, most with fun names like Dinotors, Asgard, Dragon's Teeth, and Lizard's Eye. Many of the established rock climb-ing routes on the tors are off the

Asgard Tors.

main trail. Use the *Fairbanks Area Climbing Guide* (see Appendix B) to get detailed information on specific routes.

The trail can be very wet from the trail shelter to mile 9 (km 14.5) but especially through mile 8 (km 12.9). This is the easiest place to lose the trail, especially when it is foggy. Trekkers without route-finding abilities (and even those with them) should use caution and consider returning on the same trail if foggy conditions exist. The first set of tors is at mile 7.5 (km 12.1). They are intriguing, but larger and even more spectacular formations lie ahead. Off to the south, at mile 8 (km 12.9), the Asgard Tors will be in view. The trail runs right by the next set, called Second Coming, around mile 8.5 (km 13.7). The trail dips into a forested saddle before coming back up to a barren bench.

Just past mile 9 (km 14.5) is Low Tors, which offers plenty of climbing opportuni-ties. The trail gently heads downhill and veers more northerly. The last set of tors,

Lizard's Eye and Rock 1, are at mile 10 (km 16.1). These are called the Near Tors, because they are just 5 miles (8 km) from the trailhead using the East Valley Trail. Since these are the easiest tors to reach, they have several established routes.

Past the Near Tors, the trail descends steadily and at times steeply. The fire was large and fierce, and the landscape it left behind is impressive. Vegetation recovers quickly after fires, but the more severe a fire, the slower the recovery process. The rejuvenation process here will be interesting to watch. Once off the ridge, the trail follows a boardwalk through a black spruce muskeg for a mile (1.6 km) or more. Near the end of this section, the 3-mile loop trail to the West Ridge Trail (see above) comes in from the right (north). The main (East Valley) trail takes you back to where it meets the West Ridge Trail near the beginning. Head west (straight) back along the levee to reach Chena Hot Springs Road and the parking area.

ALL ROUTES BE AWARE: Rock climbing is an inherently dangerous sport; please use caution. Use of the trail shelter is on a first-come, first-served basis, so do not rely on being able to use it. The trail between miles 7 and 9 (km 11.3 to 14.5) is usually very wet. Above tree line there are places where it is possible to lose the trail, especially if fog sets in. Some wooden tripods have been set up to help guide your way. If you are uncomfortable with route finding and a fog sets in, your best bet is to return the way you came in. A parking fee or Alaska State Park Parking Pass is required at the Granite Tors trailhead.

MORE ADVENTUROUS? The tors have rock climbing routes for all abilities, so go see what you are made of—just be sure to be on belay. Try checking out the North Tors from the spur trail at mile 5.5 (km 9), adding another mile (round trip) to the trek. This trail can be followed for more than 6 miles (9.7 km) (round trip) to another set of small tors. Alternatively, try the hike on snowshoes in March or April (or even May in some years). The Chena Hot Springs area offers a wide array of adventures. Check out some of the other nearby trails. Grapefruit Rocks (Trip 36) and the Mount Prindle area (Trip 29) also offer great rock climbing opportunities.

DIRECTIONS: Take Steese Highway (Alaska 2) north out of Fairbanks. The first exit ramp is to Chena Hot Springs Road. Take this exit and follow the road east to milepost 39.5. Turn left into the Granite Tors Trail Campground, and park in the day-use parking lot. To reach the trailhead, you need to cross the Chena Hot Springs Road bridge over the Chena River (it has a pedestrian path) and then cross Chena Hot Springs Road. There are metal guardrails on both sides, which makes it more difficult with small children or dogs. Traffic comes quickly around the curve so please pay close attention. The trail is wide and follows along the river to start.

20 ANGEL ROCKS AND ANGEL ROCKS TO CHENA HOT SPRINGS TRAILS

Angel Rocks

R/T DISTANCE: 2.5–3.5 miles (4–5.6 km)

DURATION: 1 to 4 hours

HIGH POINT: 1,990 feet (606 m)

TOTAL ELEVATION CHANGE: 2,000 feet (609 m)

DIFFICULTY: Easy to moderate

ROUTE TYPE: Established trail (nonmotorized)

Angel Rocks to Chena Hot Springs

ONE-WAY DISTANCE: 8.7 miles (14 km)

DURATION: 3 to 8 hours

HIGH POINT: 2,580 feet (786 m)

TOTAL ELEVATION CHANGE: 3,180 feet (969 m)

DIFFICULTY: Moderate

ROUTE TYPE: Established trail (nonmotorized)

BEST SEASON: May to September, but can be done the year round

USGS MAPS: Circle A-4, A-5

LAND MANAGER: Alaska Department of Natural Resources (Fairbanks), 907-451-2705

Angel Rocks is probably the most popular trail in the Interior. It is great for people of all ability levels, whether it is to stroll with the family or set up ropes for a difficult rock climb. It is also fairly close to town, but far enough away that you feel like you are definitely out of town. The rock formations are interesting to see and even better to scramble around on. The great views of

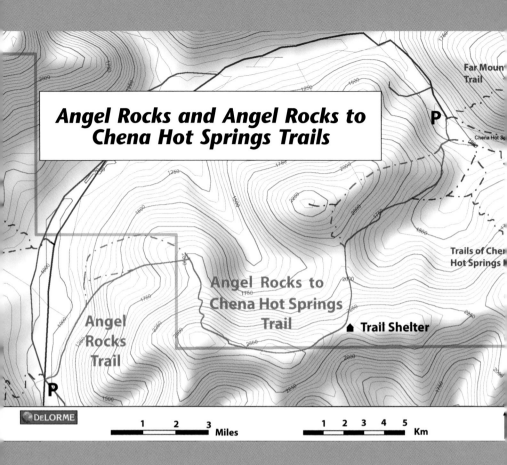

Angel Rocks and Angel Rocks to Chena Hot Springs Trails

Chena Dome (Trip 21) and Angel Creek valley (Trip 22) add to this trip and make for a nice picnic spot.

The two trails (Angel Rocks and Angel Rocks to Chena Hot Springs) are the same for the first 1.2 miles (1.8 km) and begin at the Angel Rocks Trail parking lot. The trail is wide and well maintained at first but quickly turns into a typical footpath. It follows the banks of the upper Chena River for about three-quarters of a mile (1.2 km) before heading up a slope. Though relatively steep, the slope does not last long. Many social trails lead off the main trail but most lead to Angel Rocks. The park has rerouted and shortened part of the trail before the main ascent begins. This cutoff will be on your right and is lined with boardwalk. Hopefully, it will cut down on the number of social trails. The old trail, also known as the "horse trail," continues following the river and meets the new trail just before the steeper parts.

Here, among the rolling hills of boreal forest, are a series of towering rock outcrops that provide great places to catch your breath. The stunning views from Angel Rocks take in Angel Creek valley and the ridge that Chena Dome Trail follows. Watch your footing as you admire the view; many of the outcrops have dangerous drop-offs.

These outcrops are a fun place to boulder and rock climb. The rock is brittle and sharp, which limits the number of rock climbers. There are more than a dozen established routes ranging from 5.5 to 5.11. Check out Stan Justice's *Fairbanks Area Climbing Guide* (see Appendix B) for all the details you will need to know for technical rock climbing.

At the top, 1.2 miles (1.8 km) from the trailhead, the trail crests the ridge. This is a great place for a picnic or to set some rock climbing routes. Search around to find the small cave in the rocks. Most hikers do not go beyond here, simply returning the way they came. Angel Rocks trail is officially a loop and is identified as such at the trailhead, but finding the rest of the trail can be difficult. At the top, the loop trail heads northwest (left). It is relatively clear at first but gets harder to find the farther you go, and it adds little to the hike. If heading back already just does not suit you, there is another option.

Where the trail crests the ridge, the Angel Rocks to Chena Hot Springs Trail continues to the southeast (right). The well-worn trail is marked with flagging, cairns, and posts. It heads up the ridge to the south through a grove of stunted aspens and past one last, small rock outcropping. The trail is a little hard to follow right at the outcropping but continues climbing uphill. With a little more effort, you climb above tree line to the top of the ridge and are rewarded with great views in all directions. On a clear day, the Alaska Range is visible to the south looming over the Granite Tors (Trip 19). The trail follows this ridge to the east. Mile markers track your progress in the alpine areas. Fall is a particularly good time for this trail, as the colors are spectacular and the trail is usually at its driest. The trail rolls gently up and down as you enjoy great ridge walking and panoramic views, including Far Mountain (Trip 24). All too quickly the trail descends a hill into a low pass covered with spruce trees. Here, at mile 5 (km 8), is the Angel Rocks shelter—a small, stout public-use cabin covered in tin. The shelter is available on a first-come, first-served basis.

From the shelter, the trail turns into an old, narrow dirt road that heads downhill through spruce forest into lovely groves of tall birches. At mile 6.5 (km 10.5) the trail splits, though both trails lead to Chena Hot Springs Resort. The lower (right) trail takes you to the resort in less distance (2.2 miles [3.4 km]) and with less hill climbing,

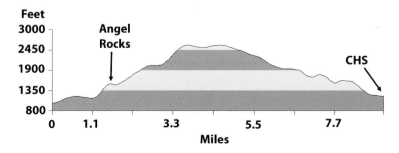

Angel Rocks at leaf-out.

but it can be wet, especially in the spring. Despite being wetter, most people take this lower trail through the muskeg because it is about a half mile (0.8 km) shorter than the upper trail. There are a number of winter trails (see Trip 23) that branch off this lower trail. Follow the homemade signs back to the resort to the west. The upper trail is drier but steeper and longer. The first half mile (0.8 km) of this trail climbs steeply toward Bear Paw Butte, which has nice views. The trail then descends steeply to meet with the lower trail just before the resort. At the resort you can end this great ridge walk with a hearty meal and a well-deserved relaxing soak in the hot springs! How can you beat that?

ALL ROUTES BE AWARE: A parking fee or Alaska State Park Parking Pass is required at the Angel Rocks trailhead. A fee is also required to use the hot springs, which are privately owned. Rock climbing and bouldering are technical and dangerous sports, so know your skill and limits. The end of Angel Rocks to Chena Hot Springs Trail meets with a jumble of other trails that are primarily maintained for winter trail use. Follow the homemade signs leading you west, back to the lodge. Staff at the resort's lodge or activities desk can help you find the trail if you want to start from the resort.

MORE ADVENTUROUS? Winter and spring trekkers can try the trip from Angel Rocks to Chena Hot Springs using skis with skins or snowshoes. In summer, instead of heading downhill at the trail shelter on the Angel Rocks to Chena Hot Springs Trail, follow the ridge east and link up with the Far Mountain Traverse (Trip 24). That will add another 25 miles (40.4 km), so be prepared! Chena Dome (Trip 21) offers a similarly rugged trip as the Far Mountain Traverse but on a well-marked trail.

DIRECTIONS: Take the Steese Highway (Alaska 2) north out of Fairbanks. The first exit ramp is to Chena Hot Springs Road. Take this exit and follow the road east to milepost 49.5. The parking lot for both trails is on the right and is well marked as the Angel Rocks trailhead. If you plan to shuttle a car or bike, take your second vehicle 6 miles (9.7 km) farther down Chena Hot Springs Road to Chena Hot Springs Resort. You can also start at the resort and finish at the Angel Rocks trailhead, but the trailhead at the resort can be difficult to find. Your best bet is to ask at the resort's lodge or activities desk.

21 CHENA DOME TRAIL

R/T DISTANCE: 30 miles (48.4 km), but shorter day trips are possible

DURATION: 2 to 3 days

HIGH POINT: 4,421 feet (1,347 m)

TOTAL ELEVATION CHANGE: 14,100 feet (4,295 m)

DIFFICULTY: Difficult

ROUTE TYPE: Established trail (nonmotorized)

BEST SEASON: May to September

USGS MAPS: Circle A-5

LAND MANAGER: Alaska Department of Natural Resources (Fairbanks), 907-451-2705

The Chena Dome Trail is a classic Interior hike. It starts in typical boreal forest, with stands of spruce, aspen, and birch in various stages of post-fire regeneration. Then it heads up to bald ridges, which are covered in alpine and offer commanding views. The loop is a demanding trip, but pleasant day hikes can be had from either trailhead.

The loop, which follows ridges that encircle the Angel Creek valley, is signed with mile markers that begin at the northern trailhead (milepost 50.5, Chena Hot Springs Road). I will describe the hike from this trailhead, though you can start at either one. The trail heads west out of the parking lot and takes you to the Chena Hot Springs Winter Trail (orange markers) after about 100 yards (meters). Veer left (south) on this trail. This section can be really wet, but it lasts only about 150 yards (meters). Turn right (west) onto the Angel Creek Trail (yellow markers, Trip 22). After about 10 yards (meters) Chena Dome Trail will break off to the north (right) along wooden planking. Signs for the trail can be in disrepair.

The first 3 miles (4.8 km) of trail gently climb westward, winding slowly through a fairly recent burn. Aspen are actively recolonizing the area and can obscure the trail. Life returns quickly to these burned areas. The trail can also be easy to lose where the fire completely denuded the slopes, especially on switchbacks.

At mile 3 (km 4.8) the trail climbs more steeply out of the boreal forest onto a rocky alpine ridge. This is a nice destination for day hikers, offering scenic vistas and rock outcrops to explore. To the east is Chena Hot Springs (Trip 23) and Far Mountain (Trip 24). To the southeast is Angel Rocks (Trip 20.)

Past mile 3 (km 4.8) the trail heads directly up some steep pitches. The substrate changes to rock, and exposed alpine ridges replace boreal forest. Beautiful, intricate, and delicate alpine flowers, such as the wooly lousewort, replace fireweed and other forest flowers as you climb higher. The pitch finally lessens and follows an open ridge with panoramic views. The summit of Chena Dome is in full view here.

The trail between mile marker 7 and 8 (km 11.3 and 12.9) may be the most difficult of the entire loop. A low saddle here creates a steep descent followed quickly by a steep, unrelenting climb. At mile 8.5 (km 13.7) remnants of a military plane crash from the 1950s are scattered about. Please do not disturb any of these artifacts. A small freshwater spring sometimes runs out of the south slope here, but the water should be treated.

Beyond the plane wreckage the trail climbs and descends each knob along the ridge, as though it were following a roller coaster track. The trail reaches the summit of Chena Dome—the highest point along the route at 4,421 feet (1,347 m)—at mile 10.5 (km 16.9). As with many domes in the Interior, the summit is marred by a communications tower and building. However, the panoramic views easily make up for this. This is a great place to stop, have lunch, and enjoy the views. Some hikers choose to return the way they came, which makes for a 21-mile (34-km) trip. Completing the loop is 9 miles (14.5 km) longer, but it offers new terrain to explore.

Miles 11–16 (km 17.7–25.8) head generally southward along the ridge. The trail here is less strenuous, being relatively flat and avoiding climbs over every knob on the ridge. At mile 14.5 (km 23.4) you will run into the Little Chena Dozer Line that was errantly put in during the record-breaking fire season of 2004 (the ridge is not vegetated here, so there was no need for a firebreak). The trail and dozer line continue south until mile 16 (km 25.8) where the trail veers off to the east, down a steep hill. The dozer line continues south, eventually hooking up with the Compeau Trail (Trip 16). The dozer trail also continues past mile 14.5 (km 23.4) to the west.

A public-use trail shelter sits at the bottom of a saddle at mile 16.75 (km 27). The building is small and somewhat drafty, but it offers decent protection during inclement weather. It can sleep two comfortably, four in a pinch, and has a woodstove, though wood is scarce nearby. The shelter is available on a first-come, first-served basis. Do not rely on using it.

Leaving the shelter, the trail follows a series of ups and downs. The bottoms of the saddles are forested, where game trails intersect the main trail perpendicularly. At mile 22.9 (km 37) a spur trail heads steeply down 1.5 miles (2.4 km) to the upper Angel Creek Cabin (Trip 22). This marked trail allows access to the cabin in summer, as the valley trail is typically too wet. Just past the spur trail intersection is probably the steepest part of the main trail, though this section is mercifully short. The summit of this knob, at mile 23.5 (km 37.9), is 3,400 feet (1,036 m) and offers great views of Chena Dome and the surrounding area. This summit is a good destination for a long day hike (13 miles [20.9 km]) from the southern trailhead. Bald outcrops at miles 26.5 and 27 (km 42.8 and 43.6) also offer good views. These are about 3 miles (4.8 km) from the southern trailhead, making for good destinations for day hikers. By mile 28 (km 45.2) you are back in the deciduous forest.

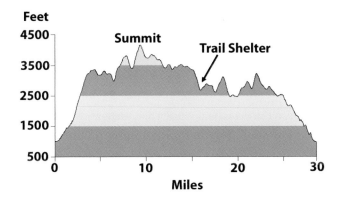

Long stretches of ridge walking.

The trail seems to split here. Follow the left fork, as the right one quickly disappears. The trail slowly continues downhill and may be a bit overgrown in places. The last 2 miles (3.2 km) of trail seem to wander aimlessly at an unnecessarily low gradient. Eventually, the trail crosses a small stream and shortly after that the Chena River comes into view. The trailhead is just ahead. The northern trailhead is 1.5 miles (2.4 km) up Chena Hot Springs Road at milepost 50.5.

The trail shelter during an unusually warm May.

BE AWARE: Watch the weather carefully when ridge hiking. Rogue storms can quickly roll into the region, bringing sleet, snow, rain, or hail—sometimes all of them. Whiteout conditions, from either snow or clouds, are common in the alpine. Only people experienced in using a compass and map should take on an adventure like this. Water is often scarce along this trail. Small springs may be found at miles 8.5 and 14.5 (km 13.7 and 23.4).

Patches of snow or small pools created by melting snow can often be found between miles 9 and 18 (km 14.5 and 29), but these water sources are not guaranteed. The earlier in the year the adventure is attempted, the greater the likelihood of finding water. However, in late spring and early summer the weather is harsher and the ridges could have too much snow. Plan carefully. This is a difficult trail with lots of ups and downs, so be prepared for a strenuous hike. Consider a relaxing soak at Chena Hot Springs Resort to ease your aches!

The summit of Chena Dome from the southeast.

MORE ADVENTUROUS? This is a tough trip, but if you want more try doing the entire loop in a day. Experienced, light, and fast uber-athletes can complete the loop in a grueling sixteen-hour day. If you can handle that, you might be ready to check into the Alaska Mountain Wilderness Classic race series. Another idea is to bushwhack over to the Stiles Creek Trail (Trip 18) and complete your adventure on that trail. Bald ridges beckon adventurers in many directions. The north ridge off of Chena Dome offers good hiking. The Far Mountain Traverse (Trip 24) may also be appealing. You can also follow the Little Chena Dozer Line and connect to the Compeau Trail (Trip 16).

DIRECTIONS: Take the Steese Highway (Alaska 2) north out of Fairbanks. The first exit ramp is to Chena Hot Springs Road. Take this exit and follow the road east to milepost 50.5. Signs direct you to the trailhead. The far end of the loop is at milepost 49. This trailhead is not as well marked. You can stash another vehicle or bicycle there to save you the walk back to the start, or you can use this trailhead to start the loop. Day hikes can be started from either trailhead.

22 ANGEL CREEK TRAIL

R/T DISTANCE: 7.2–13.4 miles (11.5–21.6 km)

DURATION: 3 to 7 hours or 2 to 3 days

HIGH POINT: 1,400 feet (426 m)

TOTAL ELEVATION CHANGE: Up to 1,000 feet (305 m)

DIFFICULTY: Easy to moderate

ROUTE TYPE: Established trail (motorized allowed)

BEST SEASON: September to May

USGS MAPS: Circle A-5

LAND MANAGER: Alaska Department of Natural Resources (Fairbanks), 907-451-2705

Angel Creek Trail is a winter trail up the valley encircled by the Chena Dome Trail (Trip 21). It parallels Angel Creek its entire length and winds through a typical boreal forest in various stages of post-fire regeneration. The bottomlands have stunted black spruce, but drier areas have nice groves of birch and white spruce. The trail gently gains elevation over its course but never reaches the bald ridges of the Chena Dome Trail. Angel Creek Trail is easily cross-country skied, hiked, or snowshoed. It is primarily one snowmachine track wide, so is not good for skate skiing. The trail is good for a day ski trip, but by staying at one or both of the public-use cabins along the trail you can extend your trip.

The trail heads west out of the parking lot and takes you on the Chena Hot Springs Winter Trail (orange markers) after about 100 yards (meters). Head south (left) on this trail for about 150 yards (meters). Turn right (west) onto the Angel Creek Trail (yellow markers).

The trail is in a bowl surrounded by the bald ridges, which make for nice views. The scenery and forest get nicer the farther you go. There is a public-use cabin at mile 3.6 (km 5.8), just off the north side of the trail. It is small for four people but has a woodstove and is comfortable. Wood from standing dead trees nearby can be

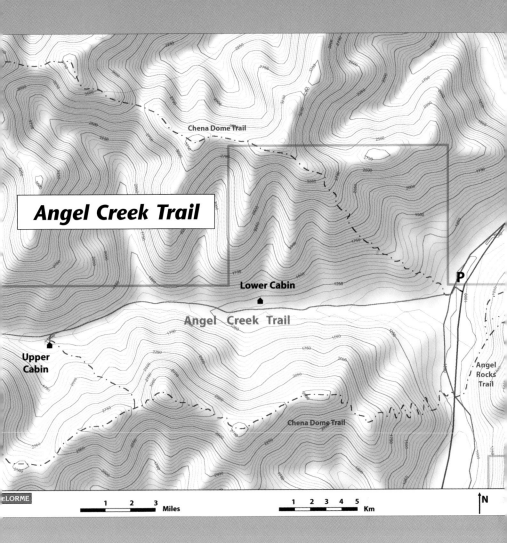

Angel Creek Trail

Chena Dome Trail

Lower Cabin

Angel Creek Trail

Upper
Cabin

Chena Dome Trail

P

Angel
Rocks
Trail

DELORME

1 2 3
Miles

1 2 3 4 5
Km

N

used for fuel. The cabin is right off the trail so be careful with children and loose dogs, as snowmachiners and dog teams can be traveling fast down the trail.

The trail receives slightly less use farther up and thus conditions are often not as smooth as below. The trail is also steeper and has more ups and downs, but it is still relatively flat and easy going. At mile 6.4 (km 10.4) a spur trail turns off and goes about a quarter mile (0.4 km) to reach the upper cabin. Use the reroute to the west to avoid overflow and a stream crossing by using the beaver dam. Please use this spur trail only if you have reserved the cabin or have an emergency. Privacy helps preserve the remote character and wilderness setting of this cabin. The spur trail continues past the cabin reaching mile 22.9 (km 37) of the Chena Dome Trail (Trip 21), but the 1.5-mile (2.4-km) climb to the ridge is steep. The main trail continues past the junction and eventually dead-ends up the valley. To return, simply follow the trail back to the trailhead.

Sunrise along Angel Creek.

BE AWARE: Watch for snowmachines and dog teams on this narrow, multiuse trail. Clear the trail if you see a dog team coming. Keep track of your dogs if they are loose. Temperatures in the valley can drop dramatically overnight. Heavy snowfalls can also make traveling much slower. Pay attention to the weather. Angel Creek may be frozen. Do not rely on it for water. Be prepared to melt snow. Of course, beware the yellow snow! Note: this trail is going to be renamed the Angel Creek Valley Trail. A new, year-round, sustainable trail is being built along the hillside called the Angel Creek Hillside Trail. The existing winter trail will be renamed the Angel Creek Valley Trail.

MORE ADVENTUROUS? The Chena Dome Trail (Trip 21) can be reached from the upper cabin, though the climb is very steep. Snowshoes or crampons may be needed. Experts may want to head west, cross the Chena Dome Trail, and connect with the Colorado Creek Trail (Trip 16). For a longer outing, the Chena Hot Springs Winter Trail (orange markers) can be followed northeast to the Chena Hot Springs Resort, about 6 miles (9.7 km), or southwest all the way to Two Rivers. For longer adventures, try out the White Mountains (Trip 34).

DIRECTIONS: Take the Steese Highway (Alaska 2) north out of Fairbanks. The first exit ramp is to Chena Hot Springs Road. Take this exit and follow the road east to milepost 50.5. Signs direct you to the trailhead.

23 TRAILS OF CHENA HOT SPRINGS RESORT

R/T DISTANCE: Up to 5 miles (8 km) or more if linking trails

DURATION: 1 to 4 hours

HIGH POINT: 2,600 feet (792 m)

TOTAL ELEVATION CHANGE: Up to 2,600 feet (792 m)

DIFFICULTY: Easy to moderate

ROUTE TYPE: Established trails (mix of motorized and nonmotorized)

BEST SEASON: November to March

USGS MAPS: Circle A-5

LAND MANAGER: Chena Hot Springs Resort, 907-451-8104 or 800-478-4681

The Chena Hot Springs Resort has a number of trails that are best suited for classical skiing and snowshoeing. Walkers and leashed dogs are also welcome. The various trails wind through birch hillsides, streams lined with white spruce, stunted black spruce stands, and muskegs. The trails can be linked to make for longer outings. The opportunity to soak in the hot springs after you are done makes this a great winter outing regardless of the temperature.

To reach most of the trails head south past the lodge and the pool building. Cross the creek on one of the bridges and follow the trail to the left (southeast). The Ridge Trail, best suited for snowshoeing (or hiking in summer), breaks off just past the old ski hill to the right (south). Look for small wooden signs. Do not head toward the old ski hill. The Ridge Trail, marked with red markers, is at first a dirt road that climbs somewhat steeply. After about 100 yards (meters) the trail breaks from the road and heads south. It is signed where the road veers sharply to the right (west). After a short stretch, the Hillside Cutoff Trail breaks to the south. To stay on the Ridge Trail veer right (southwest) and uphill. It continues a steady ascent until reaching the summit of Bear Paw Butte about 2 miles (3.2 km) from the start. There are nice viewpoints all along the trail. The condition of the trail in winter depends

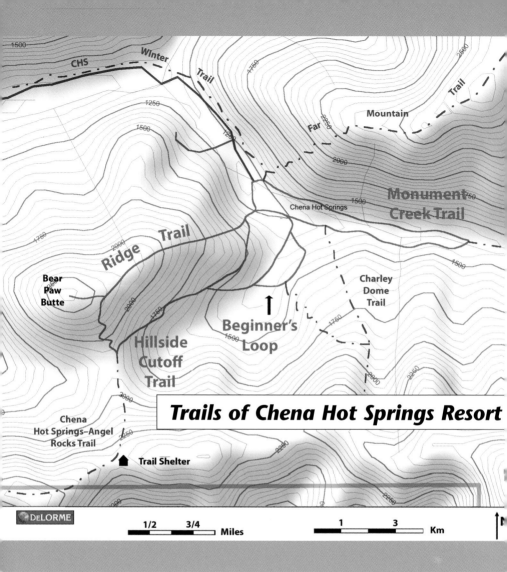

Trails of Chena Hot Springs Resort

| 1/2 | 3/4 | Miles | 1 | 3 | Km |

on how many people have used it. It may be packed or covered with loose snow. From the top, at 2,465 feet (751 m), are good views of the upper Monument Creek valley and Far Mountain (Trip 24). The last section to the top is used less and not well marked so it may require some route finding. This should be fairly easy, barring fog or a whiteout.

To return you can retrace your steps or continue following the Ridge Trail off the summit to the south. The trail heads steeply downhill for about a half mile (0.8 km) before coming to a trail junction. The trail to the right (south) is the Angel Rocks to Chena Hot Springs Trail (Trip 20). A public-use trail shelter is a mile (1.6 km) up this route. To the left, the trail heads east down the Hillside Cutoff Trail. This trail passes through extensive stands of towering birches before dropping into lower and

Snowshoeing up to Bear Paw Butte.

flatter areas just before rejoining the Ridge Trail. About halfway down the Hillside Cutoff Trail is a link to the Beginner's Loop trail.

The Beginner's Loop is more popularly reached from the Monument Creek Trail about a quarter mile (0.4 km) past where the Ridge Trail breaks from it. Like the Ridge Trail, the Beginner's Loop also breaks from the Monument Creek Trail to the right (south). The trail is best suited for classical skiing and is relatively flat. It traverses black spruce stands and muskegs for about a 1-mile (1.6 km) round trip. As noted above, the Hillside Cutoff Trail can be reached from the southwest corner of the loop.

The relatively flat Monument Creek Trail runs along the base of the hills and parallels Monument Creek. It makes for a good walk, snowshoe, or classical ski. It goes past the Charley Dome Trail for about 1.5 miles (2.4 km), where it crosses the creek via a bridge. On the other side of the creek the trail splits. One leg generally heads east farther up the valley for miles. The other leg loops back to the resort on the north side of the creek, passing Far Mountain Trail (Trip 24). Re-cross the creek on the road bridge. Once back, it is great to go for a soak to warm those cold bones.

BE AWARE: Charley Dome Trail and the yurt on the ridge is for use only by resort clients. Check with the Activities Desk about their use. Snowmachines are allowed on some trails. Dog mushers also use these trails. Try to get off the trail to allow them by, especially if you have a dog with you. These trails are generally too wet to use during the summer season. However, the Ridge and Hillside Cutoff trails can be dry enough to be hiked in the summer. A fee is required to use the hot springs. Staff can help you find trails and supply trail maps.

MORE ADVENTUROUS? Try snowshoeing the Angel Rocks to Chena Hot Springs Trail from Angel Rocks (Trip 20). The Chena Hot Springs Winter Trail (orange markers) runs the length of the recreation area to the resort. It parallels Chena Hot Springs Road but is usually far off the road. Walkers, dogs, and skiers can use the multiuse trail, which is frequently used by dog mushers and snowmachiners. If you are looking for a longer, wilder ski trip, try the White Mountains (Trip 34). During summer, the Angel Rocks to Chena Hot Springs Trail and the Far Mountain Trail and Traverse (Trip 24) are great options. Truly intrepid hikers, with very good navigational and backcountry skills, may want to hike all the way to Twelvemile Summit, which is on the Steese Highway.

DIRECTIONS: Take the Steese Highway (Alaska 2) north out of Fairbanks. The first exit ramp is to Chena Hot Springs Road. Take this exit, and follow the road east until you reach Chena Hot Springs Resort at the road's terminus (milepost 56.5).

24 *FAR MOUNTAIN TRAIL AND TRAVERSE*

Far Mountain Trail

R/T DISTANCE: 5 miles (8 km)

DURATION: 2 to 5 hours

HIGH POINT: 2,700 feet (823 m)

TOTAL ELEVATION CHANGE: 3,000 feet (914 m)

DIFFICULTY: Moderate

ROUTE TYPE: Established trail (motorized allowed)

Far Mountain Traverse

R/T DISTANCE: 26 miles (42 km)

DURATION: 2 to 4 days

HIGH POINT: 4,694 feet (1,430 m)

TOTAL ELEVATION CHANGE: 14,600 feet (4,447 m)

DIFFICULTY: Difficult to expert

ROUTE TYPE: Route (nonmotorized)

BEST SEASON: May to September

USGS MAPS: Circle A-4, A-5

LAND MANAGERS: Chena Hot Springs Resort, 907-451-8104 or 800-478-4681; Alaska Department of Natural Resources (Fairbanks), 907-451-2705

The Far Mountain Trail is a short, steep trail that runs from spruce forest through birch stands and eventually up to sweeping vistas in the alpine. Atop the climb are some small but interesting tors. The traverse takes adventurers beyond the trail along a primarily alpine route to the summit of Far Mountain (4,694 feet [1,430 m]). The route continues past the mountain and completely encircles the Monument Creek watershed, returning back to

Far Mountain Trail and Traverse

Far Mountain Traverse

Far Mountain

CHS
Winter
Trail

Far
Mountain
Trail

CHS
Road

Chena Hot Springs

Monument Creek Trail

CHS–Angel
Rocks Trail

Far Mountain Traverse

DeLORME

1   3   Miles

1   3   5   Km

the start. The traverse has some spectacular alpine ridge walking, but it is an extremely strenuous trip with lots of big ups and downs.

From the Chena Hot Springs Resort parking lot, head toward Chena Hot Springs Road. Go over the Monument Creek bridge and take a right onto the dirt road just before the resort entrance. Turn left after about 20 yards (meters) onto Chena Hot Springs Winter Trail (orange markers) and Far Mountain Trail. Going straight on the road will put you on Monument Creek Trail. After about 50 yards (meters) on Chena Hot Springs Winter Trail, Far Mountain Trail breaks away to the right (northeast).

The trail heads uphill and has some steep pitches. Some of the steepest are right at the beginning, which reduces the number of people on the trail. Turn around as you catch your breath, as good views of the Chena Dome (Trip 21) area arrive quickly. The climb up to the ridge is 1,600 vertical feet (487 m), so you may have to catch your breath a lot. The spruce thin out as you go, giving way to more birches and then shrubs. The gradient moderates, but it is still steep. After about 2 miles (3.2 km), the trail forks in front of a large rock outcrop. This is a good place to stop and soak in the sights or take a lunch break. The left (west) trail heads toward the North Fork of the Chena River. The Far Mountain Trail heads right (east) and reaches a set of interesting tors, another great spot for lunch or rock climbing. Be sure to have the proper gear, training, and expertise for the latter activity. The views from here are great. You can see the entire Monument Creek watershed to the south and east, Chena Dome to the west, and the upper North Fork of the Chena River, the Birch Creek (Trip 31) drainage, and even Pinnell Mountain (Trip 32) far off to the north. This is a good spot to turn around for a day trip.

The Far Mountain Traverse follows the trail to the northeast. The trail peters out, but the going is good as you are in the alpine much of the time. There are plenty of ups and downs but nothing more than a few hundred feet. Past Peak 2842, there is a flattish, burned-over area with toppled trees that can slow you down. Beyond here trees are found only in troughs between minor peaks and are scattered enough that they should not inhibit your progress too much. The next two peaks (3602 and 3415) can be skirted by side-hilling, which saves a lot of climbing. However, the south sides of both are pretty steep and covered with loose boulders, so you may want to stay on top. The views along this alpine ridge are fantastic. Rugged, remote country is all around.

Past Peak 3415 (mile 5.5 [km 9]) the slopes are steep, so you should stay on the ridgetop. At mile 10 (km 16) the ridge ascends to the southeast, providing views of the upper Middle Fork of the Chena River, the upper Salcha River, and even into Yukon–Charley Rivers National Preserve. At mile 10.5 (km 16.7) the ridge drops down to 4,000 feet (1,218 m). Then the ridge turns south, climbs to 4,400 feet (1,340 m), and heads southwest. There are a couple of small drops before the final climb to the summit at mile 13 (km 21). The views in all directions are fantastic. The Alaska Range can be seen to the south, Chena Hot Springs and Chena Dome to the west, the Pinnell area to the north, and the remote, rugged country of the upper Salcha River to the east. Unfortunately, because of Far Mountain's commanding position, the summit has a fairly large communications facility.

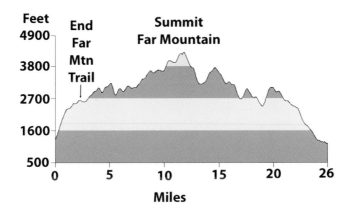

The top of the Far Mountain Trail.

Like the first part of the hike, the second half of the route has plenty of ups and downs, but these are tougher. These climbs feel like going over separate peaks, rather than hiking over a series of knobs along a ridgetop. From the summit, follow the west-trending ridge for about a half mile (0.8 km). Turn south and drop down to the low, rocky saddle 1,200 feet (365 m) below the summit. An old mining road leading from Monument Creek over to Ottertail Creek crosses the saddle at its low point. Just beyond the road, the saddle has interesting rock formations and small tors. If you are low on water, this is a good place to refill. Small depressions in the rocks may have water, or you can use the road to hike down to one of the creeks.

From the saddle, there is a steady 700-foot (213-m) climb past a series of rock outcrops to the summit of Peak 4127 at mile 16 (km 25.8). Take in views of the Granite Tors (Trip 19) as you rest for the next set of ups and downs. Head south off this peak for about 1.5 miles (2.4 km), descending down to 3,400 feet (1,036 m) and then back up to 3,900 feet (1,188 m) at mile 17.5 (km 28.2). The ridge veers west at this point. The route drops to 2,900 feet (883 m) at mile 18.5 (km 29.8) before climbing back to 3,400 feet (1,036 m) at mile 19 (km 30.6). From here the route descends down to 2,500 feet (661 m) at mile 20.5 (km 33) and gets back into the trees. Be prepared for some minor bushwhacking. You also want to prepare for the nearly 1,000-foot

(305-m) climb to the next summit. At this stage, your legs will probably be tired, and this moderate climb may feel like scaling Denali.

It is nearly all downhill from Peak 3327 at mile 22 (km 35.5), though there are a couple very small climbs. After another mile down the ridge you can see the Charley Dome Trail, which is part of Chena Hot Springs Resort winter trail system (Trip 23). The yurt atop the ridge is open only to resort guests and then only from November to March. Follow Charley Dome Trail from the yurt down to the valley floor, which can be very wet. Turn left (west) when you intersect the wide trail coming in from the east. Stay on the main trail (road) and the resort will be about a half mile (0.8 km) ahead of you.

ALL ROUTES BE AWARE: The traverse is a "route" and should only be attempted by people with backcountry skills and stout legs. Spring can come a bit later to Chena Hot Springs than to Fairbanks and snow patches can persist well into summer in places along the traverse. I would recommend bringing snowshoes if you are going to attempt the traverse early in the season. Water can be scarce in mid- and late summer for long stretches. A couple of short stretches require bushwhacking.

MORE ADVENTUROUS? You need help. The Chena Dome Trail (Trip 21) offers a similar type of challenge but is not more adventurous. You may want to check out Appendix A, "Expert Interior Favorites to Discover on Your Own", at the end of the book.

DIRECTIONS: Take the Steese Highway (Alaska 2) north out of Fairbanks. The first exit ramp is to Chena Hot Springs Road. Take this exit and follow the road east until you reach Chena Hot Springs Resort at the road's terminus (milepost 56.5).

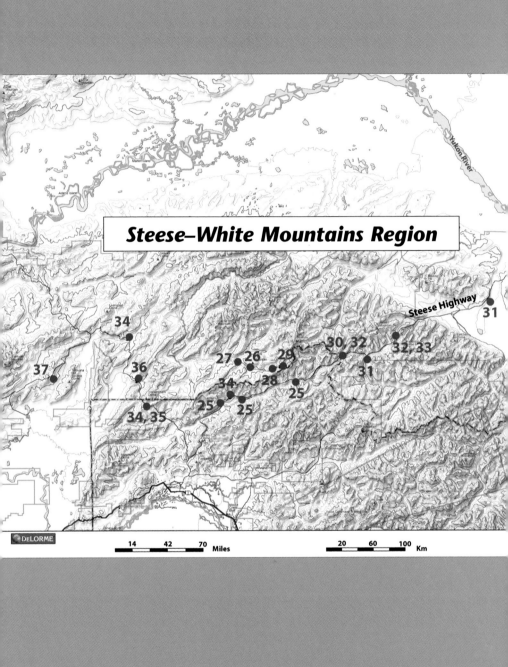

Steese–White Mountains Region

Steese–White Mountains Region

The Steese National Conservation Area (NCA)
and White Mountains National Recreation Area
(NRA), both overseen by the federal Bureau of
Land Management, comprise the majority of
land in this region, though some trips described
are on state land. The White Mountains NRA
is widely known for its lengthy multiuse trails
used especially by snowmachiners and mushers.
However, these trails and the extensive public-
use cabin system are great for intrepid cross-
country skiers. While lesser used in summer,
the White Mountains also offer great hiking
opportunities and a float down Beaver Creek, a
National Wild and Scenic River. The Steese NCA
has a National Wild River, Birch Creek, and the
Pinnell Mountain Trail, probably the best-known
hike in the Interior. Only one to two hours away
from Fairbanks, the Steese–White Mountains
region offers a slew of great hikes, floats, and
skis, as well as probably the best and most
accessible rock climbing in the region. I have
included Tolovana Hot Springs in this section,
even though it is not in the area, because the
White Mountains are its nearest neighbor.

25 CHATANIKA RIVER

ONE-WAY DISTANCE: 10–60 miles (16–97 km) with many options

DURATION: 3 hours or up to 3 to 4 days

HIGH POINT: 1,400 feet (426 m)

TOTAL ELEVATION CHANGE: up to 850 feet (259 m)

DIFFICULTY: Moderate

ROUTE TYPE: Float (class I, a few class II spots in high water), suitable for canoes, rafts, or kayaks (motorized allowed)

BEST SEASON: May to September

USGS MAPS: Circle A-6, B-5, B-6; Livengood A-1, A-2

LAND MANAGERS: Alaska Department of Natural Resources (Fairbanks), 907-451-2705; Bureau of Land Management (Fairbanks), 907-474-2200

The Chatanika River offers a variety of options, from half-day to multiple-day floats. The river parallels and crosses the Steese Highway. The primarily class I waters are lined with towering white spruce. Hillsides covered in birch trees drop right down to its banks. The float options are surprisingly diverse in their scenery and technical difficulty. Although the road is close to the river in a number of spots, the river has a fairly wild feel to it. The number of sweepers, strainers, logjams, and sharp turns keep you vigilant throughout most of the float and make it interesting for intermediate paddlers.

The Upper Chatanika River State Recreation Site at milepost 39, Steese Highway, is a popular place to launch a float trip. From here to the Elliott Highway bridge is 19 river miles (30.7 km). The gradient is about 12 feet per mile (2.3 meters per km) over this stretch, so the water can be moving fast, especially in the spring or at other high-water times. The 19 miles (30.7 km) can be done in as little as four hours with some paddling during high water, but plan for about eight hours during "normal" conditions.

There is often a logjam right at the Steese Highway bridge that has to be portaged on the river right (north side). The first few turns out of the campground can be

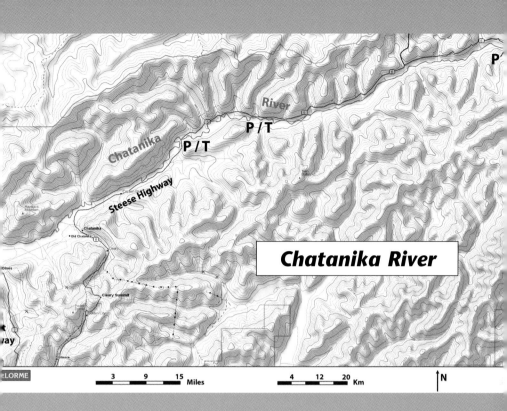

Chatanika River

3   9   15
Miles

4   12   20
Km

↑N

tricky, and sweepers spanning the entire river can be found for the first 6–8 miles (10–13 km), especially early in the season before people clear them. The river is cutting new paths for itself, so the ability to read the river is essential. During high water, a few short sections of riffles can be class II. About 5 river miles (8 km) from the bridge is a roadside turnout (milepost 34.8) that can be used as a put-in or take-out to make for shorter trips. A bridge near river mile 8 (km 13) spans the river, and a couple of houses can be seen near Chatanika. After that, the river feels fairly remote and you should not see too many structures until just before the Elliott Highway bridge. The official take-out is on river right (north) but the south side may be better at high water levels.

Further upstream, the stretch between Long Creek and the recreation site is about 11 river miles (17.7 km). Although the gradient is a little less here, the river is still moving pretty fast. This stretch is a little less technical than just below the recreation site put-in and tends to have fewer logjams and sweepers. Even though the stretch is almost entirely flat water, the numerous big turns keep you on your toes. Depending on water conditions and how much you like to paddle, this section can take three to six hours.

Loading up for a spring float.

The Chatanika can be floated from as high upriver as milepost 60, Steese Highway (Cripple Creek Campground). These upper 30 miles (48.4 km) of river are for more experienced paddlers only. The river is narrower, which increases the possibility of downed trees spanning the river. In all but the highest water levels, you will likely have to drag or line boats in places. To counterbalance these negatives, the river is seldom used this high and has more of a wild feel.

BE AWARE: There are many sweepers, strainers, and logjams; this float is not for beginners. Although the river is primarily class I, obstacles in the river require constant attention for almost the entire float. There is frequently a large logjam just below the Upper Chatanika River State Recreation Site that needs to be portaged (river right, north side). Fallen trees can span the river and require portaging elsewhere as well. There are a couple of private houses on the riverbank near Chatanika and a couple of private cabins along the way, but most of the sections have a pretty wild feel to them. Please respect private property.

MORE ADVENTUROUS? Keep floating past the Elliott Highway bridge for another 30 miles (48.4 km) or so. At that point you reach the end of the 14-Mile Trail, a rough dirt road that starts at milepost 14 of Murphy Dome Road. Allow two to three days to reach there from the Elliott Highway bridge. The 14-Mile Trail is very bumpy and unmaintained. Be sure to have a really good four-wheel-drive vehicle for the shuttle.

If that adventure is still not enough, you can continue on the Chatanika River. It flows into the Tolovana River, which dumps into the Tanana River, where you can get out at Manley Hot Springs. The gradient of the Chatanika River drops to almost nil in the Minto Flats, just past 14-Mile Trail, so be prepared for slow going and route-finding challenges. Allow three to five days to cover the 45 miles (73 km) or so from 14-Mile Trail to Manley.

Another alternative is to float in a packraft from the Elliott Highway bridge to Murphy Dome Trail (Trip 6), just before the 14-Mile Trail terminus. From there hike to the top of Murphy Dome.

DIRECTIONS: Take the Steese Highway (Alaska 2) north out of Fairbanks to the town of Fox, 11 miles (18 km) away.

If you plan to drop off a car at the Elliott Highway bridge: In Fox, go straight past the weigh station and you will be on the Elliott Highway (still Alaska 2). The Chatanika River bridge is at milepost 11. The Lower Chatanika State Recreation Area (LCSRA) is just after the bridge on the left (west) and has a parking area for river access. During high-water levels that parking area may be flooded, so it may be best to park on the south side of the bridge. To get there, turn off the Elliott about 100 yards (meters) before (south of) the bridge to the west (right heading south from the LCSRA or left heading north from Fox). After dropping your shuttle vehicle, head back to Fox.

To get to the Steese Highway put-in: Turn east (right from the south, left from the north) in Fox to get on the Steese Highway (now called Alaska 6, but miles are counted from Fairbanks—I can not explain). There are many places to put in or take out along the Steese: milepost 34.8 (large turnout on north side; bring boats upstream 50 yards to avoid the steep bank and swift current); milepost 39 (Upper Chatanika State Recreation Site); milepost 45.5 (Long Creek Trading Post; park here and line your boat south on Long Creek through the large culvert under the Steese Highway to the Chatanika); milepost 55.9 (gravel pit); and milepost 60 (Cripple Creek Campground).

26 TABLE TOP MOUNTAIN TRAIL

R/T DISTANCE: 3 miles (4.8 km)

DURATION: 1 to 3 hours

HIGH POINT: 3,130 feet (953 m)

TOTAL ELEVATION CHANGE: 2,400 feet (731 m)

DIFFICULTY: Easy

ROUTE TYPE: Established trail (nonmotorized)

BEST SEASON: May to September

USGS MAPS: Circle B-6

LAND MANAGER: Bureau of Land Management (Fairbanks), 907-474-2200

Table Top Mountain is a pleasant day hike for all age groups, and it offers sweeping views of the Nome Creek and Beaver Creek (Trip 27) valleys. The trail does not reach the summit, but with a slight detour you can get there to enjoy great views of the Mount Prindle (Trip 29) area to the east and the jagged limestone peaks of the White Mountains (Trip 34) to the west.

The hike begins at a signed location off the Nome Creek Road. The trail is not a true loop, but the two trailheads are only about 100 yards (meters) apart. Nothing is gained or lost by starting at one trailhead or the other, but the parking area is larger at the western one farther along Nome Creek Road. I will describe the trip from there.

The trail climbs moderately through forest burned in 2004 during a record-breaking fire year. It will be interesting to return to this trail and see how the vegetation recovers. The fire left plenty of standing dead spruce, so be careful of falling and fallen trees. The climb is steady but not difficult. In wetter places, the fire did not damage the forest. The juxtaposition of large spruce and completely denuded slopes is fascinating. Keep your eyes open for hawk owls on the prowl. After less than a mile (1.6 km) of generally heading north and uphill, the trail turns southeast and levels out. Here it follows the base of a steep hill before eventually heading down.

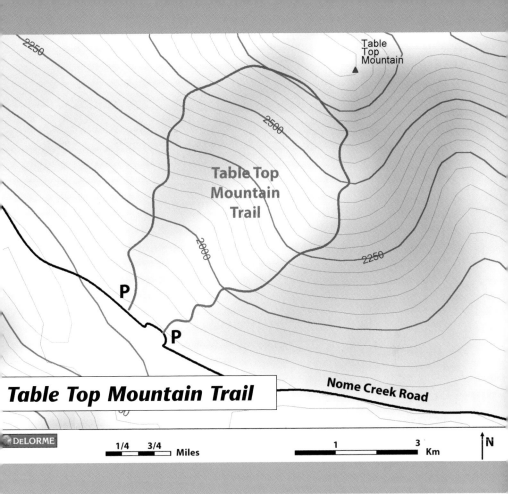

Those who are adventurous and confident they can find their way back to the trail should climb this hill to reach the top of Table Top Mountain. Though apparently flat when viewed from afar, the top has two separate summits with the southeastern one being about 50 feet (15 m) higher. The top of the mountain is treeless and offers great views in all directions, making for a wonderful lunch spot. Retrace your steps from the summit to get back to the trail.

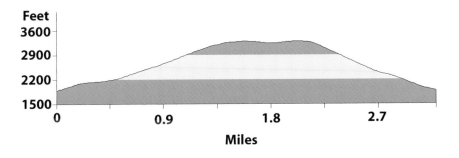

View northeast from the summit.

The relatively flat portion of the trail heads southeast for about a half mile (0.8 km) before heading south, just below the summit of the mountain. The path heads downhill less steeply than the portion of the trail on the other side. Like the climb up, the climb down winds through burned and unburned boreal forest, offering nice views of Nome Creek.

BE AWARE: The fire of 2004 left tons of standing dead trees, so be on the lookout for falling and fallen trees. In some areas, the fire burned so hot that all the vegetation was burned, making it possible to lose the trail. Vegetation recovers very quickly after wildfires, so this will likely not be a factor for very long—or at least until it burns again! U.S. Creek Road, the road that connects the Steese Highway to Nome Creek Road, is open only during the summer season.

MORE ADVENTUROUS? This is a gentle outing. For something more challenging head up Nome Creek valley and check out the Mount Prindle area (Trip 29) or the Quartz Creek Trail (Trip 28). Farther down Nome Creek Road a 7-mile (11-km) hike up the Bear Creek Trail will get you to Richard's Cabin, a public-use cabin. The trail is pretty muddy in places, so it sees little use in summer.

DIRECTIONS: Take the Steese Highway (Alaska 2) north out of Fairbanks to the town of Fox, 11 miles (18 km) away. Turn right to stay on the Steese Highway (now Alaska 6). At milepost 57.1, there is a BLM White Mountains sign. Turn left onto U.S. Creek Road. This dirt road is unmaintained (not open) in winter. Check its status with the BLM, especially its opening in spring. Follow this road for about 6.7 miles (11 km). Veer left (north) at the fork in the road and cross the Nome Creek bridge. Turn left (west) at the "T" intersection just ahead, and drive for about 8.5 miles (13.7 km) until you see the signs for the Table Top Mountain Trail.

27 BEAVER CREEK

To the Elliott Highway via the Summit Trail

ONE-WAY DISTANCE: 30-mile (48.4-km) float and 20-mile (32.3-km) hike

DURATION: 2 to 4 days

HIGH POINT: 3,207 feet (977 m)

TOTAL ELEVATION CHANGE: 7,300 feet (2,223 m)

DIFFICULTY: Difficult

ROUTE TYPE: Float (class I; packraft only) and established trail (float motorized; 15 horsepower engines or less; hike nonmotorized)

To the Yukon River Bridge

ONE-WAY DISTANCE: 360 miles (580 km)

DURATION: 18 to 24 days

HIGH POINT: 1,650 feet (502 m)

TOTAL ELEVATION CHANGE: 1,250 feet (371 m)

DIFFICULTY: Difficult

ROUTE TYPE: Float (class I); suitable for rafts or canoes (motorized allowed; 15-horsepower engines or less for first 125 miles [202 km], unrestricted after that)

BEST SEASON: June to September

USGS MAPS: Livengood A-3 (only necessary for trip including Summit Trail), B-1, B-2, C-1, C-2, D-1, D-5, D-6; Circle C-6, D-5, D-6; Fort Yukon A-5, A-6, B-5, B-6; Beaver A-1 to A-5, B-1 to B-3 (these cover the float from Nome Creek to Yukon River Bridge)

LAND MANAGERS: Bureau of Land Management (Fairbanks), 907-474-2200; Yukon Flats National Wildlife Refuge (Fairbanks), 907-456-0440; Alaska Department of Natural Resources (Fairbanks), 907-451-2705

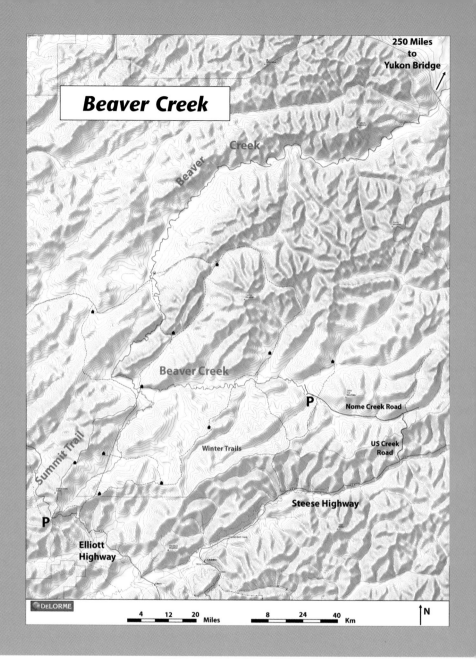

Beaver Creek

250 Miles
to
Yukon Bridge

Beaver

Creek

Beaver Creek

P

Nome Creek Road

Summit Trail

Winter Trails

US Creek
Road

Steese Highway

P

Elliott
Highway

DeLORME

| 4 | 12 | 20 |
Miles

| 8 | 24 | 40 |
Km

↑N

The most popular way to float Beaver Creek National Wild and Scenic River is to drive to Nome Creek, float Nome and then Beaver creeks for 110 miles (177 km) down to the Victoria Creek confluence, and then get flown out. However, there are two ways to make the Beaver Creek trip from road to road. Both are arduous and require good backcountry skills, conditioning, and experience.

The first way requires the use of a packraft, a small, one-person raft light enough (about 5 pounds) to carry in your pack while hiking. Adventurers can float 30 miles (48.4 km) from the Nome Creek put-in to the Borealis–LeFevre Cabin, then hike the 20-mile (32.3-km) Summit Trail back to the Elliott Highway. The trail is on the opposite shore of Beaver Creek from the cabin.

The other road-to-road option is to float 278 miles (448 km) from the Nome Creek put-in to where Beaver Creek empties into the Yukon River. Then float the Yukon to the Yukon bridge on the Dalton Highway, for a total of 360 miles (580 km).

While these trips are known as Beaver Creek floats, the put-in is on Nome Creek, an area that saw nearly a century of gold mining dating back to the 1890s. The creek is shallow and may require dragging boats over gravel bars in low-water levels. Nome Creek dumps into Beaver Creek just under 3 miles (4.8 km) downstream. This is river mile 6 (9.7 km), according to the BLM, because the National Wild and Scenic River designation begins at the confluence of Bear and Champion creeks, the start of Beaver Creek. So, floating distance is about 3 miles (4.8 km) shorter than river miles on the BLM brochures. I use only float distances in this description, not the BLM river miles. This area at the start is surrounded by low rolling hills, but the White Mountains can be seen in the distance to the west. The first major side drainage is O'Brien Creek, about 9 miles (14.5 km) into the float. Trail Creek comes in around mile 12 (km 19.4), where dragging becomes less and less common. The river continues to wind its way west through boreal forest and shrub tundra until about mile 30 (km 48.4). Here, on the north bank of the river, sits the easy-to-miss public use Borealis–LeFevre Cabin. Check with BLM to make reservations.

For those in packrafts planning to hike to the Elliott Highway, your float is done here. Your hike starts on the opposite shore of the creek as the cabin. Follow the trail to the southwest; it can be very wet. After a quarter of a mile (0.4 km) the trail will split. The Big Bend Trail comes in sharply from your right (west). You will want to stay on the Wickersham Creek Trail so continue straight (south). You will gain about 500 feet (152 m) in just over another mile (1.6 km). The trail will get drier as you go. The Wickersham Creek Trail continues south, but you will want to turn right (west) and gain the Summit Trail, a smaller, nonmotorized trail. The trail will take you over a series of bald knobs that have great views of the White Mountains and surrounding area. Between knobs you can find yourself on alpine benches, in mixed forest, or even in boggy spruce stands. The wettest areas generally have boardwalk.

Some 12 miles (19.4 km) from the Borealis–LeFevre Cabin is the Summit Trail shelter. This snug little cabin makes for a great lunch spot for speedy hikers or a good place to sleep. The shelter is cozy for two but could squeeze four if necessary. It is available on a first-come, first-served basis only, so bring a tent just in case. From the shelter, the hike is another 8 miles (13 km) back to the parking area at milepost 28

Packrafting down Beaver Creek on a warm late May day.

of the Elliott Highway. There are great views and hiking along this stretch, which takes you over Wickersham Dome (Trip 34).

For those floating the entire river, the benefits of not peeling off at the Summit Trail show themselves shortly. First, the river braids a bit after the cabin. Watch for new channels, sweepers, and other dangers. The braids come back together just before Big Bend, where the river makes a radical turn to the northeast. The river swings around the southern end of the White Mountains, giving you a spectacular, up-close look at the jagged limestone peaks. Look for Dall sheep and peregrine falcons. Stunning views of the peaks continue for miles.

Private cabins can be seen along the banks of the river following Big Bend; please respect their privacy. Across from the private cabin at the mouth of Fossil Creek (mile 43 [km 69]), the Fossil Gap Trail leads to the public-use Caribou Bluff Cabin, an 8-mile (13-km) round-trip hike. The trail can be very wet at times, but the views and cabin are great. Another place to get out and stretch your legs is at mile 51 (km 82). Here, the Colorado Creek Trail can be followed east to the public-use Wolf Run Cabin, a 3-mile (4.8-km) round-trip hike. This trail also can be very wet, as well as tussocky. This cabin has great views of the White Mountains right through its windows.

Past here, the river moves away from the White Mountains and can get braided. At mile 69 (km 110) is the Serpentine Slide Research Natural Area. A massive landslide exposed gray-green rock here. This unique environment provides habitat for unusual, but scarce, vegetation. Please do not disturb this area. Past the slide the flow quickens some before reaching Victoria Creek at mile 108 (km 174). Most boaters get picked up here by bush planes, which land on gravel bars just past Victoria Creek at mile 110 (km 177).

The river exits the White Mountains National Recreation Area at Moose Creek at about mile 114 (km 184) and enters the Yukon Flats National Wildlife Refuge. The first 15 miles (24.2 km) within the refuge can be fast, with braided channels, sharp turns, and sweepers. After that, the river gets out of the hills and dramatically changes character. The National Wild and Scenic River corridor ends here at mile 124 (km 200), and the river slows way down. It stays slow for 140 miles (226 km), where it reaches Beaver Creek Slough at mile 265 (km 428). The pace quickens some until you reach the Yukon River after some 278 miles (448 km) of floating.

The Yukon is a huge river. Its fast-moving, silt-laden, cold waters are dangerous. Unexpected high winds can cause waves large enough to swamp or capsize small boats. Be on the lookout for logs and motorboats. The float is 84 miles (135 km) from the confluence of Beaver Creek and the Yukon to the Yukon River bridge at mile 360 (km 580). The take-out is on the right (north) side.

ALL ROUTES BE AWARE: U.S. Creek Road is open only during summer. The dates at which it is passable, both in early and late summer, are highly weather dependent. Contact BLM about road conditions.

Beaver Creek is not truly "wild," as motors under 15 horsepower are permitted on the river when launched from the Nome Creek valley. Do not be surprised if you hear engines. Motorboats can be seen upstream in some places and also on the lower river where the flow is very slow.

The river is still actively cutting new channels, which can be dangerous, as sweepers may span an entire channel. Get out and scout the river if you are unsure. Sweepers are a hazard along many stretches of the river. You may have to drag your boat for short sections of shallow water. The Borealis–LeFevre Cabin is just off the river and can reserved at the BLM office in Fairbanks.

The river is very slow from mile 114 (km 184) shortly (15 miles [24 km]) after leaving the Recreation Area and remains so for about 150 miles (242 km). Private property lines the bank in places (above mean high water); be sure to check with the BLM about the location of private property. The bugs can be hideous on this float; be prepared.

On the Yukon River, be on the watch for motorboats and debris. Do not miss the Dalton Highway bridge over the Yukon; there is not another road crossing the entire

The view of Beaver Creek and the limestone jags hiking out the Summit Trail.

length of the river. Rampart, the next town past the bridge, is another 50 miles (80 km) downriver. The Summit Trail can be brushy and difficult to follow in places.

MORE ADVENTUROUS? If you are looking for other long float trips, try the Chena River (Trips 7 and 15), Birch Creek (Trip 31), Tanana River (Trips 8 and 48), or the Yukon River from Eagle (Trip 51). If you are looking for more trips to combine hiking with pack-rafting, the Arctic has plenty of options, including Trips 55 and 56 or the Chatanika River from the Elliott Highway back up to Murphy Dome (Trip 6).

DIRECTIONS: Take Steese Highway (Alaska 2) north out of Fairbanks to the town of Fox, 11 miles (18 km) away. Turn right to stay on Steese Highway (now Alaska 6). At milepost 57.1, there is a BLM White Mountains sign. Turn left onto US Creek Road. This dirt road is unmentioned (not open) in winter. Check its status with the BLM, especially its opening in spring. Follow this road for about 6.7 miles (11 km) where you need to veer left (north) at the fork in the road to cross the Nome Creek bridge. Turn left (west) at the "T" intersection, and drive for about 11 miles (18 km) until you see the turnout on the left (south) side of the road. A small sign marks Beaver Creek access (though the put-in and first couple of float miles are on Nome Creek). Drive downhill about 100 yards (meters), and park in the large lot. This put-in adds 2 miles (3.2 km) to the float. Ophir Creek Campground is another mile (1.6 km) down the road past the turn-off and is where the mileages start.

To reach the take-outs, go straight in Fox to get on the Elliott Highway (Alaska 2). Packrafters should leave a shuttle vehicle at milepost 28. There is a large, well-marked BLM parking area on the right (east) side of the highway. For those heading to the Yukon River bridge, go past milepost 28 until you reach milepost 73, where the Dalton Highway (Alaska 11) meets Elliott Highway. Take the Dalton by heading straight at the intersection. The pavement ends here, though some stretches farther north are paved. Park on the left (west) side of the road just after the Yukon River bridge at milepost 56.

28 *QUARTZ CREEK TRAIL*

R/T DISTANCE: 14 miles (22.5 km)

DURATION: 5 to 10 hours hiking or 3 to 8 hours biking

HIGH POINT: 3,250 feet (990 m)

TOTAL ELEVATION CHANGE: 3,500 feet (1,066 m)

DIFFICULTY: Moderate to difficult

ROUTE TYPE: Established multiuse trail (motorized allowed)

BEST SEASON: May to September

USGS MAPS: Circle B-6

LAND MANAGER: Bureau of Land Management (Fairbanks), 907-474-2200

The Quartz Creek Trail is a rugged but easy to follow trail on the eastern side of the White Mountains National Recreation Area. Primarily an ATV trail, it is suitable for hiking and mountain biking. Bikers should be experienced, as the trail can be very steep in places with loose gravel or cobble substrate. The trail provides access to wild country and has great views of the Mount Prindle area (Trip 29). The many rugged peaks around can easily make people forget that they are in the middle of the Interior. To the east of the trail, Mount Prindle, at 5,286 feet (1,610 m), towers over the Steese National Conservation Area.

The start of the trail weeds out most self-powered adventurers. The trail is steep, with loose gravel that can be tough to gain traction on. The pitch is fairly unrelenting, climbing 800 vertical feet (244 m) in about a mile (1.6 km). As the trail nears the summit of a pass, the gradient moderates and the footing gets better. There are good views of Nome Creek valley even from here. An ATV trail leads to the summit of Peak 3544 to the west. (Motorized use is allowed off-trail on this side of the Quartz Creek Trail.) With a little bushwhacking, hikers can reach the summit of Peak 4315 to the north. The latter has great views of upper Nome Creek valley and Mount Prindle.

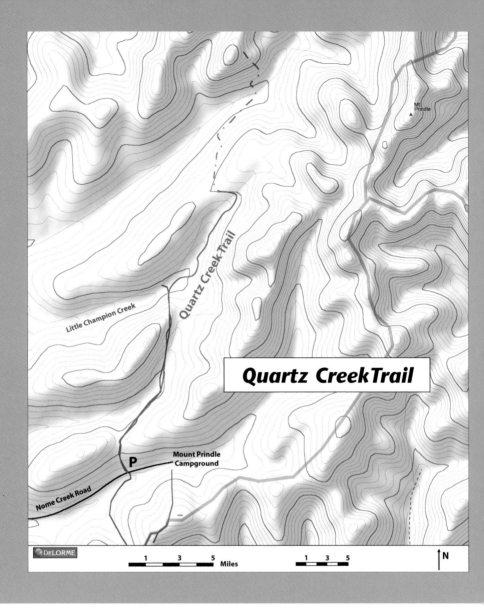

Quartz Creek Trail

Little Champion Creek

Quartz Creek Trail

Mt Prindle

Mount Prindle
Campground

P

Nome Creek Road

DeLORME

| 1 | 3 | 5 |
Miles

| 1 | 3 | 5 |

↑N

After the pass, Quartz Creek Trail gently descends for about a mile and a half (2.4 km) to a bald knob, just above and left (west) of the trail. While the gradient is gentle, the trail is a bit rough for cycling in places. The knob makes an excellent destination or lunch spot. It is perched just above a steep drop in the trail.

The trail then makes a steep, 300-foot (91-m) drop taking you into a forest of hardwood and spruce. After crossing a couple of small streams, the trail levels out. These streams can be slightly more challenging to cross during high-water levels. The trail does not become flat, as it hugs the west flanks of the mountains. The peaks of these mountains extend up to 4,700 feet (1,432 m) and become more visible the farther you go.

After a couple more miles, the trees fade away, and you reach Little Champion Creek at 7 miles (11.3 km). The views are great, and Dall sheep might be seen to the southeast. Most self-powered adventurers will turn around here. For some, Quartz Creek, which is 10 miles (16 km) farther, will call to them. Those who continue will be rewarded with more alpine terrain, wild country and creatures, and spectacular views of the mountains.

BE AWARE: This trail is primary an ATV trail, so expect traffic—especially during weekends and hunting season. The first hill is steep, long, and full of loose rock. Bikers should strongly consider walking their bikes both up and down this stretch. Plastic mesh blocking has been put down in wet areas to control trail erosion (and expansion). The blocking can be very slick when wet for both hikers and cyclists. Bikers should consider walking their bikes across these. U.S. Creek Road is open only during the summer.

MORE ADVENTUROUS? A round trip from the trailhead to the trail's end at Quartz Creek and back is 35 miles (56 km). This makes for a nice multi-day hike or very long mountain bike. The mountainous views seem to get better the farther you go. From the end of the trail, near Peak 4501, adventures into the seldom-visited northern parts of Steese National Conservation Area and White Mountains National Recreation Area can be launched. Rocky Mountain (Lime Peak) lies some 10 miles (16 km) farther to the northwest. Heading in the other direction (east), you can follow the ridge that veers off to the south after a couple of miles and head up Mount Prindle. By cutting through the pass at Little Champion Creek you can have easier access to Mount Prindle (see Trip 29).

DIRECTIONS: Take the Steese Highway (Alaska 2) north out of Fairbanks to the town of Fox, 11 miles (18 km) away. Turn right to stay on the Steese Highway (now Alaska 6). At milepost 57.1, there will be a BLM White Mountains sign. Turn left onto U.S. Creek Road. This dirt road is unmaintained (not open) in winter. Check its

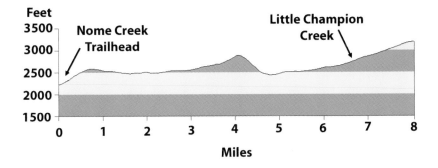

117

An alpine section of the trail overlooking the White Mountains.

status with the BLM, especially its opening in spring. Follow this road for about 6.7 miles (11 km), veer left (north) at the fork and cross the Nome Creek bridge. Turn right (east) at the "T" intersection and drive for about 3.3 miles (5.3 km) until you reach the Quartz Creek Trail turnout. If you reach the Mount Prindle Campground, you have gone too far.

29 *MOUNT PRINDLE*

R/T DISTANCE: 19 miles (31 km)

DURATION: 2 to 3 days

HIGH POINT: 5,286 feet (1,610 m)

TOTAL ELEVATION CHANGE: 8,400 feet (2,559 m)

DIFFICULTY: Difficult

ROUTE TYPE: Route (nonmotorized)

BEST SEASON: May to September

USGS MAPS: Circle B-5, B-6

LAND MANAGER: Bureau of Land Management (Fairbanks), 907-474-2200

Upper Nome Creek valley is the place you did not think existed in the heart of the Interior. There are seemingly endless hiking, backpacking, and climbing opportunities in the area due to a rugged group of peaks over 4,000 feet (1,219 m) high. At 5,286 feet (1,610 m), the barren and craggy Mount Prindle is the crowning peak. This rugged area dispels the myth that the Interior is nothing but endless rolling hills.

The first part of the trip has a couple of stream crossings, which discourages many people. From the parking lot at the Prindle Campground, follow the main social trail east to Nome Creek's west bank. Follow the bank upstream about 10 yards (meters) and cross the creek. Another good crossing is about 50 yards (meters) or so farther upstream on the west bank. After crossing Nome Creek, follow the obvious social trail on the edge of the east bank upstream for about 75 yards (meters). The trail will turn right (east) as another creek comes in from that direction. (This is where you should hit the social trail if you followed the west bank social trails farther before crossing Nome Creek.) The trail follows the southern bank of this new creek for about 25 yards (meters), then turns north and crosses it. Both of these "little" creeks can swell during high water and make the crossings very tough. Nome Creek has completely washed out the campground during storms in the spring and is one of the reasons there is not a bridge here.

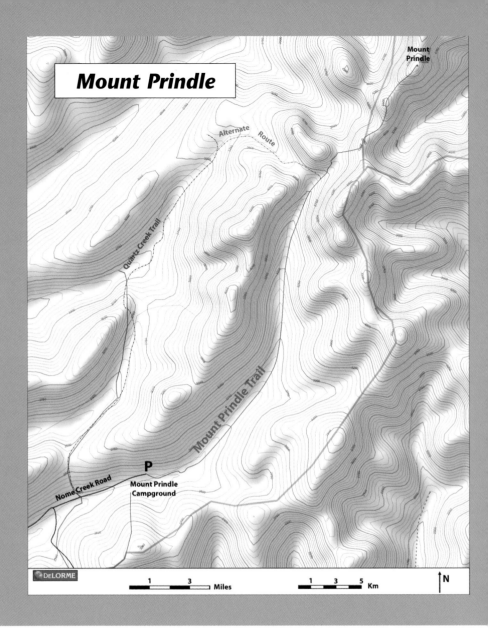

Mount Prindle

Mount Prindle

Alternate Route

Quartz Creek Trail

Mount Prindle Trail

P

Nome Creek Road

Mount Prindle Campground

DeLORME

1   3   Miles

1   3   5   Km

N

Once on the north side of the second creek, the going is much easier. The trail heads out of the riparian zone and quickly into shrub tundra. The brush is a bit scratchy, so you may want to wear pants even on a hot day. The brush in this tundra is only about knee-high. Stay on the northbound social trail the best you can. For the most part it is obvious, and most deviations just bring you back to the main trail. Once up on the bench, you will be able to take in the full glory of upper Nome Creek valley. The mountains are larger and more rugged the farther you get, and the valley closes in. The trail gently gains elevation, so the going is easy. About a mile (1.6 km) along the trail, it forks. The left fork heads straight but actually leads you lower and is harder to follow. The right fork seems to head too far east, but it comes back to a more northerly heading and is easier to follow.

Looming in front of you is a dark, unnamed mountain rising to 5,043 feet (1,536 m). It is a good destination for a rigorous, stand-alone day hike or as an excursion from a base camp. As you approach its flanks, some 4 miles (6.4 km) into the hike, you will probably think about hiking on the other (west) side of the creek. You can do that, but the tundra there is much wetter with lots of puddles and ponds to walk around. The east side requires more up and down, as well as side hilling, but has better walking conditions.

The next mile (1.6 km) is steeper than the previous and takes you into a bowl. This is a good place for a campsite. Water is available and will be hard to come by higher up, plus several day hikes can be done from here. The vegetation quickly changes from tundra to alpine as you gain elevation.

From the bowl, head north, aiming for the nearest small rock outcrop. Once on top of the ridge, head east up a steep rise. From here, you can get glimpses of Mount Prindle in the distance. From the top of this rise about 6 miles (9.7 km) in, your path becomes obvious and there will be sets of small tors. You will head uphill to the northeast then north, eventually aiming for the larger, more distant peak hiding behind a closer one.

After topping the hill, you will have a view of the spectacular northeast-trending ridge. It has a series of unforgettable tors at ridgeline that are quite photogenic and make for great rock climbing. (See *Mount Prindle Area Climbing Guide* [Appendix B] for specific rock climbing routes.) Each set of tors seems more amazing than the next. This is a fine destination in its own right. Enjoy the views of American Creek valley to the east or the rugged skyline to the southeast.

After the last set of tors, the route gets steep and boulder-strewn as it climbs a peak. You might be tempted to skirt the peak, but the slopes are rugged and steep, so the best course is to go over the top. From the top, the trail drops about 500 feet (152 m)

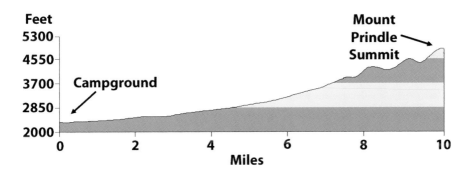

The main tors rising from the rugged ridgeline.

to an elevation of about 4,500 feet (1,372 m). Catch your breath here before making the steady climb to the summit of Mount Prindle at 5,286 feet (1,610 m). From the top the views of the surrounding area are stunning. Dall sheep are often seen in the area. Rock climbers use the sides of Mount Prindle as a playground. From the summit, the main wall they use is visible to the east, in the headwaters of American Creek. The ridge continues north into the wild, beckoning more adventurous souls. For mere mortals, retracing your steps is no loss as the tors are just as awe-inspiring the second time around.

BE AWARE: This is a route, so you (or at least one of your partners) need to be skilled and experienced in backcountry travel. Water is tough to come by past the bowl at about mile 5 (km 8) of the trek; top off your water before getting on the ridge. Camping is not allowed in the Mount Prindle Research Natural Area, which includes the ridgeline with the tors and the summit. Dall sheep are frequently seen in the region; please watch them from a respectful distance. If they start moving away from you, you have gotten too close. Leash dogs in the Little Champion Creek pass (see "More Adventurous?"), as the possibility of sheep being present is high. The U.S. Creek Road is open only during summer. Those interested in rock climbing should purchase the *Mount Prindle Area Climbing Guide* (Appendix B), which details specific routes and their ratings. If you choose to try rock climbing, remember that it is inherently dangerous. Please be very careful. Help is a long way away.

MORE ADVENTUROUS? You have come to the right spot. There are so many opportunities in this region that you could write a book about them. (Stan Justice wrote an entire guidebook—the *Mount Prindle Area Climbing Guide*—just for the rock climbing and mountaineering routes in the region.) The Mount Prindle hike can be done in a very long day. Experienced uber-athletes can make the round trip in about seven hours.

A couple of hiking options include returning via the Quartz Creek Trail (Trip 28). The first option is to continue hiking north past the summit of Mount Prindle. The Quartz Creek Trail can be reached by heading west along the first major ridgeline some

4 miles (6.4 km) north of the summit. Alternatively you could continue ridge walking 7 miles (11.3 km) north of the summit and then head northwest. This would place you near Peak 4501, which is about 6 miles (9.7 km) from the remote Rocky Mountain (also known as Lime Peak).

The rocky ridgeline route.

A shorter route using the Quartz Creek Trail is to make for the Little Champion Creek pass, which is just prior to reaching the first, small tors of the Mount Prindle hike. Hike on the northeast side of the pass. The cliff area near the lakebed on the southwest side has a mineral lick that wildlife should be able to reach unhampered. Please leash your dogs in this area. Past this area, travel on the south side of the creek, which has good walking conditions. The Nome Creek valley is lined with several mountains reaching 4,000 feet (1,218 m) and more, making it a good area for peak bagging. Peak 5043 can be a good destination for a long day hike, or it can be a great add-on to a Mount Prindle hike.

DIRECTIONS: Take the Steese Highway (Alaska 2) north out of Fairbanks to the town of Fox, 11 miles (18 km) away. Turn right to stay on the Steese Highway (now Alaska 6). At milepost 57.1, there will be a BLM White Mountains sign. Turn left onto U.S. Creek Road. This dirt road is unmaintained (not open) in winter. Check its status with the BLM, especially its opening in spring. Follow this road for about 6.7 miles (11 km), veer left (north) at the fork and cross the Nome Creek bridge. Turn right (east) at the "T" intersection, and drive for about 4 miles (6.4 km) until you reach the Mount Prindle Campground. There is a place for hikers to park vehicles at the northeast corner of the campground.

McMANUS MOUNTAIN

R/T DISTANCE: 6 miles (9.7 km)

DURATION: 3 to 6 hours

HIGH POINT: 4,250 feet (1,295 m)

TOTAL ELEVATION CHANGE: 2,900 feet (883 m)

DIFFICULTY: Moderate

ROUTE TYPE: Route (nonmotorized)

BEST SEASON: May to September

USGS MAPS: Circle B-4, B-5

LAND MANAGER: Alaska Department of Natural Resources (Fairbanks),
907-451-2705

You will not find McManus Mountain named on any maps. I gave it that moniker, because the USGS survey monument near the summit has that name. This alpine hike offers great views of the Pinnell Mountain National Recreation Trail (Trip 32) and the White Mountains (Trip 34). People enjoy walking this ridge even though it is not an established trail. Search around while hiking, and you will find social trails, small cairns, and even rock shelters along the way. The crisp days of fall are an ideal time to do this hike because of the vibrant colors.

The easiest way to start this hike is to follow the Pinnell Mountain Trail boardwalk from its Twelvemile Summit trailhead. After about a half mile (0.8 km), the trail starts heading to the northeast. Veer off the trail here, making your way through knee-high willows, heading northwest to the top of the knoll not far away. After cresting the knoll, follow the broad ridge to the west. This alpine ridge has good footing and views of mountains in all directions. After about a half mile (0.8 km) you will descend about 300 vertical feet (100 m), but you will have left most of the willows behind. From the bottom of the descent, the summit is a short but relatively steep climb up to the southwest, which requires a bit of scrambling over broken rocks. This rock field is pretty loose so watch your footing and balance. Light rain

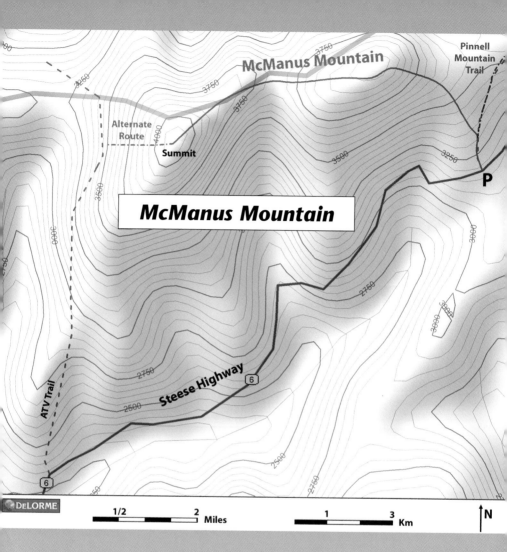

McManus Mountain

Alternate Route

Summit

McManus Mountain

Pinnell Mountain Trail

P

ATV Trail

2750

2600

Steese Highway 6

6

DeLORME

1/2   2 Miles

1   3 Km

N

or even high humidity can make the black lichens coating these rocks extremely slick. This route basically follows a portion of the Fairbanks North Star Borough boundary. The hike to the summit is about 3 miles (4.8 km), with great views of the White Mountains and the Pinnell Mountain Trail area. After you are done enjoying the views, just head back the same way you came.

For an alternate route, park in the turnout where Montana Creek crosses the Steese Highway at milepost 80.1. Follow the ATV trail north for about 1.5 miles (2.4 km), then veer off it to the northeast. The summit is another mile away. This route is shorter than the first, but it is steeper and the ATV trail could have traffic.

BE AWARE: This is a route, not a trail, so route-finding skills are required. The weather in the mountains can change rapidly. Whiteout conditions can develop

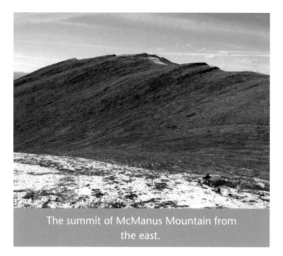

The summit of McManus Mountain from the east.

in any season, making route finding difficult for even experienced orienteers. Follow previously developed social trails and walk on exposed rock as much as possible to minimize damage to fragile vegetation. While Pinnell Mountain Trail is nonmotorized, ATVs use the trail portion of the alternate route, though not to the summit of McManus Mountain.

MORE ADVENTUROUS? Instead of turning around at the summit of McManus Mountain, follow the ridgeline west and then southwest for another 4 miles (6.4 km) to where the Faith Creek Road spurs off from the Steese Highway. Experts may want to consider following the ridges all the way to the Nome Creek valley and Mount Prindle (Trip 29).

For mountain bikers, there are a couple of ATV trails south of the Twelvemile Summit parking lot that go on for miles. The ATV trail that heads southeast is the 55-mile (89-km) Circle–Fairbanks Historic Trail, which ends near Cleary Summit a few miles from Fox. Have at it!

DIRECTIONS: Take the Steese Highway (Alaska 2) north out of Fairbanks to the town of Fox, 11 miles (18 km) away. Turn right to stay on the Steese Highway (now Alaska 6). The Steese is paved until milepost 62.5, and the dirt portion is generally in good shape until milepost 126. Park at milepost 85.5 in the parking lot on the right (south) side of the road. This is Twelvemile Summit, which is the southwestern terminus of the Pinnell Mountain Trail (Trip 32). The trail is on the north side of the road.

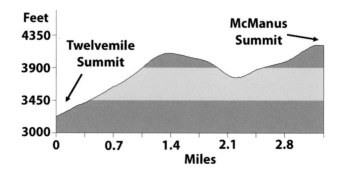

126

31 *BIRCH CREEK*

ONE-WAY DISTANCE: 107 miles (172 km) but also 18- and 125-mile (29- and 201-km) options

DURATION: 4 to 8 days (40 to 55 hours on the river)

HIGH POINT: 1,950 feet (594 m)

TOTAL ELEVATION CHANGE: 1,250 feet (381 m)

DIFFICULTY: Moderate

ROUTE TYPE: Float (class I but short class II and III rapids); suitable for canoes or small rafts (no motorized access)

BEST SEASON: late May to September

USGS MAPS: Circle B-1 to B-4, C-1

LAND MANAGERS: Bureau of Land Management (Fairbanks), 907-474-2200; Alaska Department of Natural Resources (Fairbanks), 907-451-2705

Birch Creek National Wild River bisects the southern unit of the Steese National Conservation Area. At the trip's start, the river flows immediately away from the road, providing a wilderness trip until the last few miles where the river comes back to the Steese Highway. Bounded by mountains 3,000 to 4,000 feet (913 to 1,218 m) high on either side, numerous rapids punctuate this wild float. You exit the hills 30 miles (48.4 km) from the end of the float. Here, the river slows, but this section is relaxing and beautiful in its own way. Only paddlers experienced with remote rivers and wilderness camping should attempt the upper portion of this float.

The put-in is at the confluence of Birch and Twelvemile creeks. The water is generally really clear and shallow, but the current is fast. During low water, boats may have to be dragged much of the first 9 miles (14.5 km) until the Harrington Fork of Birch Creek enters. Even with moderate water levels, there are plenty of places where boats have to be dragged or lined. The creek is narrow enough that sweepers and logjams can span from bank to bank. Be very vigilant in these upper waters. The creek heads pretty much due south until it reaches the Harrington Fork. Here, the creek turns

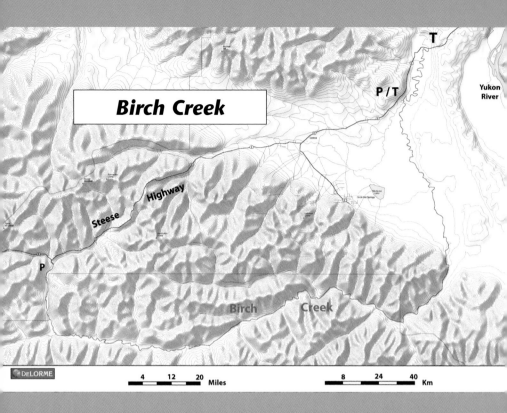

DeLORME

Birch Creek

```
        4    12   20                8    24   40
        |====|====|                |====|====|
             Miles                       Km
```

to the east and generally has enough water to float in. However, there will likely be spots where you have to drag until you reach Clums Fork at mile 33 (km 53).

Shortly after McLean Creek, you should hear falling water. The first rapid is a short drop (typically class II–III) between two calm stretches. It should be scouted and can easily be portaged on the river left (the north side). After about another mile, near mile 39 (km 63) but before Wolf Creek, you should hear rushing water again. Just up ahead is Shotgun Rapids. This curving drop (class III rapid) should be portaged, although experienced paddlers may want to run the rapid in their empty boats. Many boats have been swamped or damaged here, so be careful and wear your life jacket (as always). The rapid spits you out into calm waters, but it's also a very narrow, cliff-lined canyon so it's not as easy to deal with a capsized boat as the previous rapid. It is, however, one of the most picturesque spots along the river. Camping spots are plentiful, so the more adventurous may want to run either or both sets of rapids more than once.

Harrison Creek comes in from the north at mile 54 (km 87). At its mouth is Pitka's Bar, named after Pitka Pavaloff, a Russian miner who helped spark the Birch Creek gold rush in 1894. Old miner and trapper cabins, as well as numerous other artifacts of that era, can be seen along the creek's shores here in particular. Enjoy the history, but please leave the structures and artifacts as you found them for others to enjoy.

The South Fork of Birch Creek enters at mile 67 (km 108). The creek grows with each mile and becomes more like a river; however, the river can get wide and shallow, grounding even those picking the best lines. You leave the hills at mile 77 (km 124), with Beauty Dome on your left (west), and the wide, flat Yukon River valley opens up before you.

Past Beauty Dome, the river becomes more sinuous and slow, but still has long stretches of quick-moving water. Large stands of birch, as well as muskegs, line the shores. Be prepared to go slow or paddle plenty—likely both. These last 30 miles (48.4 km) are made for relaxing, but only the las 15 miles (24.2 km) are particularly slow. The take-out is not obvious, so scout it out when you drop off your shuttle vehicle. Traffic is very light this far up the Steese Highway, so you may not hear road noise. As you approach the take-out, the hills will get pretty close on the left (west) side. You will see a small dirt ramp leading to the parking lot on the left (west) side. The take-out is on river mile 107 (km 172) and at Steese Highway milepost 140.5. The National Wild River corridor ends here, as do most trips.

However, another take-out spot is 18 miles (29 km) downriver at the Steese Highway bridge. Paddlers can decide to take out at the bridge for a 125-mile (201-km) float, or they can put in at this take-out and float to the bridge. This 18-mile (29-km) stretch is perfect for an easy family outing. The only real hazard is motorboat traffic. The section, with a slow 1–2 mph current (1.6–3.2 km/h), can be done in five hours with steady paddling. However, it is probably best done as an easy overnighter, taking up to twelve hours on the river. (A north wind can slow you down, increasing this time greatly.) This shorter float is a beautiful fall trip, with the expansive birch stands glowing yellow.

BE AWARE: The take-out is not very obvious. When you drop off your shuttle vehicle, make sure to walk out to the river and note the characteristics of the take-out area. Usually, it is marked with flagging. The small dirt ramp on the left (west) side of the river is easy to spot as you float by. If you do overshoot a little, the river is slow and shallow enough here that you should be able to get to shore and back to the ramp.

The beginning of the upper portion of the float is very shallow until Harrington Fork at 9 miles (14.5 km). During low water you may have to drag your boat a lot over this stretch. Even at moderate water levels you will have to drag in places. Be on the lookout for sharp turns. Also watch for sweepers and logjams that can span the entire creek. These are less of a problem later in the year, because boaters often cut them out. Low water can be a problem all the way to mile 33 (km 53) at Clums Fork. The rapids between McLean and Wolf creeks (class II–III) should be scouted and can be portaged on the river left side. Experienced boaters may want to portage gear and run the rapid, generally on the right (south) side. Thrill seekers may want to run

Reflections on the lower stretches of Birch Creek.

and re-run these sections. Be sure to have your life jackets on and spotters with throw ropes on the banks. The water slows after the rapid, so swamped canoes can be recovered fairly easily, but tall and steep rock walls may hinder efforts after Shotgun Rapids. Sweepers become less of a problem this far down, but always keep watch for them. The creek slows way down after exiting the hills. The last 15 miles (24.2 km) are very slow going. Prepare to do some paddling. The USGS topographic maps for this area have not been updated since the mid-1950s. The creek has altered its course in places—most notably just as you come out of the hills and into the flats. The amount of flow is determined by rainfall, except for late May snow runoff. Knowing ahead of time when high flows are going to be available on the creek is not easy. While on the river, be careful where you camp, as water levels can rise quickly. Moose-hunting season is probably the busiest time on the river. If you are interested in skiing the river, note that snowmachines are allowed in the river corridor during winter.

MORE ADVENTUROUS? Other great float trips include the Chena River (Trips 7 and 15), Beaver Creek (Trip 27), Tanana River (Trips 8 and 48), Delta River (Trip 44), Gulkana River (Trip 45), Fortymile (Trip 50), and the Yukon River (Trip 51).

DIRECTIONS: Take the Steese Highway (Alaska 2) north out of Fairbanks to the town of Fox, 11 miles (18 km) away. Turn right to stay on the Steese Highway (now Alaska 6). The Steese is paved until milepost 62.5, and the dirt portion is generally in good shape until milepost 126.

To get to the put-in: At milepost 94.0, turn right (south), following the signs for Birch Creek access. The road heads downhill for about a quarter mile (0.4 km) to a large parking lot. Boats need to be carried about 40 yards (meters) to the launch, which is near the southeast corner of the lot.

To reach the take-outs: The main take-out is at milepost 140.5, Steese Highway, on the right (east) side and is marked. A 50-yard (meter) trail leads from the parking lot to the river. Use this as a put-in if you want to float the lower section on the river to the bridge at milepost 147.1. Parking spots on the right (south) side of the road can be found on both sides of the bridge (mileposts 147.0 and 147.2, respectively). The parking area on the far side of the bridge is larger and more accessible.

32 PINNELL MOUNTAIN TRAIL

ONE-WAY DISTANCE: 27.3 miles (44 km)

DURATION: 2 to 5 days

HIGH POINT: 4,934 feet (1,503 m)

TOTAL ELEVATION CHANGE: 9,400 feet (2,863 m)

DIFFICULTY: Moderate to difficult

ROUTE TYPE: Established trail (nonmotorized)

BEST SEASON: May to September

USGS MAPS: Circle B-3, B-4, C-3, C-4

LAND MANAGER: Bureau of Land Management (Fairbanks), 907-474-2200

The Pinnell Mountain National Recreation Trail is probably the best known Interior trail outside of the region. The trek is entirely above tree line and offers sweeping views of the White Mountains and Steese National Conservation Area. The trail is rugged and remote. The remarkable wildlife and ancient rocks (some of the oldest exposed in Alaska) add to the area's feeling of wilderness. This trek, part of the National Recreation Trail system, is not to be missed.

Most hikers begin at the 3,624-foot (1,104-m) Eagle Summit trailhead, as it is 500 feet (152 m) higher than the Twelvemile Summit trailhead. Mile markers begin from this location, so my description will as well. The trail is obvious and leads north out of the parking area toward a hill. A short climb warms you up, and then the trail wraps around to the north side of the hill. A side trail leads to the top of the hill, but the main trail skirts around it. Because the trail is on the hill's north side, this is one of the last places snow patches persist along the entire trail. Caribou from the Fortymile Herd are often seen in this area, so keep watch for them.

The trail flattens out for a short while and is somewhat protected from the wind—which makes this a good place to find the bug dope. The trail eventually trends west, but first it reaches the ridgeline by climbing north and somewhat east. This climb

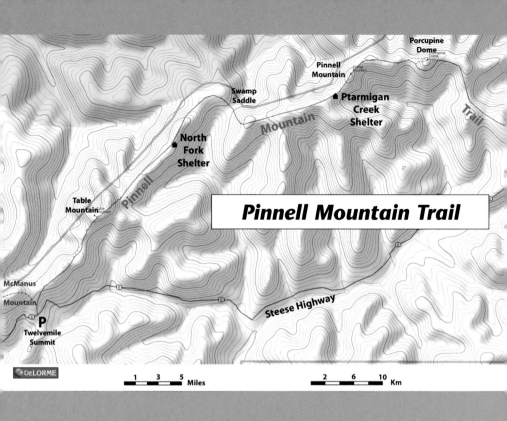

Pinnell Mountain Trail

begins just before mile 3 (km 4.8) and tops out around mile 4 (km 6.5), making it a good destination for day hikers.

Once atop the ridge, the trail veers to the west with Porcupine Dome looming directly in front of you. The trail skirts around the southern slope of the dome. Those with strong legs, route-finding abilities, and a thirst for peak bagging can continue due west up the steep talus slope to the summit Porcupine Dome. The peak is at 4,915 feet (1,497 m) and has communications facilities on top, but it offers great views of the trail and surrounding area. Robert Pinnell, for whom the trail is named, died climbing Porcupine Dome, so use caution. To regain the trail, continue west and you will come back onto the trail at mile 6.5 (km 10.5).

Most hikers will want to stay on the main trail. On the far side of the dome, Pinnell Mountain at 4,934 feet (1,503 m) will come into full view. Its top is worn and weathered, its slopes cracked and splintered. Scanning lower, among the vegetated slopes, you can see examples of solifluction lobes. Appearing like wavy curtains, these formations are where the topsoil and its vegetation slid downhill over the bedrock.

The climb from the far side of Porcupine Dome at mile 6.5 (km 10.5) to the summit of Pinnell Mountain at mile 9 (km 14.5) is one of the longest on the trail.

A strong wind usually scours the peak of Pinnell, but its rocky top offers lots of spots to duck out of the wind so you can admire the scenery, enjoy lunch, catch a nap, or spot wildlife. Also, if bad weather rolls in, you are only about a mile (1.6 km) from the Ptarmigan Creek Trail Shelter. The slope down to the shelter is fairly moderate and the footing is good. The shelter is just off the trail and would be hard to miss in all but the foggiest conditions. It operates on a first-come, first-served basis. It has a water catchment system with a cistern for drinking water. Treat the water before drinking.

The next few miles past the shelter are really enjoyable. You pass many interesting rock formations, and the White Mountains are in full view in front of you. These miles go quickly not only because of the scenery but also because they gently descend. Soon the Swamp Saddle, with its swampy marshes, comes into view. To see so much vegetation again seems almost strange. At mile 13.2 (km 21), the trail descends more steeply into the saddle, which bottoms out at 3,500 feet (1,066 m). The descent, the saddle, and the climb out all have boardwalk, as the area really is a swamp. The climb from the bottom of the saddle to the ridge ahead is about a mile (1.6 km) and 500 vertical feet (152 m). The plateau can also be very wet and is dominated by tundra. It gently climbs for about another mile (1.6 km).

Reaching dry ground at mile 15.5 (km 25) also means another climb. This lesser peak tops out at mile 16.7 (km 27) and is more than 1,000 feet (300 m) above the Swamp Saddle. The descent from this peak is steep and boulder-strewn. In this saddle, a side trail heads south to the North Fork Trail Shelter at mile 17.5 (km 28). The shelter is a great place to get out of the elements for a while or spend the evening. However, it operates on a first-come, first-served basis. It also has a water catchment system with a cistern for drinking water. Treat the water before drinking.

The main trail skirts the northwest slope of the next hill for some reason, making for some side hilling. The trail then makes its way back up to the ridgeline near mile 18 (km 29). The next few miles trend downhill with good footing, but there are ups

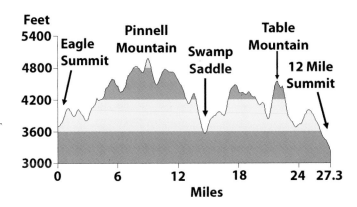

Porcupine Dome from the slopes of Pinnell Mountain.

and downs. Unfortunately for weary hikers, the steepest descent occurs around mile 19.5 (km 31.4)—just before the mile-long (1.6-km-long), 700-foot (213-m) schlep to the summit of Table Mountain. This summit, at 4,472 feet (1,362 m), is a great destination for day hikers who start at the Twelvemile Summit trailhead, making for a 10-mile (16-km) round trip. The flat top of this peak is a fun place to take a break and look around. It is also so large and flat that it is an easy place to lose the trail in fog. Large cairns and wooden posts help hikers find their way.

The steep hike off Table Mountain is often covered with abundant wildflowers. One final, small ascent from mile 23 to 24 (km 37 to 38.6) awaits, so this is a good place to stop, smell the flowers, and power up for the last hill. From mile 24 (km 38.6), the trail is generally downhill with fairly flat sections. Eventually, you will be out of the rocky terrain and back into tundra. Boardwalk lines the last part of the trail. Please stay on it to protect this fragile vegetation. The parking area for the Twelvemile Summit trailhead is across the Steese Highway and down a small embankment. Watch for traffic.

BE AWARE: This area is higher than most of the surrounding region. It can get socked in with fog or low clouds, making it difficult to navigate. Be sure to have your maps, compasses, and the skills to use them. Due to the higher elevations, the area is usually colder than Fairbanks and sees a fair bit of strong rain showers. Be prepared for these conditions. The trail shelters snugly fit four people but are on a first-come, first-served basis. Do not rely on them being available. The shelters are each equipped with a rain catchment system that collects drinking water. The water needs to be filtered or boiled before use. For some reason, there are marmots desperately seeking to wrest control of these shelters—beware the marmots!

The view west from the summit of Pinnell Mountain.

MORE ADVENTUROUS? Rather than heading to the parking lot at Twelvemile Summit, continue along the ridge to McManus Mountain (Trip 30). You can continue past there along ridges and make your way to the Mount Prindle area (Trip 29). The Circle–Fairbanks Historic Trail heads southwest out of the Twelvemile Summit parking lot. It dips down into lower elevations in some areas before reaching Fairbanks some 55 miles (88 km) away. These trips should be undertaken only by very experienced adventurers. Uberathletes with plenty of outdoor experience may be able to cover the length of the Pinnell Mountain Trail in one arduous fourteen-hour day.

DIRECTIONS: Take the Steese Highway (Alaska 2) north out of Fairbanks to the town of Fox, 11 miles (18 km) away. Turn right to stay on the Steese Highway (now Alaska 6). The Steese is paved until milepost 62.5. Turn right into the Twelvemile Summit parking lot at milepost 85.5. Leave your shuttle vehicle here. Continue on the Steese Highway until milepost 107.3, where you will turn left (north) into the Eagle Summit parking area. The trail starts at the north end of the parking lot. Just past the parking lot a side trail heads directly up a steep rocky outcrop for people to get views, but the main trail skirts this knob to the right (northeast).

33 *MASTODON DOME*

R/T DISTANCE: 11 miles (17.7 km)

DURATION: 3 to 6 hours

HIGH POINT: 4,418 feet (1,346 m)

TOTAL ELEVATION CHANGE: 2,700 feet (822 m) or 4,200 feet (1,279 m) if you go over first hill

DIFFICULTY: Easy to moderate

ROUTE TYPE: Route (nonmotorized)

BEST SEASON: May to September

USGS MAPS: Circle B-3

LAND MANAGER: Alaska Department of Natural Resources (Fairbanks), 907-451-2705

The hike out to Mastodon Dome is one of the most enjoyable around. The area is remote enough that few hikers come this far and the vast majority who do choose to hike the Pinnell Mountain National Recreation Trail (Trip 32). The trek to Mastodon Dome gives you stunning views of the Pinnell Mountain Trail area to the northwest, the Crazy Mountains to the northeast, and Birch Creek drainage (Trip 31) to the south. The wildflowers can be amazing, and this dome is totally bereft of communication facilities!

The trip starts by parking at the Eagle Summit parking lot at 3,624 feet (1,104 m), where the Pinnell Mountain Trail starts. However, this hike starts on the opposite side of the Steese Highway. Your first route-finding decision comes immediately after crossing the road. Either you can climb up and over the 400-plus-foot (122-m) hill directly in front of you, or you can skirt around it. If you choose to skirt the hill, try not to lose elevation, as you will only have to gain it back. Both ways take you to a small saddle about 1.5 miles (2.4 km) from the start. The route continues to go generally southeast and steadily uphill for about a mile (1.6 km).

Make your way to the far (east) side of this plateau, as that side is much drier. Work your way south, contouring as you go. This will bring you into a very large, flat

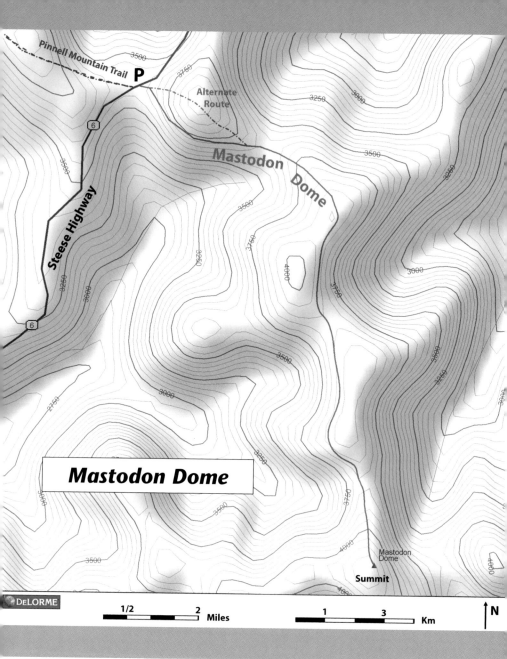

Pinnell Mountain Trail

P

Alternate
Route

Mastodon Dome

Steese Highway

6

6

3500

3750

3250

3000

3500

3250

3500

3500

3750

3250

4000

3750

3000

3500

3250

3500

3000

2750

3000

3250

3500

3750

4000

Mastodon
Dome

Summit

Mastodon Dome

| 1/2 | 2 | Miles |
| 1 | 3 | Km |

N

meadow less than 3 miles (4.8 km) from the start. It can be wet, so pick your route carefully. The beauty of the wildflowers easily makes up for the wetness. Primrose, forget-me-not, arctic poppy, whirled lousewort, and dryas flowers carpet the ground. Spin yourself around, and take in the views from all angles.

A higher route gives you better footing but fewer flowers. Descend this inclined plateau then head up the final pitch to the summit of Mastodon Dome. The pitch is

Pinnell Mountain from the summit of Mastodon Dome.

somewhat steep but not technical. The views are great, and there tends to be an upwelling wind on the summit that keeps the mosquitoes down. Retrace your steps to make your way back.

BE AWARE: This is a route not a trail, so you must be experienced and proficient at map reading and route finding. Fog can roll in fast, making those skills even more important. This route has plenty of wet tundra, so be prepared for wet feet and swarms of mosquitoes.

MORE ADVENTUROUS? The Pinnell Mountain Trail (Trip 32) starts at Eagle Summit parking lot and is an excellent backpacking trip. Many bald ridges lead off from Mastodon Dome, which invite adventurers to explore just a bit farther. Experts may want to connect ridges all the way past Ketchum Dome to Circle Hot Springs.

DIRECTIONS: Take the Steese Highway (Alaska 2) north out of Fairbanks to the town of Fox, 11 miles (18 km) away. Turn right to stay on the Steese Highway (now Alaska 6). The Steese is paved until milepost 62.5. Turn left (north) into the Eagle Summit parking area at milepost 107.3. Leave your car here and carefully cross the Steese, where this adventure begins.

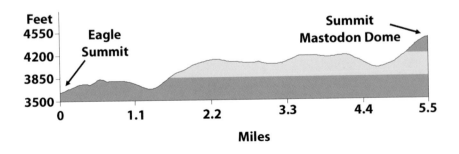

34 *WHITE MOUNTAINS*

R/T DISTANCE: 5–115 miles (8–185 km) or more

DURATION: Two hours or up to two weeks

HIGH POINT: 3,285 feet (1,001 m)

TOTAL ELEVATION CHANGE: Generally less than 2,000 feet (609 m); depends on route

DIFFICULTY: Moderate to expert

ROUTE TYPE: Established trail (motorized allowed except for Summit Trail)

BEST SEASON: November to April

USGS MAPS: Livengood A-1 to A-3, B-1 to B-3, C-1 to C-3; though the BLM map will suffice

LAND MANAGER: Bureau of Land Management (Fairbanks), 907-474-2200

The White Mountains National Recreation Area provides an extensive network of winter trails through some remote and rugged backcountry. The trails join up so extremely long trips can be put together. Shorter trips can also be done, including the 5-mile (8-km) Ski Loop Trail from the milepost 28 trailhead (Elliott Highway). A series of about ten public-use cabins are dispersed along the trail system. Many skiers use snowmachines or dog teams as support vehicles, allowing them to ski farther into the recreation area. Most people classical ski, but some sections of trails can be skate skied. There are also great snowshoeing opportunities, especially near the spectacular and jagged White Mountains themselves.

I will start by describing the shortest trail. The 5-mile (8-km) Ski Loop Trail starts by following the Summit Trail up a moderate rise. You will get views as you quickly reach alpine country. The wind often scours these knobs clean and makes the remaining snow crusty. During whiteout and fog, following the trail over this particular section can be tricky. Look for the tripods that mark the trail here. From the second minor summit the trail veers back down into the spruce. After about 1.7 miles (2.7 km) the trail hits a "T" junction. A left turn heads uphill toward Wickersham Dome

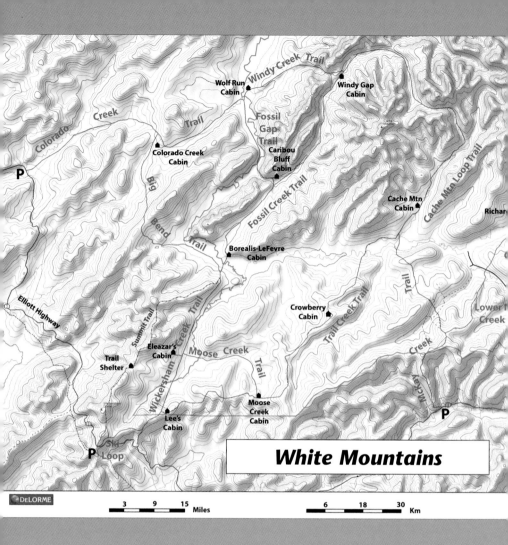

White Mountains

3   9   15
Miles

6   18   30
Km

(Trip 35). The Ski Loop Trail heads right (south) for about a mile (1.6 km), where it runs into the Wickersham Creek Trail. At the intersection, turn right (west) and the trail will take you back to the parking lot. Often, the only groomed part of the loop is the Wickersham Creek Trail.

The Wickersham Creek Trail provides the most options for skiers looking to explore the recreation area without launching a full-scale expedition. The trail rolls along a ridgeline that provides views of Wickersham Dome and the surrounding area. Portions of the trail are suitable for skate skiing. An unofficial trail comes in from the right (west) at the bottom of a steep hill. It terminates at milepost 23, Elliott Highway, and is a fairly popular shortcut. Keep heading east, and after 6 miles (9.7 km) the trail intersects with Trail Creek Trail. To get to Lee's Cabin, which sleeps up to eight and is the closest cabin to the road in the entire system, go right (east) at

Wickersham Creek Trail near Beaver Creek.

the intersection and go three-quarters of a mile (2.4 km) and then turn left (north) at the next intersection.

Nine miles (14.5 km) past Lee's Cabin, along Trail Creek Trail, is Moose Creek Cabin (sleeps six). There are a few tough climbs and hair-raising, twisting downhills. Moose Creek Trail breaks off of Trail Creek Trail here and heads north and west, dropping off the ridge to the valley below. This trail is often not as well maintained as the Trail Creek Trail. After about 9 miles (14.5 km) it runs back into Wickersham Creek Trail. Eleazar's Cabin, which sleeps four to six, is up a side trail just past the junction. If you head back south on the Wickersham Creek Trail you could have a four-to-five-day trip that covers 36 miles (58 km). It is a long steep climb from Wickersham Creek back up to the Trail Creek Trail junction, so you may prefer to do this loop in the opposite direction.

Heading north on Wickersham Creek Trail will lead you past ungroomed Summit Trail (see Trip 35). From here you will have great views of the limestone cliffs of the White Mountains and Beaver Creek to the north. About 9 miles (14.5 km) from Eleazar's Cabin is Borealis–LeFevre Cabin, which sleeps eight and sits on the north bank of Beaver Creek, 20 miles (32.3 km) from the trailhead. Between Summit Trail and Beaver Creek is a junction with Big Bend Trail. Big Bend does not see as much use as other trails, but it has great views of the west flanks of the White Mountains. About

141

Snowshoeing near Beaver Creek.
Photo by Shawn Wiegand.

16 miles (26 km) up Big Bend Trail is Colorado Creek Cabin (sleeps six).

The trail heading north from Borealis–LeFevre Cabin is Fossil Creek Trail. At mile 10 (km 16) it meets Fossil Gap Trail. To reach Caribou Bluff Cabin (sleeps four), turn left (northwest) onto the Gap trail and then take your first right (northeast) after crossing Fossil Creek. The cabin sits at the southern end of Limestone Gulch. Fossil Gap Trail is about 8.5 miles (13.7 km) long and ends where it enters mile 22 (km 35.4) of the Colorado Creek Trail. Fossil Creek Trail continues northeast for another 10 miles (16 km) where it reaches Windy Gap Cabin, which sleeps six and is 20 miles (32.3 km) from Borealis–LeFevre Cabin.

Windy Gap Cabin has sweeping views of the jagged White Mountains and is close to Windy Arch, the most spectacular of the natural arches in the vicinity. There are also numerous caves in the area. Just past the cabin is Fossil Creek Trail's intersection with Windy Creek Trail, which turns to the west and bisects the White Mountains. This trail reaches Wolf Run Cabin (sleeps four to six) after about 9 miles (14.5 km).

If you do not turn west at the intersection, you will be on Cache Mountain Loop Trail. (Fossil Creek Trail ends at the intersection.) It goes over Cache Mountain divide at 3,285 feet (1,001 m), which is the high point on the trail system and a place where the weather can be nasty. The trail goes for 26 miles (42 km) before reaching Cache Mountain Cabin (sleeps eight). The stretch from the divide to the cabin is also known as O'Brien Creek Trail. South of the cabin, you are back on Trail Creek Trail, about 23 miles (37.1 km) northeast of Moose Creek Cabin. Halfway between Cache Mountain and Moose Creek cabins is Crowberry Cabin, which burned down in 2005 but was rebuilt in 2007.

About 4 miles (6.4 km) south of Cache Mountain Cabin, Trail Creek Trail meets McKay Creek Trail. McKay Creek Trail heads south for 17 miles (27.4 km), where it reaches the parking area at milepost 42.5, Steese Highway. The last 4 miles (6.4 km) of the trail descend pretty steeply, making for a long uphill if you start at the Steese Highway. Lower Nome Creek Trail breaks off the McKay Creek Trail 8.5 miles (13.7 km) from the Steese Highway trailhead. Richard's Cabin (sleeps six) is 10.5 miles down this trail (which turns into Bear Creek Trail after crossing Nome Creek Road), making for a 19-mile (30.6-km) trip from the Steese trailhead.

The Colorado Creek trailhead is at milepost 57, Elliott Highway. Colorado Creek Cabin is 14 miles (22.5 km) down this relatively flat trail. Near the cabin, Big Bend Trail breaks off and heads to the south, meeting Wickersham Creek Trail after about 13 miles (21 km). This trail is hilly and often is the last to be broken or groomed. Colorado Creek Trail heads northeast from the cabin and intersects with Fossil Gap Trail at mile 22 (km 35.4). Just a mile (1.6 km) farther is the Wolf Run Cabin, which burned in 2004 and was rebuilt.

The recreation area gets much less use in summer as many of the trails are very wet. Most summer users head up Wickersham Dome via the Summit Trail (Trip 35), but a few enjoy trips to Lee's Cabin. Another trip is to take the Bear Creek Trail from Nome Creek Road to Richard's Cabin. McKay Creek Trail is an ATV trail that can be hiked or biked. After 5.5 miles (9 km) of steady but not overly steep uphill, you get good views of the White Mountains.

BE AWARE: None of the trailheads have plug-ins, so use good judgment about parking during winter travels and be prepared to thaw frozen vehicles. As always, check weather conditions before departing but especially on long outings! Trips beyond Lee's Cabin should be done only by people in excellent physical condition who have winter camping experience. The White Mountains National Recreation Area is prone to wildfires. While this creates an abundance of firewood for cabins in some areas, the fires have also claimed cabins and bridges. Contact the BLM about trail and cabin conditions (or existence!). Overflow, creek crossings, and open water can be very hazardous; use caution. Fees are required to use the cabins overnight. Make reservations at the BLM office in Fairbanks. Snowmachiners and dog mushers use these trails, so watch for them, especially on weekends in March.

MORE ADVENTUROUS? You are kidding, right? No? All right, then you might want to try some wilder routes to Tolovana Hot Springs (Trip 37). Also consider expert-only trips such as Hutlinana Hot Springs, Kanuti Hot Springs, or Chena Hot Springs to Circle Hot Springs (Appendix A).

DIRECTIONS: For the Elliott Highway trailheads: Take the Steese Highway (Alaska 2) north out of Fairbanks to the town of Fox, 11 miles (18 km) away. Go straight here, which actually takes you off the Steese Highway and onto Elliott Highway (however, still highway Alaska 2). At milepost 28, a large, signed parking area is on the right (northeast) side of the road. Wickersham Creek Trail leaves from the east side of the lot. The nonmotorized Summit Trail leaves from the northwest side. The Ski Loop Trail starts and ends at these two trailheads. Farther on the Elliott Highway, parking for Colorado Creek Trail is near the Tolovana River bridge at milepost 57.

For the Steese Highway trailhead: Turn right in Fox to stay on the Steese Highway (now Alaska 6). Drive to milepost 42.5. The McKay Creek Trail and parking area are on the left (north) side of the road.

35 *WICKERSHAM DOME AND SUMMIT TRAIL*

Wickersham Dome

R/T DISTANCE: 6.5 miles (10.5 km)

DURATION: 2 to 5 hours

HIGH POINT: 3,207 feet (977 m)

TOTAL ELEVATION CHANGE: 2,800 feet (853 m)

DIFFICULTY: Easy to moderate

ROUTE TYPE: Established trail (nonmotorized)

Summit Trail

R/T DISTANCE: 16 miles (26 km) but can be extended to 40 miles (64.5 km)

DURATION: 4 to 10 hours or up to 2 to 3 days

HIGH POINT: 3,207 feet (977 m)

TOTAL ELEVATION CHANGE: 4,100 feet (1,249 m) or more

DIFFICULTY: Moderate

ROUTE TYPE: Established trail (nonmotorized)

BEST SEASON: June to September, but there are year-round opportunities

USGS MAPS: Livengood A-3, B-2, B-3

LAND MANAGER: Bureau of Land Management (Fairbanks), 907-474-2200

Wickersham Dome via the Summit Trail offers easy access to alpine country. It is far enough from Fairbanks to get that out-of-town feeling, but it is close enough that it does not have to take all day. Because of these characteristics this hike is fairly popular, but you should not see crowds like at Angel Rocks (Trip 20). The trip to Wickersham Dome offers a mix of wet spruce forests and alpine country, along with good views of the White Mountains National Recreation Area (Trip 34). It can be hiked, skied, or snowshoed.

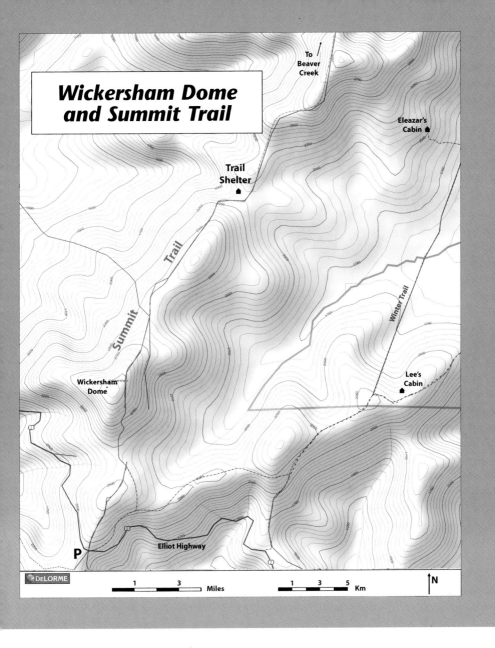

Most people turn around at Wickersham Dome, but Summit Trail continues on, rolling through alpine knobs and spruce forests. Some 8 miles (13 km) from the start is a stout public-use trail shelter, which makes for another great destination. The trail goes beyond here, too, for a total of 20 miles (32.3 km) one-way—all the way to Beaver Creek and the Borealis–LeFevre Cabin.

Summit Trail, starting at 2,200 feet (670 m), climbs steadily from the parking lot through diminutive spruce trees. Your first taste of alpine country and scenic vistas

The trail to Wickersham Dome provides easy access to the alpine.

comes swiftly. The trail skirts the top of a squat, bald dome before dropping back into spruce forest. The area is wet, but the trail has boardwalks through this section. After heavy rainfall, some of the boardwalks may be underwater. After 1.7 miles (2.7 km) the trail reaches a "T" intersection. The Ski Loop Trail (Trip 34) heads off to the right (southeast) and is usually wet in the summer. Summit Trail heads left (north) at this intersection to Wickersham Dome.

The trail gently climbs out of the spruce forest, but it gets steeper as you transition from tree line to brush line. Just ahead the trail levels out, and you find yourself back in alpine country once again. The summit of Wickersham Dome will be visible off to the left (west) on a clear day. Summit Trail, oddly enough, does not head to the summit. The summit has several communication facilities. You can make your own way to the summit but respect the facilities.

A better choice is to continue along the trail for another half mile (0.8 km) to reach a nice rock outcrop just off the left (west) side of the trail. This spot has good views and makes for a great destination and lunch spot. Most people choose to turn around here.

For a longer trip, stay on the Summit Trail heading northeast. The trail drops off Wickersham Dome and rolls along this northeast-running ridge. The trail is generally in good shape, but there are short stretches of wet areas. The trail alternates between alpine knobs and saddles of mixed forest. Most of the wetter areas have

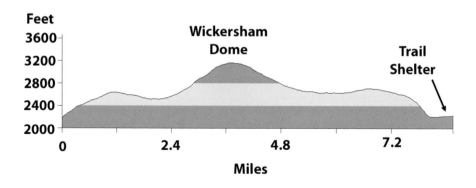

Summit Trail in fall.

boardwalk. The spectacular colors make fall an ideal time to hike this trail. Around mile 7 (km 11.3) the trail drops out of alpine country into a dense spruce stand. This area, nearly a mile (1.6 km) long, is wet but has boardwalk. A short climb takes you out of the spruce and reveals the public-use Summit Trail shelter nestled between two knobs. This pretty, 10 x 10-foot (3 x 3-m) trail shelter at mile 8 (km 13) is a good overnight destination. The use of the trail shelter is on a first-come, first-served basis, so be prepared to camp out. There are plenty of great camping spots before and after the shelter.

BE AWARE: Like many domes in the Interior, the summit has communication facilities. There is very little access to water along the trail, so be sure to bring enough. The trailhead has no plug-ins, so use good judgment about parking during winter travels. The trail can be hard to follow after fresh snow or during low clouds. If the trail is obscured and you are not adept at route finding, try another time when the weather is more cooperative. The trail shelter does not have a stove but is quite comfortable. It sleeps two, four if necessary.

MORE ADVENTUROUS? The Summit Trail runs 20 miles (32.3 km) from the trail-head to the Borealis–LeFevre Cabin on Beaver Creek, making for a 40-mile (64.5-km)

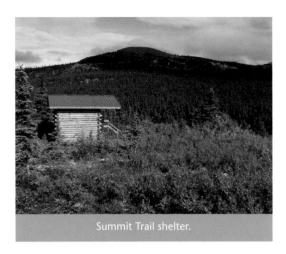

Summit Trail shelter.

Rolling terrain of the Summit Trail.

round trip. Past the shelter at mile 8 (km 13), the trail climbs to 3,100 feet (944 m) before diving back into spruce forest for a couple of miles. Then it climbs to 2,500 feet (761 m) before the steady descent to Beaver Creek. The trail can be wet, brushy, and difficult to follow in places. At mile 18 (km 29), Summit Trail connects with Wickersham Creek Trail. Turn left (north). Wickersham Creek Trail here can be pretty wet. After another mile (1.6 km) Big Bend Trail comes in from the northwest. Take the right (northeast) fork to stay on Wickersham Creek Trail, past Wickersham Creek, to reach Beaver Creek, which is about a mile (1.6 km). The Borealis–LeFevre Cabin is on the far side of the river. Crossing the river can be dangerous, especially at high water. Scout for the best spot to cross, and know proper river crossing techniques (see page xxiii). An exciting alternative is to packraft Beaver Creek (Trip 27) to the cabin, and then hike the 20 miles (32.3 km) to the trailhead. Summer hikes are limited in the western part of the White Mountains, but trips to Lee's and Moose Creek cabins are possible (Trip 34).

DIRECTIONS: Take the Steese Highway (Alaska 2) north out of Fairbanks to the town of Fox, 11 miles (18 km) away. Go straight here, which actually takes you off the Steese Highway and onto Elliott Highway (however, still highway Alaska 2). At milepost 28, a large, signed parking area is on the right (northeast) side of the road. Summit Trail trailhead is on the near (northwest) side of the parking area. The trailhead on the east side of the lot is for the Wickersham Creek Trail.

36 *GRAPEFRUIT ROCKS*

R/T DISTANCE: 1.1 miles (1.8 km)

DURATION: 1-hour hike, but enough rock climbing routes for days

HIGH POINT: 1,450 feet (442 m)

TOTAL ELEVATION CHANGE: 900 feet (274 m)

DIFFICULTY: Moderate but short hike; rock climbing routes of all levels

ROUTE TYPE: Social trail (nonmotorized)

BEST SEASON: April to September

USGS MAPS: Livengood B-3

LAND MANAGER: Alaska Department of Natural Resources (Fairbanks),
907-451-2705

Grapefruit Rocks is *the* rock climbing spot in the Interior. It is relatively close to Fairbanks, and has easy road access with a wide array of rock climbing routes. The area is bisected by the Elliott Highway, which separates the upper (east) and lower (west) areas of Grapefruit Rocks. Upper Grapefruit Rocks has more climbing terrain and routes. Hikers can also just enjoy the view or watch climbers in action. *Fairbanks Area Climbing Guide* by Stan Justice (see Appendix B) details individual routes.

Many social trails lead to Upper Grapefruit Rocks, but there are two (the North and South trails) that receive the majority of use; try to limit the number of social trails by sticking to the more established ones. Upper Grapefruit has about fifty established rock climbing routes on numerous outcrops. It offers more climbs, outcrops, and opportunities for beginners than Lower Grapefruit. Some of the outcrop names are Lowest Rock, Gorilla's Head, Twin Towers, Morning Wall, Beggar's Canyon, and Falcon Rock.

The first five of these outcrops are best reached using the steep South Trail. Lowest Rock will be the first to appear on the left (north) side of the trail. It has a couple of routes ranging from 5.6 to 5.9. Next up is Gorilla's Head with a 5.7 route and a couple of 5.10s. Farther up, but before Twin Towers, is an area for bouldering—though top roping is recommended due to the steep hillside below.

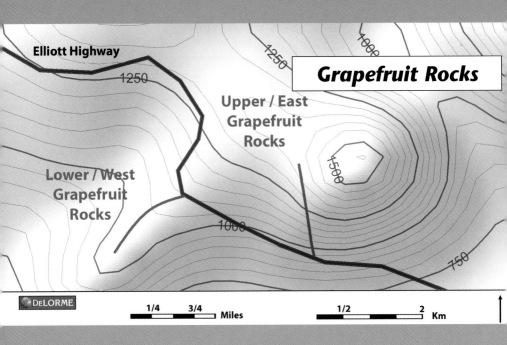

Elliott Highway

1250

1250

Upper / East
Grapefruit
Rocks

1000

1500

Lower / West
Grapefruit
Rocks

1000

750

DeLORME

1/4   3/4   Miles

1/2   2   Km

Farther up still is Twin Towers and Morning Wall. These two outcrops offer many routes and the greatest spread of ratings. The dozen or so established routes range from 5.4 to 5.11, with many routes for novices. From Twin Towers, you can head north over to Falcon Rocks or pass by Morning Wall and crest the hill. Following an indistinct trail to the northeast you will come to Beggar's Canyon. This area has about ten climbs ranging from 5.8 to 5.10.

Falcon Rocks is most easily reached by taking the steep North Trail from the parking area. Falcon Rocks outcrop is divided into three areas: Hole in the Wall, Peanut Butter, and Refrigerator Crack. This outcrop has the most established routes (eighteen) in the Grapefruit Rocks area with routes ranging from 5.7 to 5.12.

To reach Lower Grapefruit Rocks, follow the jeep trail (see "Directions" below) west about a quarter mile (0.4 km) until it ends. Lower Grapefruit generally has fewer and harder routes. First Crag should be visible from the end of the jeep trail. The ten or so routes here range from 5.4 to 5.11. Head to the left (north) side of First Crag to reach Second Crag. This outcrop has three established routes ranging from a difficult 5.9 to 5.12.

Another section of Lower Grapefruit Rocks called the Lost 5.10 Crack Area offers routes ranging from 5.8 to 5.10. However, this spot can be hard to find. Adventurous souls seeking this outcrop should consult Stan Justice's guide or climbers who have been there before. If you are not sure what all these 5-something ratings mean, you should find an expert to literally show you the ropes!

Rock climbing at Upper Grapefruit.

BE AWARE: Rock climbing is an inherently dangerous sport; please use caution and a helmet. Mosquitoes and sunshine can both be powerful at Grapefruit Rocks; be prepared. Cold temperatures and snow can persist here into April and May. Expect large trucks on Elliott Highway, which is part of the route to the Prudhoe Bay oil fields.

MORE ADVENTUROUS? Mount Prindle (Trip 29) and Granite Tors (Trip 19) also offer great rock climbing opportunities, but their remote locations also provide a wilderness experience.

DIRECTIONS: Take the Steese Highway (Alaska 2) north out of Fairbanks to the town of Fox, 11 miles (18 km) away. Go straight here, which actually takes you off the Steese Highway and onto Elliott Highway (however, still highway Alaska 2). At milepost 39, just after the Globe Creek bridge, there is a turnout on the right (north) side of the road. The turnout is actually a short, rough gravel road paralleling the highway. Park at the far end of this turnout to reach Upper Grapefruit Rocks.

To reach Lower Grapefruit Rocks, continue on the Elliott for about a half mile (0.8 km). On the left (south) side of the highway is another pullout. Park here to get to Lower Grapefruit Rocks. Park in the turnout, not on the jeep trail heading toward the rocks. Both sets of Grapefruit Rocks are visible from the Elliott Highway as you drive north.

37 *TOLOVANA HOT SPRINGS TRAIL*

R/T DISTANCE: 22 miles (35.5 km)

DURATION: 2 to 3 days

HIGH POINT: 2,120 feet (645 m)

TOTAL ELEVATION CHANGE: 7,300 feet (2,224 m)

DIFFICULTY: Moderate

ROUTE TYPE: Established trail (motorized allowed)

BEST SEASON: October to April

USGS MAPS: Livengood B-4, B-5

LAND MANAGER: Tolovana Hot Springs, Ltd., 907-455-6706

Use of the hot springs, cabins, and surrounding area is by reservation and fee payment only.

Few things capture the imagination of Interior adventurers more than a winter trip that ends with a soak in a natural hot springs. Tolovana Hot Springs offers a vastly different experience than Chena Hot Springs. It is remote and far less developed. The trail to it rolls through quintessential Interior forests and hills. The hot springs is on the wooded south slopes of Tolovana Hot Springs Dome. This winter trip is best suited for classical skiers, but often the trail is packed enough by snowmachines that hikers have no problems.

The trip begins relatively high off the Elliott Highway in a nice grove of birch trees. The trail then quickly and steeply drops through ever-shrinking trees and a series of old burns. The drop is steep enough that you can sled down the hill if you are pulling one. Just be careful not to gain too much speed, go careening off the trail, and injure yourself. The descent mellows after the first mile (1.6 km). The next couple of miles take you through a typical black spruce lowland bog. The trail is usually well packed and frozen, but this area can have wet or overflow conditions and stretches of open water. On the other side of the bog the trail again changes

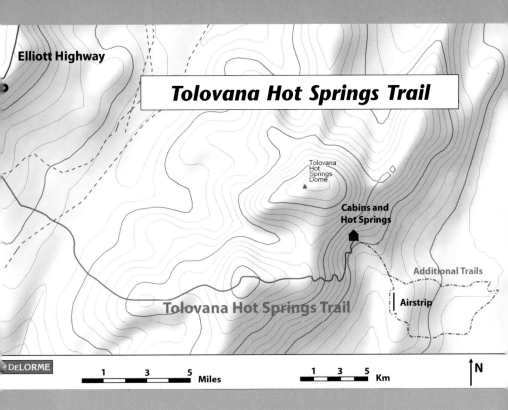

Tolovana Hot Springs Trail

Tolovana
Hot
Springs
Dome

Cabins and
Hot Springs

Additional Trails

Tolovana Hot Springs Trail

Airstrip

DeLORME

1   3   5
Miles

1   3   5
Km

↑N

character, climbing steadily for about 1,000 feet (305 m) before leveling out. The level area is short-lived, as there is another pitch that rises 500 feet (152 m) to the "Top of the Dome"—but not Tolovana Hot Springs Dome, which is to the northeast.

The views from the Top of the Dome, at about mile 8 (km 13), can be spectacular as the trees thin out and give way to wide-open vistas. To the northwest are the rugged peaks of Wolverine and Sawtooth mountains. To the south and southeast are the expanses of the Minto Flats State Game Refuge. On clear days you can even make out Wickersham Dome (Trip 35) in the distance to the east. However, the top can be windy or fogged in. This is about the only spot where finding the trail might be difficult. If you are not experienced at route finding and the top is fogged in, consider heading back rather than having to bivouac in the snow.

Descending off the dome, you traverse an old, inactive airstrip. Watch for moose here, as the browse is great for them. Just past the runway is the steepest part of the trail. To the northeast, the hot springs area can be seen on the south slopes of Tolovana Hot Springs Dome. This part of the trail is another fun place to ride the sled rather than dragging it behind you. Mind your speed. At the bottom of this long descent, a short, gentle uphill is all that is left before reaching the springs. The first cabin you come

The tub at the hot springs.

to is private property and not part of the hot springs development. The hot springs area consists of three rustic but well-maintained cabins, a couple of hot tubs along the creek, and a natural cold spring for fresh water. As of this writing, only two of the cabins were available for rent: the small frame cabin and a larger log cabin. The woods surrounding the hot springs burned a few years ago, so there is ample firewood. Logs can be found near the cabins that can be sawed to woodstove length and split. Water jugs, saws, axes, and pretty much everything you will need is provided.

Once you manage to pry yourself from the hot springs, just head back out the way to you came. But remember that you will have two hills to climb on the way back!

BE AWARE: Again, use of the hot springs, cabins, and surrounding area is by reservation only. The cabins are stocked with cook gear, propane, a propane stove and lights, an ax, a saw, a woodstove, and excess foam pads, so you can travel light if you want. The small cabin can fit four people, but it is a squeeze. The cabins are not right next to the tubs, so be prepared for a 75- to 150-yard (meter) walk to and from the tubs. If someone has not used the tubs in a while, there could be quite a buildup of algae. Be prepared to drain and clean the tub or just put up with some slime. No soaps are allowed in the hot springs or creek. Dogs cannot be loose; this is to minimize

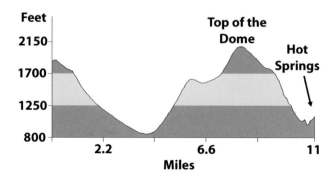

damage of the fragile ecosystem and to avoid trouble between pets and dog teams.

Snowmachines and dog teams use this trail, so watch for them. When the trail is well packed, the going is easy, but be prepared for much slower going if you have to break trail. The trail is often difficult to find at the top of the dome because of drifting snow or low clouds.

Wolf tracks with Sawtooth Mountain in the background.

MORE ADVENTUROUS? After an 11-mile (18-km) up-and-down hike, most people like to just soak in the warm waters. If you have lots of energy or plan to stay in the area for a few days, there are a few side trips you can make. You can climb Tolovana Hot Springs Dome, at 2,386 feet (727 m), or follow trails southeast away from the springs for an 8-mile (13-km) loop. Watch for open leads of water. There are other, longer trails that reach the hot springs. These trails start near Livengood (26 miles [42 km]) and Murphy Dome (50 miles [81 km]). One also starts from Nenana. These trails are used mostly by snowmachiners and mushers, but highly experienced backcountry skiers could use them for an extended trip. Another idea is to go down the Elliott Highway a little farther to Hutlinana Hot Springs Trail (see Appendix A).

DIRECTIONS: Take the Steese Highway (Alaska 2) north out of Fairbanks to the town of Fox, 11 miles (18 km) away. Go straight here, which actually takes you off the Steese Highway and onto Elliott Highway (however, still highway Alaska 2). The pavement ends at milepost 73, past Livengood. Here the Elliott meets the Dalton Highway. At this intersection, turn left to stay on the Elliott. (Continuing straight puts you on the Dalton Highway.) Park at milepost 93.1 in a turnout on the left (south) side of the highway. There is no sign at the turnout, but Tolovana Hot Springs Dome will be visible to the southeast. The trail, which starts as a road, is on the west side of the turnout. After about 30 yards (meters) there will be a sign noting that you are on the Tolovana Hot Springs Trail.

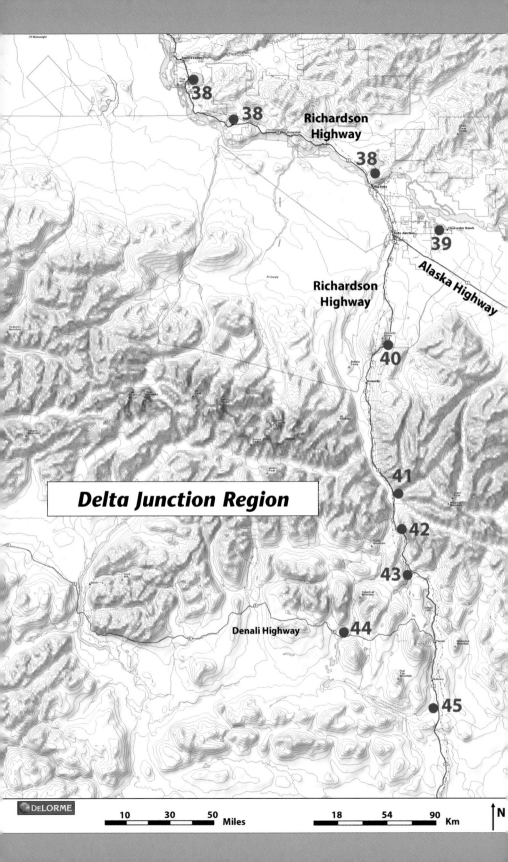

Delta Junction Region

Richardson Highway

Richardson Highway

Alaska Highway

Denali Highway

38 38 38 39 40 41 42 43 44 45

DeLORME

10 30 50
Miles

18 54 90
Km

N

Delta Junction Region

Just 15 miles (24 km) north of the towering Alaska Range, the Delta Junction region offers easy access to strenuous hikes and scenic floats. In stark contrast to the mountains are the extensive agricultural fields in the area. Delta Junction is about 100 miles (160 km) southeast of Fairbanks, about two hours by car. Some of the land between Delta Junction and the mountains to the south belongs to Fort Greely (permission is required to use much of these lands). This area has many technical mountaineering trips, as well as wilderness epics (e.g., the Alaska Mountain Wilderness Classic traverse from Black Rapids to Denali National Park). The adventures I have described for this region are less demanding than those, but they are still challenging trips. The number of hikes in the region is limited only by your imagination. The area also has several excellent floats with unbeatable scenery. A couple of the adventures described here are south of the Alaska Range; I include them because of their popularity with Interior residents.

38 HIGHWAY LAKES—Harding, Birch, and Quartz

R/T DISTANCE: Up to 3 miles (5 km)

DURATION: Up to 2 to 3 hours

HIGH POINT: 1,100 feet (335 m)

TOTAL ELEVATION CHANGE: Less than 100 feet (30 m)

DIFFICULTY: Easy

ROUTE TYPE: Established trail or float (flat water); suitable for canoes, rafts, and all kayaks (mix of motorized and nonmotorized)

BEST SEASON: May to September

USGS MAPS: Big Delta B-6, A-4

LAND MANAGER: Alaska Department of Natural Resources (Fairbanks), 907-451-2705

South of Fairbanks are a series of lakes along the Richardson Highway that have state recreation areas. They all offer opportunities to get out for a canoe ride, have a picnic, or go for a stroll. Harding Lake is the closest to Fairbanks, next comes Birch Lake, and then Quartz Lake. Quartz Lake is just a few miles north of Big Delta at the confluence of the Tanana and Delta rivers (Trips 39, 44, and 48).

Harding Lake, along with Chena Lake, is widely used by Fairbanksans as their beach. You can use canoes here, but during nice summer days motorboats dominate the lake. There is a state recreation area on the west side of the lake with a boat launch and a short, quarter-mile (0.4 km) nature trail.

The Birch Lake Recreation Area has a designated swimming area, but the area's primary function is as a boat launch. Birch Lake is smaller than the other two highway lakes, so it receives somewhat less motorboat traffic. There are no hiking trails here.

Quartz Lake offers the most variety of the three highway lakes. First, there are actually three "lakes" at the Quartz Lake State Recreation Area: Quartz Lake, Lost

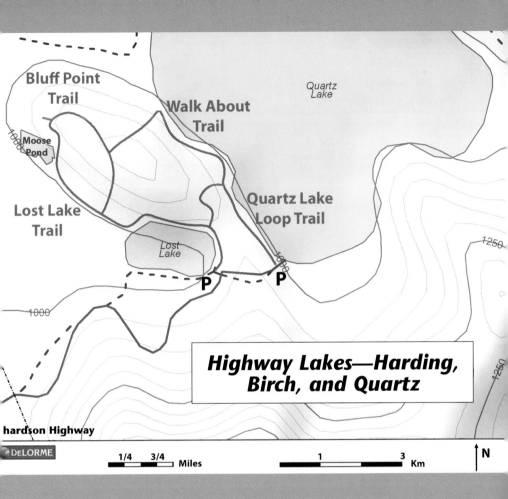

Lake, and Moose Pond. Quartz Lake is large and receives a lot of motorboat use. Lost Lake is much smaller, but only nonmotorized craft are allowed on it, making it an ideal spot to paddle your canoe. Swans and ducks are often swimming among the pond lilies. The lake is stocked with rainbow trout, so try your hand at fishing. Moose Pond can be found by following one of the area's nature trails. There are a series of trails that each make for a nice walk: Quartz Lake Loop Trail (1.8 miles [2.9 km]), Lost Lake Trail (1.3 miles [2.1 km]), and Bluff Point Trail (3 miles [4.8 km]). Two public-use cabins are available for rent here the year round. Quartz Lake Cabin, right at the campground parking lot, is 10 x 16 feet (3 x 5 m), sleeps three, and is car accessible. Glatfelder Cabin can be reached by trail or by Quartz Lake. The lake route requires a half-mile (0.8-km) paddle, but when the lake freezes solid you can walk or ski to the cabin. Glatfelder Cabin is 15 x 20 feet (5 x 6 m) and sleeps four.

BE AWARE: The recreation areas have fees. The larger lakes have lots of motorboat traffic. Avoid the Bert Mountain Trail at Quartz Lake. It is not a mountain, it is

Ice remnants on Birch Lake in May.

barely a trail (thorny roses have taken over), and the overlook was completely overgrown (as of 2004).

MORE ADVENTUROUS? If you enjoy these lake recreation areas and are heading farther east, check out Fielding Lake (Trip 43) down the Richardson Highway or Moon Lake Recreation Area at milepost 1332 of the Alaska Highway (Alaska 2). Moon Lake is about 15 miles (24 km) northwest of Tok.

Also check out Bluff Cabin Trail for a relatively easy, 7-mile (11.3-km) round-trip hike near Delta Junction. Route-finding skills are important on this trail as it has many side trails, which can be wet in summer. To get to the Bluff Cabin Trail trailhead, turn left (north) onto Tanana Loop Extension at milepost 271.8 of the Richardson Highway. Stay on Tanana Loop for 1.3 miles (2.1 km), then turn right (east) at the intersection. Follow that road 2.3 miles (3.7 km) until you see the trailhead on the left (north) side.

Follow the multiuse trail north for nearly a mile (1.6 km), until the intersection at Fourmile Hill. Turn right (east) and follow the trail to the northeast for about a half mile (0.8 km). A side trail to the bluff's namesake cabin departs to the right (east), but the cabin was destroyed as of 2004. Go to the next intersection a quarter mile (0.4 km) distant and take the trail to the right (east), which will lead you up the ridge and eventually to two lakes. The farther lake is 3.5 miles (5.6 km) from the start. It is larger, has fish, and is called Bluff Cabin Lake. While this is a nice hike on a ridge, leaves usually block the views in the summer.

DIRECTIONS: Take the Richardson Highway (Alaska 2) southeast out of Fairbanks. To reach Harding Lake State Recreation Area, turn left at milepost 321. Signs will lead you the short distance to the recreation area.

Birch Lake abuts the Richardson Highway, but the road to the boat ramp and swimming area is a little farther down the highway. At milepost 305, turn left (north) on the dirt road.

To reach Quartz Lake State Recreation Area, turn left (north) on the gravel road at milepost 278. Follow it about a mile (1.6 km) to reach Lost Lake, or keep going another quarter mile (0.4 km) to reach the large parking area for the Quartz Lake boat launch and hiking trails.

39 *CLEARWATER AND TANANA RIVERS*

ONE-WAY DISTANCE: 12 miles (19 km) to Clearwater Lake or 28 miles (45 km) to Richardson bridge

DURATION: 3 to 6 hours to the lake or 5 to 10 hours to the bridge

HIGH POINT: 1,050 feet (320 m)

TOTAL ELEVATION CHANGE: Less than 75 feet (23 m)

DIFFICULTY: Easy to moderate

ROUTE TYPE: Float (class I); suitable for canoes and river kayaks, rafts if going to bridge (motorized allowed)

BEST SEASON: April to September

USGS MAPS: Big Delta A-3, A-4

LAND MANAGER: Alaska Department of Natural Resources (Fairbanks), 907-451-2705

Willow buds sprouting, squadrons of geese flying overhead, days growing longer, and canoes plying the waters of the Clearwater: these are the rites of spring in the Interior. The Clearwater River offers boaters one of the earliest spring opportunities to dust the cobwebs from the canoe. Also known as the Delta Clearwater River, it is the largest spring-fed tributary of the Tanana River. The river is about 20 miles (32 km) long, with water as clear as can be, hence its name. This trip is a great first adventure of the season to shake off winter and enjoy the spectacle of thousands of migrating waterfowl. However, it is a nice float in summer and early fall as well.

The launch is at a state recreation site. Soak in the sites of the crystal-clear water and the towering white spruce trees. Many birds are attracted to the open water; after a long winter it is nice to hear their songs again. The river winds its way through woods, but plenty of houses and cabins dot the shore, so do not expect a wilderness experience for the first few miles. On longer straightaways you will catch glimpses of the snow-covered Alaska Range looming in the south.

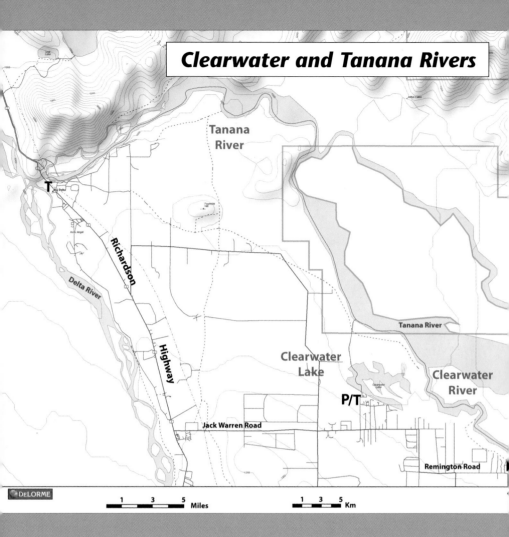

Clearwater and Tanana Rivers

Tanana
River

Richardson

Delta River

Highway

Tanana River

Clearwater
Lake

Clearwater
River

P/T

Jack Warren Road

Remington Road

DELORME

1   3   5
Miles

1   3   5
Km

The current is steady but not strong. There are no rapids and only occasional maneuvers are required: a good place to learn your strokes or shake off the rust. The river has places to pull over for lunch, but be mindful of private property.

All too swiftly the 8-mile (13-km) stretch of the Clearwater is behind you. The water becomes cloudy as you enter the Tanana River and the vegetation changes from towering trees to colonizing willows and other earlier successional species. It is here that the proverbial fork in the road lies.

If your destination is the boat launch at Clearwater Lake, then stay to the left (as you are looking downstream, south side). There will be a river entering from this side. It is the outlet to Clearwater Lake and will be clear and dark, but not cloudy. There is a sign marking the outlet but floodwaters from the Tanana have a tendency to keep it in disrepair, so do not count on it being visible. The outlet is slow-moving, but the current is steady with the first quarter mile (0.4 km) being the toughest. Two good paddlers can make their way upstream without too much effort, but this part of the trip may be more challenging for smaller or less experienced folks, especially with a headwind. Portaging or lining your boat would be difficult and is not recommended. Larger trees will again line the shore. The paddle up the outlet stream is about 1.5 miles (2.4 km) long. Most people choose this as their destination, as during peak migration thousands of golden eyes, mergansers, mallards, swans, and geese gather here. The take-out is on the southwestern shore, about 12 miles (19.4 km) from the trip's start.

The put-in on the Clearwater in mid-April.

Be mindful of waves on the lake if the wind kicks up.

For those who scratch their heads in disbelief that people actually paddle upstream, then continuing past the Clearwater Lake outlet may be the better option. The Tanana River is a big Alaskan river; only experienced paddlers should attempt this float. However, the western channels of the river tend to be pretty quiet (when the river is not acting up). The river is wide and straight enough that most sweepers should be relatively easy to avoid. There are many miles without roads, houses, and power lines. The calming influence of being in the wild has time to set in.

The river has several camping spots for those wishing to make the float into a weekend excursion. The farther you go, especially past the outlet of the Goodpaster River, the more signs of civilization you will see. Houses become more frequent, especially on the southern bank. In just a few more miles the Trans-Alaska Pipeline and the Richardson Highway bridge will come into sight. The landing is between the pipeline and the bridge on the left (facing downstream, south side), 28 miles (45 km) from the start. The trip will leave you wanting more; the good news is that the season of summer adventures has just kicked off.

BE AWARE: The Tanana is a large, cold, silty, and powerful river. Only experienced canoeists and kayakers should travel on rivers of this size and speed. The journey to Clearwater Lake involves paddling upstream. The current is not very strong but is steady. If the wind picks up, substantial waves can form in the lake. This can make the traverse of the lake to the take-out treacherous. Mid- to late April is the peak of the spring migratory season, so be prepared for plenty of company on weekends. Keep a good distance from the birds; many still have a long way to go. If they move away from you, you have gotten too close.

MORE ADVENTUROUS? The sky is the limit, or rather the river is. The Tanana River parallels the Richardson Highway and can take you as far as Fairbanks, Nenana, or even Manley Hot Springs if you have a couple of weeks. You can also put in farther upriver. The Tanana can be accessed at many locations upriver as far as Northway Junction (Trip 48). Paddlers should be experienced, as there are rapids and other serious river hazards.

DIRECTIONS: Head south on the Richardson Highway (Alaska 2) to milepost 275. There is a dirt parking lot on the far (south) side of the bridge on your left (east). It is right next to the Trans-Alaska Pipeline. Drop a shuttle vehicle here if you plan to float back down to the bridge; otherwise continue south on the Richardson for an additional 7 miles (11.3 km) to Jack Warren Road (milepost 268). Take a left onto Jack Warren, eastbound.

If you plan to use Clearwater Lake as your take-out, turn left (north) onto Triple H Road after about 3 miles (4.8 km). Please be aware that the Triple H Road sign is often missing. Take Triple H north for about three-quarters of a mile (1.2 km), past Olmstead Road. Triple H will turn into Clearwater Avenue. Turn left, following the signs for the launch. The boat launch is about a half mile (0.8 km) past where Triple H becomes Clearwater and has a large area for parking a shuttle vehicle.

To get to the put-in, get back out on Jack Warren Road. Continue east, and the road will curve to the right (south) and change its name to Southrada Road. Continue on the main road by turning left onto Remington Road, which again feels more like a curve than a turn. The turn for the Clearwater State Recreation Site, which has the boat launch, is on the left after about a mile (1.6 km) and is well signed.

To get to the put-in from the east side of Delta Junction, turn right (north) on Clearwater Road about 7 miles (11.3 km) before Delta Junction. This will take you to Remington Road. Turn right on it and the recreation site will be just ahead on the left.

40 *DONNELLY DOME*

R/T DISTANCE: 3 miles (4.8 km)

DURATION: 2 to 5 hours

HIGH POINT: 3,910 feet (1,188 m)

TOTAL ELEVATION CHANGE: 3,800 feet (1,157 m)

DIFFICULTY: Moderate

ROUTE TYPE: Social trail (nonmotorized)

BEST SEASON: May to September

USGS MAPS: Mount Hayes D-4

LAND MANAGER: U.S. Army, Fort Greely (visitors' center), 907-873-3660

Donnelly Dome rises out of the flats like a lone sentinel in front of the mighty Alaska Range. The dome is steeply walled on all sides, so there is no easy route to its summit. Although steep, the hike is short and provides great views of the flats to the north, the Delta River, and the Alaska Range to the south.

From the parking area, follow the gravel jeep trail west for about a quarter mile (0.4 km). Here the jeep trail veers back to the south toward the highway. Break away from the jeep trail, to the northwest, following a well-worn social trail. Dwarf birch scratch at your legs, but generally the social trail is easy to follow. However, it quickly loses its easygoing nature and heads right up the dome. The trail is steep and covered with loose, sharp rock fragments. It is pretty much unrelenting for 1,400 vertical feet (426 m). The higher you go, the better the views become—so enjoy the scenery and catch your breath. Spring crocus (pasque flowers) will greet early season hikers, as will scores of ground squirrels. Scan the valley as well; moose and caribou are frequently seen in the open shrub and tundra countryside.

The trail can split with many legs petering out in places; just keep heading uphill if you can not find it again, but it is likely you will. The pitch lessens as you near the top. Though still uphill, the last 200 yards (meters) will feel flat in comparison to the hill you have just climbed. The summit is a great place to soak in the 360-degree

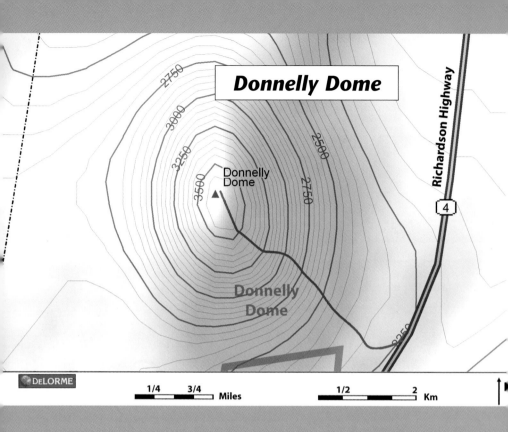

Donnelly Dome

Richardson Highway

4

Donnelly
Dome

▲

Donnelly
Dome

DELORME

1/4   3/4 Miles   1/2   2 Km

views and enjoy your lunch. When you are ready, retrace your steps back to the
road. Take your time, as the steep, loose trail is more treacherous going down than
coming up.

BE AWARE: This trip is on Fort Greely. You should probably check in at the visitors' center to see if anything is going on, such as military exercises. A Recreational
Access Permit (RAP) is required if you are going hunting or fishing on the base (as
it is with other bases in the state). Army representatives have said RAP cards are not
necessary to park for this hike, but you may see signs that state otherwise. The visitors' center at Fort Greely is open Monday through Friday, 6 a.m.–3:30 p.m., but is

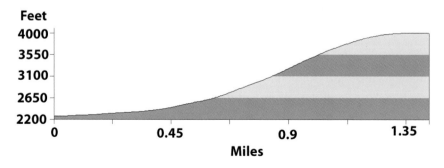

Caribou grazing north of Donnelly Dome.

closed on weekends. However, the one at Fort Wainwright (Fairbanks) is open 24 hours a day, every day (907-353-6144). Personnel there can answer some questions and issue RAPs, which are good for two years. The hike is very steep and the trail consists mainly of loose, sharp rock. I recommend bringing hiking poles to help you keep your balance, gaiters to keep rocks out of your shoes, and leather gloves to protect your hands on the way down.

MORE ADVENTUROUS? The Alaska Range beckons in the distance to the south. Castner Glacier (Trip 41) and Rainbow Ridge (Trip 42) offer adventurers more challenging hikes into wilder country. If that sounds too hard-core but you are still looking to walk around some more, try the tundra around Tangle Lake (Trip 44).

DIRECTIONS: Head southeast on the Richardson Highway (Alaska 2) out of Fairbanks. In Delta Junction, veer to the south (right) to stay on the Richardson (now Alaska 4). Follow this until you reach milepost 246.5. There is a small dirt turnout on the right (west) side. There is a smaller turnout at milepost 247, but the trail there is less distinct and even steeper, so I do not recommend it. The Fort Greely Visitors' Center is 4.5 miles (7.3 km) south of Delta Junction on Highway Alaska 4. Turn left (east) and follow the signs to the red building. It is not open on weekends.

41 *CASTNER GLACIER*

R/T DISTANCE: Up to 16 miles (26 km)

DURATION: 2 to 3 days, but day trips are possible

HIGH POINT: 4,500 feet (1,370 m)

TOTAL ELEVATION CHANGE: 4,000 feet (1,218 m)

DIFFICULTY: Moderate to difficult

ROUTE TYPE: Route (nonmotorized)

BEST SEASON: June to September for hikers, mid-March to early May for skiers

USGS MAPS: Mount Hayes B-4

LAND MANAGER: Alaska Department of Natural Resources (Fairbanks), 907-451-2705

Castner Glacier spills out of an amphitheater of rugged mountains. Devil's Thumb and Mount Silvertip crowd the northern rim while the west ridge of Triangle Peak encases the valley to the south. This trip takes you from the terminus of Castner Glacier onto its vegetated cover, and into the heart of the Alaska Range. Day hikes of any length provide spectacular views, but the views get better the farther you go. Longer trips make for great overnighters or weekend backpacking trips. This trip requires backcountry experience, route-finding abilities, and knowledge of glacier travel.

From the turnout off the Richardson Highway, follow the social trail through the alders heading east. The trail is cut out so traveling is good here on the terrace above the river. After about 100 yards (meters) the trail drops out of the alders and down to the lower riverbank. Stay on the south bank and close to the creek, which can be thundering at times. The going is mostly good, but you have to contend with some side hilling, narrow ledges, short stretches of bushwhacking, and talus. This section is quite fun for those who enjoy route finding over advanced terrain. For skiers, the route finding is much less challenging because snow covers many obstacles.

After about a mile (1.6 km), when you are even with the rock outcrop on the ridge to the south, you should see a large, squarish boulder about 6 x 12 feet (2 x 4 m). This

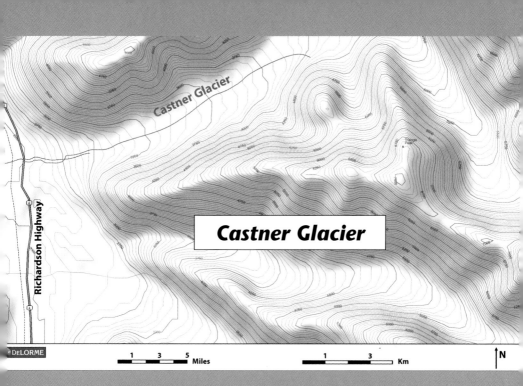

Castner Glacier

Richardson Highway

1 3 5 Miles

1 3 Km

↑N

•DeLORME

can be a good place to cut across a small braid of the main creek and reach the toe of the glacier. The glacier is vegetated, but the brush is mostly sparse and knee-high. On warmer days, the "ground" can be spongy as the glacier heats up. The hiking is good, and views are hard to beat. There are short ups and downs, but generally the hike is a gradual uphill. Good campsites can be found all along the glacier's edge. At the head of the valley, glaciers spill off steep mountainsides in three directions, forming the Castner Glacier. This is a great spot to stop and enjoy the sights or plot out adventures to hit the high peaks.

BE AWARE: This trip is on an active glacier—albeit a glacier covered by vegetation. Good route-finding abilities and a knowledge of glaciers are required. Glaciers present many obstacles, such as crevasses and tricky footing; know your abilities and stay within your comfort zone. Conditions can vary dramatically over the season and even throughout the day. On warm days, the "ground" may be soft, leading to spongy hiking conditions. High winds can arrive seemingly out of nowhere and last for days; expect them. Snow cover varies greatly from year to year; hikes in early June may be fine, but a foot of snow may remain from winter. That can be good for late-season skiers, but be mindful—this is definitely avalanche country.

MORE ADVENTUROUS? The Alaska Range looms all around. Peak baggers with mountaineering experience can head south to tackle Triangle Peak—its 7,368-foot (2,244-m) summit is only a couple of miles away—or north to climb Mount Silvertip

River beauty and peaks surrounding Castner Glacier.

(9,400 feet [2,863 m]). The least technical route up Triangle Peak is to follow Castner Creek to the rock outcrop on the mountain's west ridge. A short but arduous quarter-mile (0.4-km) uphill bushwhack through alders will take you into alpine country and a moderately pitched route to the summit. Other routes up Triangle Peak and any route up Mount Silvertip require mountaineering equipment and experience. Donnelly Dome (Trip 40) and Rainbow Ridge (Trip 42) offer other great hiking experiences in the area that are not as daunting. Other options? Look around, there are plenty of adventures for you to discover on your own. Highly experienced white-water kayakers and packrafters may want to float the fast class III waters of Castner Creek back to the bridge. Helmets, life jackets, and dry suits are necessary, as is a thorough scouting effort. There are few spots to pull out, adding to the skill needed for this adventure.

DIRECTIONS: Head southeast on the Richardson Highway (Alaska 2) out of Fairbanks. In Delta Junction, veer to the south (right) to stay on the Richardson (now Alaska 4). Follow this until you reach milepost 217.1. There is a small dirt pullout on the left (east) side, immediately after the Castner Creek bridge. The turnout is about 50 yards (meters) long. Try to park so that others can park and not be blocked in.

42 **RAINBOW RIDGE**

Traverse

ONE-WAY DISTANCE: 6 miles (9.7 km)

DURATION: 2 to 5 hours or up to 2 days

HIGH POINT: 3,500 feet (1,066 m)

TOTAL ELEVATION CHANGE: 1,700 feet (518 m)

DIFFICULTY: Moderate

ROUTE TYPE: Route (nonmotorized)

High Pass

R/T DISTANCE: 3 miles (4.8 km)

DURATION: 2 to 5 hours

HIGH POINT: 4,750 feet (1,447 m)

TOTAL ELEVATION CHANGE: 4,500 feet (1,371 m)

DIFFICULTY: Difficult

ROUTE TYPE: Route (nonmotorized)

BEST SEASON: June to September

USGS MAPS: Mount Hayes B-4

LAND MANAGER: Alaska Department of Natural Resources (Fairbanks), 907-451-2705

Rainbow Ridge forms an imposing wall that is memorable for most everyone traveling the Richardson Highway. Towering some 4,000 feet (1,220 m) over the road, the steep slopes of the ridge are tinted in unusual colors: bright orange lying next to rich purples. For hikers, the ridge has several options with varying degrees of difficulty. One is a 6-mile (9.7-km), one-way traverse that is relatively easy going aside from a couple of short but steep climbs. Good camping spots can be found after a few short pitches, making for

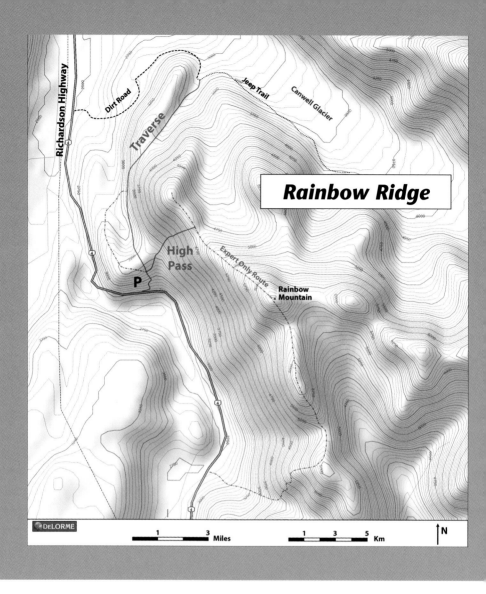

Rainbow Ridge

1   3 Miles   1   3   5 Km   ↑N

a mile (1.6 km) round trip if you are looking for something short. Or you can climb straight up the steep ridge to a high, 4,750-foot (1,447-m) pass—and even beyond.

Head east about 50 yards (meters) from the turnout, skirting a small pond. A small cairn on the north side of the pond marks the start of a social trail that heads steeply up the initial hill. The trail, aside from being steep, is a bit overgrown and lined with small, loose gravel that makes footing treacherous. The pitch is short to the first bench. It makes for a good place to catch your breath and enjoy the ever-improving views of the valley and surrounding mountains. Head for a small notch on the west side of the next pitch, as it provides the path of least bushwhacking.

The top of this second small rise marks decision time. To the east, the ridge climbs quickly and then gets steeper leading to the high pass. If you want to do the traverse, head north, where there are brushy areas interspersed with open alpine tundra. A rock wind shelter sits to the west, and the immediate area has other pleasant places to camp. If you are looking for more of a workout but still want to do the traverse, head

An overview of the traverse while climbing to the high pass.

northwest and take to the ridge. It has more ups and downs.

Continuing to head north at this decision point will give you much less climbing (and descending). After a gentle 200-foot (61-m) climb, maintain your elevation as you go between the west ridge and the towering slopes of Canwell Peak to your east. (Canwell Peak is not an official name. The peak has a USGS survey monument with that name on it.) The main valley will continue to head basically north, but after a mile (1.6 km) the slopes of Canwell Peak will form nearly a 90-degree angle and head east. Follow this slope, and climb the 200-foot (61-m) pitch to the 3,500-foot (1,066-m) pass. From here, on a clear day, you will have great views of the Canwell Glacier and your path ahead. Follow this valley down to the northeast. Stay on the east side of the creek and you will run into an ATV trail that will take you to the road. Head downhill and to the west (left) and you will shortly reach the pick-up point.

The alternative decision to hit the high pass is a decision to go vertical. Head east at the top of the second climb. The views of the Delta River valley and the Alaska Range are fantastic, but the path is steep, very steep. The footing can be tricky, as the slope is covered in a loose talus. I would recommend gaiters to keep the rocks out of your boots. Rock outcrops along the way provide respites from the talus and make fine destinations. A 4,750-foot (1,447-m) high pass provides a spectacular overlook of not only the Delta River valley but the massive Canwell Glacier and rugged peaks of the central Alaska Range.

ALL ROUTES BE AWARE: Route-finding abilities are required for this hike. There are short sections of bushwhacking, depending on route choice. The climb up Rainbow Ridge is steep and exposed. The slope is covered with loose talus, making for a "two steps forward, one step back" progression in many places. Only sure-footed and confident climbers should attempt to gain the high pass. You can get great views by just climbing a short ways. Be very mindful of creating rockslides and cascading rocks onto hikers below. High winds can arrive seemingly out of nowhere and last for days; expect them. Snow cover varies greatly from year to year; hikes in early June may be fine, but a foot of snow may remain from winter.

MORE ADVENTUROUS? From the high pass, the 5,422-foot (1,652-m) summit of Canwell Peak is only a mile (1.6 km) away to the northwest, and Rainbow Mountain (6,700 feet [2,041 m]) is less than 2 miles (3.2 km) to the southeast. Both are hard climbs. In an epic day, uber-athletes can hike the entire Rainbow Ridge, descending about 3 miles (4.8 km) south of Rainbow Mountain and following the creek west to the gravel pit at milepost 206.5. That route spans 11 miles (18 km) and is for experts only. Also from the high pass, you can descend to the northeast and reach a high alpine meadow. Descend the gentle slopes to reach the Canwell Glacier dirt road to the north (about 5 miles [8 km] oneway). Donnelly Dome (Trip 40) and Castner Glacier (Trip 41) offer other great hiking experiences nearby that are not as daunting. Other options? Look around, there are plenty of adventures for you to discover on your own.

DIRECTIONS: Head southeast on the Richardson Highway (Alaska 2) out of Fairbanks. In Delta Junction, veer to the south (right) to stay on the Richardson (now Alaska 4). Follow this until you reach milepost 209.5. There is a small dirt turnout on the left (north) side, where the hike and traverse starts.

To leave a shuttle vehicle for doing the traverse north, turn east onto a dirt road on milepost 213.5. The road is in good condition for about a mile (1.6 km). The road is rockier, but generally passable by two-wheel-drive vehicles until 3.5 miles (5.6 km) in. There is parking here, or if you have a four-wheel-drive vehicle with high clearance you can cross the creek a little farther on and head up the hill about 100 yards (meters). Park where the ATV trail breaks away to the south. Be sure to leave room for others to pass. At times the road has been blocked. If it is, you can still park at milepost 213.5; however, this would add the distance of the road to the hike.

For those attempting to hike south along the entire Rainbow Ridge, park your shuttle vehicle at a parking area on the south side of the highway at milepost 206.5, at the gravel pit.

43 *FIELDING LAKE*

R/T DISTANCE: Up to 8 miles (13 km) paddling; 3 miles (4.8 km) skiing

DURATION: Up to 8 hours

HIGH POINT: 2,973 feet (906 m)

TOTAL ELEVATION CHANGE: 0 feet (0 m) float; less than 50 feet (15 m) ski

DIFFICULTY: Easy

ROUTE TYPE: Float (flat water), suitable for canoes, rafts, and kayaks
  (motorized allowed); ski, unmaintained road (motorized allowed)

BEST SEASON: June to September (float); March to May (ski)

USGS MAPS: Mount Hayes A-4

LAND MANAGER: Alaska Department of Natural Resources (Fairbanks),
  907-451-2705

Fielding Lake is nestled high in the pass between Delta Junction and Paxson. Tundra-covered hills surround its shores. From its waters, you get nice views of the Alaska Range to the northeast. Most people use the lake to go fishing or just get out on the water. The lake is a fine place for a canoe outing, and the far (southern) shores are generally pretty quiet, making for a good overnight paddle. A public-use cabin sits on the edge of the campground north of the lake. The cabin is available the year round and is a good destination for cross-country skiers in spring. The road is not maintained, so ski the unplowed road from the Richardson Highway for 1.5 miles (2.4 km) to reach the cabin.

  BE AWARE: High winds can arrive seemingly out of nowhere and last for days; expect them. These winds can cause fairly big waves in the lake, so be careful. Snow cover varies greatly from year to year; the road may be closed into early June with a foot of snow remaining from winter. Motorboats are allowed to use the lake and are present most of the time when the lake is ice-free. This area is very popular with snowmachiners in spring. Private property is scattered about the area, especially on the lake's east shore. There are no official hiking trails and you need to cross the outlet stream to get to the hills on the west side.

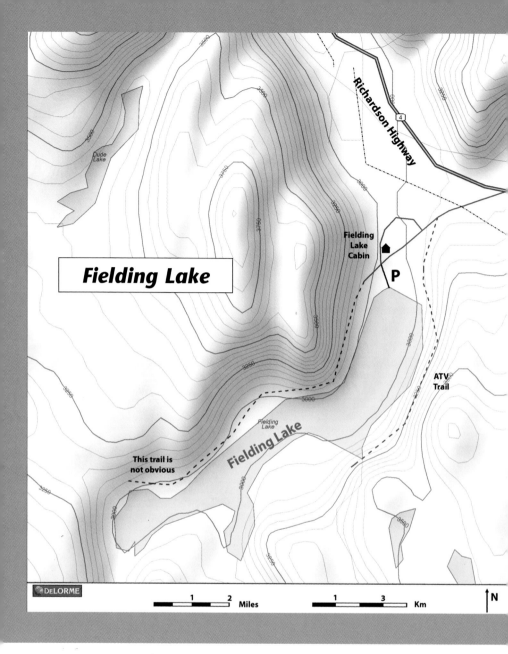

Fielding Lake

Dude Lake

Richardson Highway

4

Fielding Lake Cabin

P

ATV Trail

Fielding Lake

Fielding Lake

This trail is not obvious

DELORME

1   2   Miles

1   3   Km

N

MORE ADVENTUROUS? You can hike up the ridge on the southeast side of the lake on an ATV trail (about a mile [1.6 km] in on the road), where you can get great views of the lake and surrounding area. You can also cross the creek to explore the tundra-covered hills to the north and west of the lake. The Delta (Trip 44) and Gulkana (Trip 45) rivers are great road-to-road floats in the region. Donnelly Dome (Trip 40) and Castner Glacier (Trip 41) offer great hiking experiences close by. The Castner Glacier is also an enjoyable spring ski.

The Alaska Range as seen from the cabin.

DIRECTIONS: Head southeast on the Richardson Highway (Alaska 2) out of Fairbanks. In Delta Junction, veer to the south (right) to stay on the Richardson (now Alaska 4). Follow this until you reach milepost 200.5. Signs mark the road to the lake, which is on the west (right) side. The public-use cabin is 1.5 miles (2.4 km) down the road. The lake and boat launch are another quarter mile (0.4 km) farther.

44 *DELTA RIVER*

ONE-WAY DISTANCE: 30 miles (48.4 km)

DURATION: 2 to 3 days

HIGH POINT: 2,791 feet (850 m)

TOTAL ELEVATION CHANGE: 600 feet (183 m)

DIFFICULTY: Easy to moderate

ROUTE TYPE: Float (class I and II), suitable for canoes, river kayaks, and rafts (the lakes and the river below the take-out are motorized, but the float portion of the river is nonmotorized)

BEST SEASON: Late May to September

USGS MAPS: Mount Hayes A-4, B-4

LAND MANAGER: Bureau of Land Management (Glennallen), 907-822-3217

The headwaters of the Delta River are on the south side of the Alaska Range, but this river flows north. It has carved its way through these rugged peaks, but not before making its way through the scenic Amphitheater Mountains—helping earn its National Wild River designation. The river enters the Tanana River next to the Richardson Highway bridge near Delta Junction. Natives used this wondrous area for 10,000 years, and remnants of their use led to the creation of the Tangle Lakes Archeological District. Please do not disturb any artifacts. Gold rush miners combed through the area's hills and creeks. Some mines in the region are still active. In fact, recent discoveries of huge mineral deposits may threaten the character of this wild and scenic region. The float combines lakes, outlets, some rapids, beautiful scenery, wonderful camping spots, and the chance for great wildlife viewing. And this can all be packed into a weekend—or at least a three-day weekend.

The put-in is on Round Tangle Lake. Cool air commonly rushes down the towering peaks to the north, often creating a stiff headwind and large waves. Winds are often calmest first thing in the morning. You will paddle about a mile (1.6 km) across the

Delta River

Delta
River

Richardson

Highway

Denali Highway

2   6   10
Miles

3   9   15
Km

N

DeLORME

lake before reaching its outlet. The outlets connecting each of the Tangle Lakes can be shallow, requiring dragging during low water. The short outlet of Round Tangle Lake leads to Long Tangle Lake.

The lakeshore vegetation is tundra, which makes it easy to spot wildlife. The Nelchina Caribou Herd often frequents this region in April and September while migrating between their winter ranges and calving grounds. Individual caribou can be spotted any time of the year, but late September offers your best chance.

Setting up camp in September.

Long Tangle Lake is often so narrow it's hard to tell if it is a lake or an outlet. When it does eventually widen, it becomes Lower Tangle Lake. Where the lakes meet is a good spot to camp if you want to include hikes up Sugarloaf and Tangle mountains towering to the east. Lower Tangle is the last of the lakes. From its outlet, the river runs due north and can be either class I or II water, depending on conditions. About 2 miles (3.2 km) from the outlet of Lower Tangle Lake is a take-out on the east side (right side facing downstream). A portage starts here before the river makes a sharp turn to head due east. The portage has a small sign, but it is on the west side (river left). Do not bother going all the way across to read it, as it just states that you need to get back to the east side.

Below the take-out is a waterfall, so you must use the portage. It is actually an interesting half-mile (0.8-km) portage. You walk by cliffs and then about halfway through is a small pond. Use your canoe or raft to get to the far shore to finish the portage. The portage ends at an attractive rocky beach, which is a great spot to refuel. From here you can climb a rock pinnacle to enjoy the views (the fall colors can be spectacular) or scout the river ahead. The falls themselves make another interesting side trip.

The next mile (1.6 km) downstream is the trickiest of the trip. The rapids have large boulders and can reach class III. Under certain conditions these rapids can be tame (easy class II). Either way, if you are not confident about handling these rapids, you can line boats on the right (south) bank. Better to be safe than have your canoe wrapped around a rock. The next 13 miles (21 km) offer easygoing class

I water. Amphitheater Mountains now lay behind you, the snowcapped Alaska Range comes into better view, and the boreal forest returns.

The river changes character again at its confluence with Eureka Creek. The clear water and channeled course turn into a silty, braided river. Watch the river carefully, as it is easy to take a braid with too little water. The channels are interwoven, so you will likely get back to deeper water soon enough. The river keeps this character for the final 6 miles (9.7 km) or so until you reach the take out.

Beach at the far end of the portage.

BE AWARE: The small sign for the portage is on the west side of the river, just before the portage, and warns you to get to the take-out on the east side. Do not bother paddling all the way to the sign just to paddle back to the eastern shore. The portage is necessary, as the falls are not runnable. The river gets faster and much wilder past the take-out near Ann Creek. Only experienced (expert) rafters should attempt going farther.

MORE ADVENTUROUS? Even for more experienced rafters, the Delta River can get exciting past the Ann Creek take-out. From there, class III waters run for nearly 50 miles (80 km) before simmering down to class I for the last 20 miles (32 km) into Delta Junction. The class IV rapids above Black Rapids Glacier should be portaged. The Gulkana River offers another good road-to-road float (Trip 45). For those wishing to stretch their legs, try climbing 5,341-foot (1,629-m) Sugarloaf Mountain or Tangle Mountain to the east of Lower Tangle Lake. You can also try other Delta Junction–area hikes (Trips 40–42).

DIRECTIONS: Head southeast on the Richardson Highway (Alaska 2) out of Fairbanks. In Delta Junction, veer to the south (right) to stay on the Richardson (now Alaska 4). Follow this until you reach about milepost 212. Leave your shuttle vehicle anywhere south of Ann Creek and north of Phelan Creek. Continue south until you reach the Denali Highway (Alaska 8) at Paxson. Turn right and head west for 20 miles (32 km) until you see a sign for the Tangle Lakes boat launch and campground. Turn right (north) on the dirt road just past the bridge.

45 GULKANA RIVER

ONE-WAY DISTANCE: 45 miles (72.6 km)

DURATION: 2 to 4 days

HIGH POINT: 2,553 feet (778 m)

TOTAL ELEVATION CHANGE: 600 feet (183 m)

DIFFICULTY: Moderate

ROUTE TYPE: Float (class I–III), suitable for rafts and white-water canoes (motorized allowed)

BEST SEASON: Late May to September

USGS MAPS: Gulkana B-3, B-4, C-4

LAND MANAGER: Bureau of Land Management (Glennallen), 907-822-3217

This National Wild River is outside my definition of the Interior, but I decided to include this trip because it is so popular with Interior residents. It has road-to-road access, great fishing (king salmon in June), good scenery, challenging water, and a wild character. The float includes a large lake, a variety of fast and slow river action, and the potential to run a short, tough rapid. Most people choose to use rafts because of the long stretches of rapids, but skilled canoeists give this route a go every year.

The area around the Paxson Lake launch is incredible. The lake is about 10 miles (16 km) long, but only a half mile (0.8 km) across at its narrowest. Caribou can often be spotted swimming across the narrows in the fall. The lake offers unobstructed views of the Alaska Range. Winds often come pouring down these slopes and across the lake, creating big waves. The waves get larger at the far (south) end, where the launch is. The float starts by crossing the lake, so take care if there are waves, which will be perpendicular to your route.

The western shore offers refuge from the waves as the lake angles to the southwest. Keep heading in this direction to find the lake's outlet stream. Cabins sit on shore near the outlet and remnants of older cabins can be seen all along the stream, which was heavily used by Natives and miners over the years. The 3-mile (4.8-km)

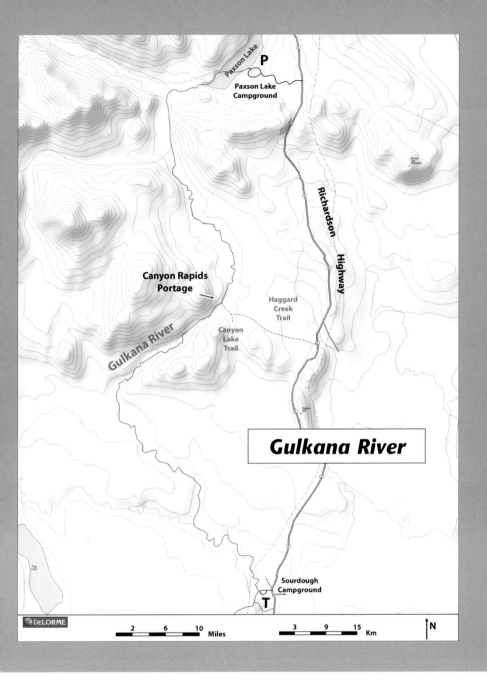

Gulkana River

| | 2 | 6 | 10 | |
Miles

| | 3 | 9 | 15 | |
Km

N

long outlet stream is narrow, shallow, and fast-moving class II water. Overhanging brush, sweepers, and frequent maneuvering will keep you on your toes down this stream.

The outlet stream spits you into the Middle Fork of the Gulkana River. A popular camping spot is on the west side of the river here. The next 15 miles (24 km) are

Ready for another set of rapids (July).

meandering class I waters. The river is deep and dark as you cut through stands of large white spruce. Stay alert for the sporadic huge boulders that will appear in your path. You may also spot one of those large king salmon that survived the gauntlet of downstream anglers.

Canyon Rapids begins at mile 18 (km 29). A sign for the portage is on the left (east) side. Everyone should get out here, even those wanting to run the rapids. Gear is easily brought to the far end of the quarter-mile (0.4-km) portage. The far end of the portage has a popular spot to camp. The rapids should be scouted, as they can be class IV. Groups may want to station people with throw ropes at the middle and end of the rapids, which could be run multiple times for fun. However, these rapids are not to be trifled with. They have ended so many trips that a rough, 6-mile (9.7-km) trail has developed back to the highway. The trail can also be used to hike to the scenic Canyon Lake, about a mile (1.6 km) away.

Though Canyon Rapids can be easily portaged, the next 8 miles (13 km) of the river is what generally dissuades people from using canoes. The river is really rocky and requires a lot of maneuvering through its primarily class II waters. Paint and aluminum marks can be seen on rocks all along this stretch. For the experienced canoeist, this can be the most fun section of the river. However, you are a long way from civilization if you wreck and have no other boats to bail you out.

The 8-mile (13-km) stretch of white water comes to an abrupt halt, where the river changes to a wide, slow-moving, class I waterway. Powerboats are allowed up to here and some come this

The Alaska Range from Paxson Lake.

far during the June king salmon run. During the next 18-mile (29-km) stretch, more and more powerboat traffic appears as you drift downstream, especially on weekends and when the kings are running. Just after passing under the Trans-Alaska Pipeline you will spot the take-out on the left (east) side at Sourdough Creek Campground (milepost 147.6).

BE AWARE: This is a very tough trip for canoeists. There are long sections of challenging rapids. Running the Canyon Rapids, even for rafters, is dangerous. The river is powerful and there are numerous rocks and cliffs to get hung up on. Wearing a helmet is a good idea. Keep watch for logjams, sweepers, and large boulders in calm water. Stay alert for overhanging brush in the Paxson Lake outlet. Motorboats use the last 18 miles (29 km) of this float.

MORE ADVENTUROUS? The Middle Fork can be reached via Dickey Lake by starting at Upper Tangle Lake. This route has additional portages, including one longer one, but you experience really remote and beautiful country. This float meets up with the float detailed above at the confluence of the Paxson Lake outlet. You can tack on another 35 miles (56 km) by floating on by Sourdough Creek Campground all the way to the Richardson Highway bridge (milepost 126.8). These 35 miles (56 km) are mostly class I and II waters that can be done as a separate float. The Delta River (Trip 44), just to the north, is another great road-to-road float.

DIRECTIONS: Head southeast on the Richardson Highway (Alaska 2) out of Fairbanks. In Delta Junction, veer off to the south (right) to stay on the Richardson (now Alaska 4). Follow this until you reach milepost 175. Turn right into the Paxson Lake Campground. The boat launch, the put-in for this trip, is about a mile down a steep hill. To drop off a shuttle vehicle, continue southbound on the Richardson until you reach Sourdough Creek Campground at milepost 147.6 on your right (west) side.

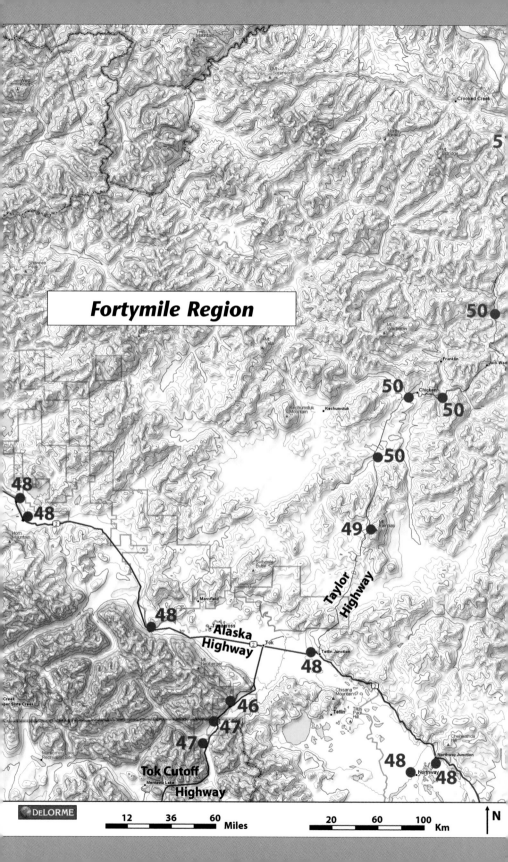

Fortymile Region

Fortymile Region

The Fortymile River received its name around 1886 because the river's mouth is about 40 miles (64.4 km) downstream of Fort Reliance, a Hudson Bay outpost. The region is rich with mining history, and gold miners are still active in the area. Eagle, on the banks of the Yukon River and close to Canada, was a bustling city at the turn of the last century and boasted Fort Egbert, a large military outpost. Eagle Trail linked this city with the port of Valdez. Currently, the town of Tok is the main hub of the area. It is the first stop for those driving up from the Lower 48 and Canada. In Tok, travelers can choose to head southwest toward Glennallen, Anchorage, and the rest of southcentral Alaska or continue west to Delta Junction and Fairbanks. The most popular trip in this region is floating the Fortymile National Wild and Scenic River. However, the area has a few worthwhile hikes and some other floats, including the spellbinding Yukon River.

46 *EAGLE TRAIL*

Nature Trail

R/T DISTANCE: 1.0 mile (1.6 km)

DURATION: 30 minutes to 1 hour

HIGH POINT: 2,000 feet (609 m)

TOTAL ELEVATION CHANGE: Less than 50 feet (15 m)

DIFFICULTY: Easy

ROUTE TYPE: Established trail (nonmotorized)

Tok River Valley Overlook Trail

R/T DISTANCE: 3.0 miles (4.8 km)

DURATION: 1 to 3 hours

HIGH POINT: 2,800 feet (853 m)

TOTAL ELEVATION CHANGE: 1,750 feet (533 m)

DIFFICULTY: Easy to moderate

ROUTE TYPE: Established trail (nonmotorized)

Clearwater Creek Trail

R/T DISTANCE: 12 miles (19 km) or more

DURATION: Up to 10 hours or overnight

HIGH POINT: Up to 3,000 feet (914 m)

TOTAL ELEVATION CHANGE: 2,000 feet (609 m)

DIFFICULTY: Moderate

ROUTE TYPE: ATV trail (motorized allowed)

BEST SEASON: May to September

USGS MAPS: Tanacross A-5

LAND MANAGER: Alaska Department of Natural Resources (Fairbanks), 907-451-2705

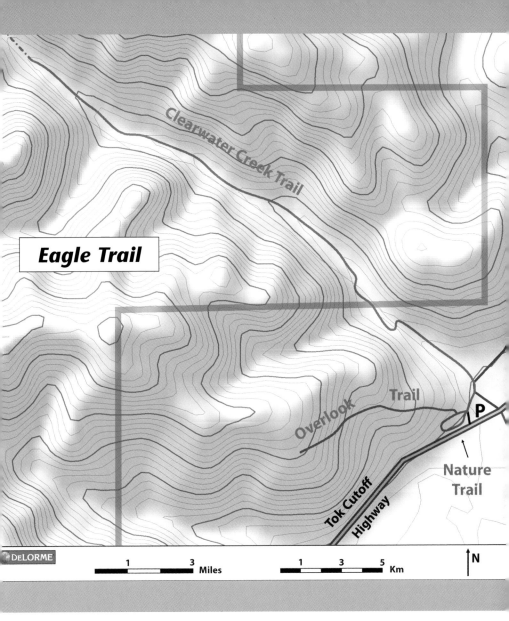

Eagle Trail

The Eagle Trail, or Valdez–Eagle Trail, was the first all-American route to the Klondike gold fields. At the time, people thought Eagle would become the center of mining activity in Alaska and so Fort Egbert was built there. Portions of the trail were upgraded for pack trains soon after, and in 1900 a telegraph line was built along the trail, providing faster communication between Eagle and Washington, D.C. The Washington–Alaska Cable and Telegraph System (WAMCATS) was 428 miles (690 km) long and its remnants can still be found.

Today, Eagle Trail offers a range of outdoor opportunities at the Eagle Trail State Recreation Site.

Nature Trail

The Nature Trail starts out on the Eagle Trail, also called Old Slana Highway. The old roadbed is lined with aspen and has placards describing the history, geology, and botany of the region. After about a half mile (0.8 km) the trail veers sharply to the left (east) and its style becomes more of a traditional hiking trail. The trail bends back toward the start, coming relatively close to the highway, making its way through large spruce.

Tok River Valley Overlook Trail

The Tok River Valley Overlook Trail breaks away from the Nature Trail after about 50 feet (15 m), going up a steep staircase to the right (west). Beyond the stairs, a well-defined trail climbs steadily up the ridge. Bluebells, soapberry, and kinnikinnick carpet the forest floor. A couple of benches early on offer a place to rest and have nice views. Aspen trees give way to spruce as you climb switchbacks. The trail drops into a small saddle before a short, steep climb to the overlook. The trail branches here into smaller social trails. One heads left (east) for about 50 yards (meters) to another overlook. Another heads right (west) and quickly peters out at a rock outcrop. The views of the Tok River valley and surrounding mountains are well worth the hike.

Clearwater Creek Trail

For longer adventures, try Clearwater Creek Trail, which makes for a good hike or mountain bike ride. To reach the trail, head to the west end of the campground. The widest trail takes you to Clearwater Creek. The creek has to be forded here to reach Clearwater Creek Trail. If this is not to your liking, then this trail probably is not for you because you will have to cross it again and again. You can avoid this first stream crossing by going back to the highway and taking your first left. On the far side of the creek is a clearing that leads to an old road. Head straight on it (north) for about 100 yards (meters), then turn left (west) onto the ATV trail (which at this point looks like a road). The valley and trail are pretty flat for many miles, though both climb slightly. Stands of large white spruce grow on the higher spots, and willows and alders grow in the more disturbed areas. The trail crosses the creek a few times and slowly gets worse the farther you go.

ALL ROUTES BE AWARE: The combination of plentiful fruiting plants and a campground can be enticing for bears. Stay alert, and make noise while hiking. Clearwater Creek Trail is an ATV trail that is used by hunters and trappers. Be prepared to see remains. Keep dogs close to avoid problems with traps and carcasses, and please respect private property. You will be able to hear road noise throughout

View from the Overlook Trail.

the Nature Trail and for sections of the Overlook Trail. There is a fee to stay at the campground.

MORE ADVENTUROUS? Clearwater Creek Trail can be used to access incredible alpine country. The valley is surrounded by many peaks, some that reach beyond 6,000 feet (2,000 m). Plenty to keep you busy. You may also want to check out Mount Fairplay (Trip 49).

DIRECTIONS: Take the Richardson Highway (Alaska 2) southeast out of Fairbanks. Stay on Highway Alaska 2 in Delta Junction. (The Richardson veers sharply off to the south here.) Highway Alaska 2 is called the Alaska Highway (and also the Alcan) east of Delta Junction. Follow this east to Tok. In Tok, turn right (south) onto the Tok Cutoff (Alaska 1). Turn right (west) at milepost 109.2, about 15 miles (24 km) south of Tok, into Eagle Trail State Recreation Site. Proceed about an eighth of a mile (0.2 km) straight ahead. The parking area will be on your left (south). The trailheads for the nature and overlook trails are at the southwest corner of the cleared area. Clearwater Creek Trail can be reached at the west (far) end of the campground.

47 TOK AND LITTLE TOK RIVERS

ONE-WAY DISTANCE: 6, 35, or 41 miles (10, 56, or 66 km)

DURATION: 2 to 4 hours or up to 2 to 3 days

HIGH POINT: 2,040 feet (621 m)

TOTAL ELEVATION CHANGE: Up to 400 feet (122 m)

DIFFICULTY: Moderate

ROUTE TYPE: Float (class I), suitable for canoes, river kayaks, small rafts, and packrafts (motorized allowed)

BEST SEASON: May to September

USGS MAPS: Tanacross A-4, A-5, B-4

LAND MANAGER: Alaska Department of Natural Resources (Fairbanks), 907-451-2705

Rugged mountains and braided rivers may not be the first thing you think of when someone mentions the Tok and Little Tok rivers, but nonetheless they are part of this float. Craggy and rugged 6,000-foot (1,827-m) peaks ring the headwaters of the rivers, providing a spectacular backdrop for a trip. You can float a short section in an afternoon or make a multi-day excursion out of this trip, depending how much effort you want to expend.

The section from the Little Tok bridge (milepost 98.1, Tok Cutoff) to the Tok bridge (milepost 103.8, Tok Cutoff) is about 6 miles (9.7 km) long and flows mostly through Native corporation land. Tall white spruce line the banks, casting shadows across the river. The combination of these tall trees and the narrowness of the river gives boaters a sense of closeness with the area. Keep watch all around; a great horned owl may be perching right above you. Since the river is narrow and the trees tall, logjams and sweepers can completely span the river, forcing you to portage over or around them. Be careful when you do; the shore is silty, and you can sink up to your knees in spots. Many trees are in the water, requiring frequent maneuvers. However, the water often moves pretty slowly, so generally there is ample time to maneuver. Breaks in the trees offer glimpses of the surrounding mountains. But you do not

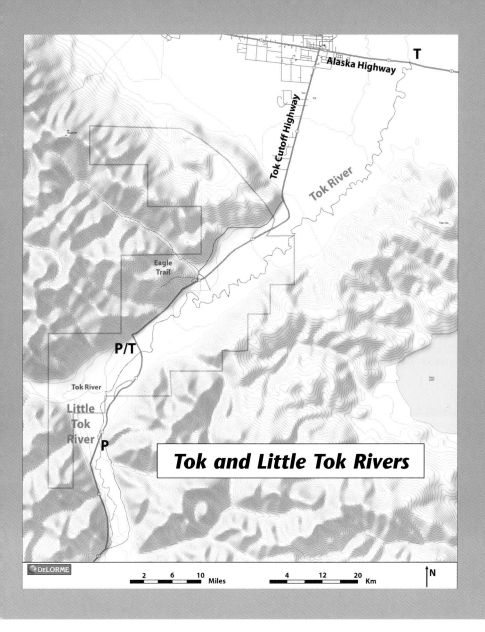

Tok and Little Tok Rivers

Miles: 2 6 10

Km: 4 12 20

N

really get the wide-open vistas of the rugged peaks until the Little Tok spills into the Tok, about 3 miles (4.8 km) into the float, when the river starts braiding. Past the confluence, the northwest side of the river has good campsites on state land. The Tok bridge is less than 3 miles (4.8 km) downriver from here. The float from bridge to bridge can be done in as little as two to four hours.

Below the milepost 103.8 bridge, the river turns to the northeast and is less braided, but large gravel bars can still be found for about 6 miles (9.7 km) downstream. Smaller gravel bars can be found for a few more miles after that (depending

Packraft at the confluence of the Tok and Little Tok rivers.

on water level), as the river trends more easterly. Views of the surrounding mountains here are still great.

About 10 miles (16 km) downriver of the bridge, the river comes close to the foothills on the east side of the valley then heads north. The large, riparian white spruce are replaced with diminutive black spruce as the valley starts to widen. Campsites get harder to find at this point. This is not entirely bad, because by 14 miles (22.6 km) downriver of the milepost 103.8 bridge you are out of the mountains, the ground is fairly boggy, and the land is again owned by a Native corporation, requiring their permission to camp. This stretch of land is 18 river miles (29 km), so get started early. You do not want to be forced to camp where you are trespassing. You can camp on gravel bars below the high-water mark, which are state property.

The stretch of river from the milepost 103.8 bridge to the Alaska Highway is about 35 miles (56 km) long. Plan on two pretty long days (eighteen to twenty-eight hours of total water time). I recommend doing one-third of the trip on the first day and two-thirds on the second. By combining the two floats (Little Tok and Tok), you can paddle for 41 miles (66 km).

BE AWARE: Much of the land abutting Tok and Little Tok rivers is owned by Native corporations. In these areas you need permission to use the land above the high-water mark, but not gravel bars below this mark. Land lining the river from the Tok Cutoff bridge of the Little Tok River (milepost 98.1, Tok Cutoff) to the confluence of the Tok and Little Tok rivers is primarily Native land. From there, state land stretches until about 14 miles (22.6 km) downstream of the Tok Cutoff bridge of the Tok River (milepost 103.8, Tok Cutoff). Campers should use this stretch of the river unless they have permission to use other areas. From 14 miles (22.6 km) past the bridge until about 2 miles (3.2 km) before the Alaska Highway bridge the land is again Native land. The water is slow here; get an early start so you can make it to the bridge before night. Contact the state Department of Natural Resources or the federal Bureau of Land Management (See Appendix B) to get accurate maps of land ownership.

The Little Tok is lined with large trees. Expect to portage around a couple of jams that may span the entire river. The Tok is braided from the confluence with the Little Tok to the bridge, so look carefully for deeper channels. The upper portions of the Tok and the start of the Little Tok are close to the road, so expect road noise. Tok River comes close to the road just south of Eagle Trail State Recreation Site (milepost 109.2, Tok Cutoff).

MORE ADVENTUROUS? With higher water or a shallow draft, boaters can put in at another Little Tok bridge at milepost 91.0 of the Tok Cutoff. The Little Tok River's course here is sinuous and fairly slow. You should expect more portaging around logjams. The 12 miles (19 km) may take as little as five hours, but plan for an overnight just to be safe. If you are looking for bigger water, you will want to check out the Tanana (Trip 48), Fortymile (Trip 50), and Yukon (Trip 51) floats.

DIRECTIONS: Take the Richardson Highway (Alaska 2) southeast out of Fairbanks. Stay on Alaska 2 in Delta Junction. (The Richardson veers sharply off to the south here.) Alaska 2 is called the Alaska Highway (and also the Alcan) east of Delta Junction. Follow this east to Tok.

The take-out for the 35- and 41-mile (56- and 66-km) floats is at the Tok River bridge on the Alaska Highway, about 4 miles (6.4 km) east of Tok at milepost 1309.2. To get to the put-ins, go back to Tok, and turn left (south) onto the Tok Cutoff (Alaska 1).

The Tok River bridge is at milepost 103.8, Tok Cutoff, about 20 miles (32 km) south of Tok. This is the put-in for the 35-mile (56-km) float and the take-out for the 6-mile (10-km) float from the Little Tok bridge. There is a place to park on the right (northwest) just before the bridge. The bank is steep here and the water fast and quick. You may want to portage boats across the road to the east side, where the bank is flatter, or to the far side of the bridge, where there is a good spot to put in on the west side but no parking. Traffic comes hurtling down the highway, so be very careful.

The farthest upriver put-in is at the Little Tok bridge (milepost 98.1). Parking is on the far side and on the left (south).

48 *UPPER TANANA RIVER*

ONE-WAY DISTANCE: 7–300 miles (11–484 km)

DURATION: 2 to 4 hours or up to 5 to 15 days (and anything in between)

HIGH POINT: 1,700 feet (518 m)

TOTAL ELEVATION CHANGE: Less than 750 feet (228 m)

DIFFICULTY: Moderate

ROUTE TYPE: Float (class I–II), suitable for rafts, kayaks, or canoes (motorized allowed)

BEST SEASON: June to September

USGS MAPS: Nabesna D-2, D-3; Tanacross A-2, A-4, B-4, B-6, C-6; Mount Hayes C-1, C-2, D-2; Big Delta A-2, A-4

LAND MANAGERS: Alaska Department of Natural Resources (Fairbanks), 907-451-2705; Tetlin National Wildlife Refuge, 907-883-5312

Nabesna and Chisana rivers come pouring out of the Alaska Range and meet near Northway to form the Yukon River's largest tributary, the Tanana River. Those same snowcapped mountains provide a splendid backdrop to any float on this fast, large, and cold river. Only the Yukon surpasses its power, and only experienced paddlers should float it. The Tanana parallels the Alaska Highway, but it has long stretches far enough from the road to give you a feeling of wild country. The upper Tanana River can be accessed in many places, which gives you options to float for a couple of hours or a couple of weeks. With trips as short as 7 miles (11.3 km) and ranging up to 300 miles (484 km) or more, the Tanana is what you make of it. Under normal water levels, the many gravel bars make ideal campsites all along the river.

Putting in on Nabesna River at Northway gives you the opportunity for the longest float. Starting on Chisana River, just before Northway, is only slightly shorter. The rivers come together within 10 miles (16 km) of either starting point. Their confluence is the origin of the Tanana River. Be careful of hydraulics where the rivers

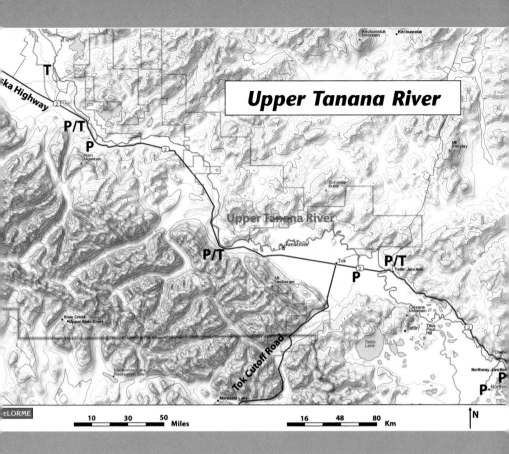

Upper Tanana River

come together. The Tanana meanders through Tetlin National Wildlife Refuge, and stays close to the Alaska Highway for about its first 15 miles (24 km). Here it turns more westward and away from the highway. It crosses the valley floor on its way over to Tetlin Hills. The river parallels the hills then makes its way north, where it crosses under the Alaska Highway at milepost 1303.4. The take-out is at the bridge, on the right (east) side of the river. The float to this bridge is about 50 miles (80 km) from the Chisana put-in and about 55 miles (88 km) from the Nabesna put-in. The distance could be covered in a very long day, but is best enjoyed as a two- to three-day trip.

The float from the Alaska Highway bridge at milepost 1303.4 to Cathedral Rapids is about 55 miles (88 km). You could cut off about 5 miles (8 km) by putting in on Tok River (milepost 1309.2, Alaska Highway) instead. From the milepost 1303.4 bridge, the river heads north before making a radical turn, after about 6 miles (9.7 km), to the southwest at Porcupine Creek. Use caution on this turn. Here, you leave the Tetlin refuge behind. The river stays on the north side of its valley, near the hills, during this next stretch. You will float by the village of Tanacross (about 40 miles [64 km] downstream from the milepost 1303.4 bridge), which is connected to the road system. After Tanacross, the river rapidly closes on the Alaska Range. In fact, this is as near to the range as you get on the river. Jagged, 6,000-foot (1,827-m) mountains loom just a couple of miles to the south. You will spot Cathedral Bluffs directly in front of you on the north side of the river, which gives you warning that the next take-out spot is close. The Cathedral Rapids take-out is hard to spot from the river. The parking for this take-out is a 75-yard (meter) walk up a right-of-away. Make sure to scout it out when you drop off your shuttle vehicle. This distance could be covered in one very long day, but is best enjoyed as a two- to three-day trip.

From Cathedral Rapids, the river heads north toward Tower Bluffs and Tower Bluff Rapids. The rapids are just after Robertson River joins the Tanana (65 miles [104 km] from the 1303.4 bridge) from the west and about 10 miles (16 km) downstream from Cathedral Rapids. Conditions are dependent on water levels, so scout the rapids before attempting to run them. After the rapids, the Tanana heads northwest into flatter country. The river passes a number of picturesque bluffs before reaching the boat launch at milepost 1385 on the Alaska Highway. The boat launch is subtle and well hidden from the river. When you drop your shuttle vehicle off, make sure to note features about the launch's location. The float from Cathedral Rapids to milepost 1385 is about 65 miles (104 km) and is best enjoyed as a two- to three-day trip.

The tail end of this section of the river can be made into a very short trip by starting at the Johnson River bridge. You will be on the Johnson River for about 2 miles (3.2 km) with a bluff in front of you and the Alaska Range behind. This float is about 7 miles (11.2 km) down to the milepost 1385 boat launch, which should take you two to four hours. If you want more float time, keep going to Cumming's Landing.

The float from the launch at milepost 1385 to Cumming's Landing is about 12 miles (19.4 km). Like the Johnson River section, on this float you have bluffs in front and the Alaska Range at your back. Plan on four to six hours for this section, or do it as an easy overnighter. Cumming's Landing to the Tanana bridge in Big Delta is about 65 miles (104 km). This float takes you past Clearwater Lake (Trip 39) and is best enjoyed as a two- to three-day trip.

BE AWARE: Tanana River is fast, powerful, and silty. Only experienced paddlers should attempt floats on this river. Always wear your life jacket. Entire trees can be washing downstream at any time of the year, so keep watch for those. Also watch for motorboat traffic, especially near launches and towns. The banks of the Tanana are owned by an assortment of people and agencies. Be sure to know the status of the land if you intend to camp or hunt. Gravel bars below the high-water mark are state land and can be used for camping. The federal Bureau of Land Management or the Alaska Department of Natural Resources can help determine land status along the

Upper Tanana River near Cathedral Rapids.

river. Strong winds can slow travel and cause dangerous water conditions. Dangerous ice conditions can last well into June; be sure to scout ahead.

MORE ADVENTUROUS? You can float past the Alaska Highway bridge at Big Delta, north of Delta Junction. Fairbanks is some 100 miles (160 km) distant, while Nenana (Trip 8) and Manley are even farther. If you are looking for great float trips on other rivers, try Chena River (Trips 7 and 15), Beaver Creek (Trip 27), Birch Creek (Trip 31), Delta River (Trip 44), Gulkana River (Trip 45), or the Yukon River (Trip 51).

DIRECTIONS: There are numerous put-in and take-out locations for the upper Tanana River. Take the Richardson Highway (Alaska 2) southeast out of Fairbanks to the Big Delta bridge at milepost 275. A dirt parking lot is on the far (south) side of the bridge on your left (east). This is the farthest downstream take-out described above.

Stay on Alaska 2 in Delta Junction. (The Richardson veers sharply off to the south here.) Alaska 2 is called the Alaska Highway (and also the Alcan) east of Delta Junction.

Turn left (north) at milepost 1392.2, Alaska Highway, on Cummings Road to reach Cumming's Landing. It is a several-mile-long dirt road just past (east of) Gerstle River. Gerstle River is generally too braided and shallow to float to the Tanana.

The next access point is at milepost 1385, where there is a steep boat launch. Turn left (north) into the marked turnout. The access is a paved road about an eighth of a mile (0.2 km) long at the east end of the turnout. There is room to park near the ramp as well. If you use this as a take-out, be sure to note downstream river features to help you find the access point while on the river. It can be hard to spot, and the current makes getting out somewhat difficult.

At milepost 1380.3 is the Johnson River. About 100 yards (meters) past (east of) the bridge, turn right (south). Turn into the gravel pit and head right (west) back to the river. A steep dirt road heading right (north) leads down to the river.

Cathedral Rapids take-out, at milepost 1338.6, has access on the right (south) side of the highway. Parking is limited. Getting to the river requires about a 75-yard (meter) portage over rocky cobble under the highway. This is a Tanacross easement with restrictions during big-game hunting seasons; please do not use it at that time.

The Alaska Highway crosses Tok River at milepost 1309.2. Parking is on the left (north) side and past (east of) the bridge.

Just a little farther, at milepost 1303.4, Tanana River crosses under the highway. Parking is on the left (north) just past (east of) the bridge.

For the farthest upriver put-ins, turn right (south) at Northway Junction, milepost 1264. About a half mile (0.8 km) down is the Chisana River bridge. A boat launch is at the bridge. Nabesna River can be reached at the end of this 7-mile (11-km) road in Northway Village.

49   *MOUNT FAIRPLAY*

R/T DISTANCE: 4 or 6 miles (6.5 or 9.7 km)

DURATION: 2 to 6 hours

HIGH POINT: 5,541 feet (1,688 m)

TOTAL ELEVATION CHANGE: 4,500 or 4,650 feet (1,371 or 1,416 m)

DIFFICULTY: Moderate

ROUTE TYPE: Route (nonmotorized)

BEST SEASON: March to September

USGS MAPS: Tanacross C-3

LAND MANAGER: Alaska Department of Natural Resources (Fairbanks), 907-451-2705

Mount Fairplay rises dramatically from a sea of spruce. It is the highest (and practically only) peak for 30 miles (48 km) in any direction. Taylor Highway takes you up out of the muskegs and spruce on the mountain's west shoulder. This trip offers great alpine hiking with stunning views of the Alaska Range to the south and the vast expanses of Fortymile country all around. Caribou can frequently be seen here in late winter or early spring.

The most direct way to tackle the summit is to start around milepost 33.2 of the Taylor Highway, just after a small draw. Head for the north side of the draw, where the brush is lower and thinner, and alpine country is easier to reach. The summit is to the southeast, but a direct route makes for a steep climb. Head due east to moderate your climb and reach alpine country quicker. This bushwhack is easy, but to avoid it you can begin your hike another half mile (0.8 km) down Taylor Highway. That starting point is actually slightly lower and farther from the summit, but from there you reach the bald crest of the ridge quicker.

Once on the ridge, the going is great, with alpine vegetation and 360-degree views. The climb is steady but not overly steep. After 1.5–2 miles (2.4–3.2 km), depending on route, you will reach a false summit at 5,120 feet (1,560 m). The views of the surrounding Fortymile country are commanding. Boulder fields are common on some of

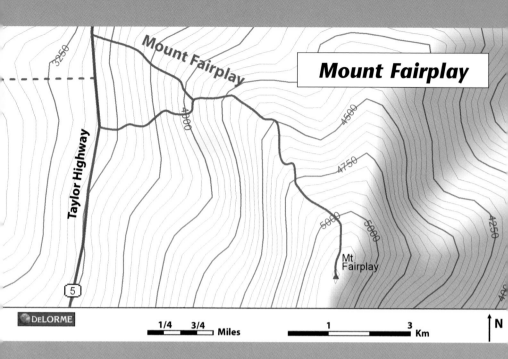

Taylor Highway

Mt Fairplay

DELORME

1/4   3/4 ⬛ Miles

1   3 ⬛ Km

↑N

the steep, north-facing slopes of the mountain. From the false peak, head southeast for a little more than a half mile (0.8 km). The summit of Mount Fairplay, 5,541 feet (1,688 m), has great views of the towering Alaska Range to the south, Prindle Volcano to the east, the Tanana uplands and Fortymile River to the north, and the Mosquito Flats to the west. Unfortunately, it also has a communications facility.

Early in the season can be an ideal time to attempt this peak for a couple of reasons. For one, members of the Nelchina Caribou Herd can often be spotted on the slopes of Fairplay in March and early April, before spring migration. The herd regularly uses the vast expanse of boreal forest surrounding Mount Fairplay as its winter range. Also, not many people are ready for hiking at this time of year, so the likelihood for solitude is increased. However, you may need snowshoes, depending on snow conditions. Also, winds can harden the snow near the summit, making crampons and an ice axe good to have, just in case. The weather can be unpredictable at this time of year. Check forecasts for cold or windy weather. If the weather is lousy or questionable, give it a go another time. Help is far away.

BE AWARE: Because Mount Fairplay towers above the flat expanses of east-central Alaska, its summit was a natural location to stick communication and weather facilities. The summit has a small building and a couple of metal towers that detract from the wilderness quality of the experience. Put your back to it, and enjoy the vast emptiness that surrounds this peak. Large trucks use Taylor Highway, so try to park as far off on the shoulder as you can. The highway is a summer-only road. However, the state plows this road, seemingly earlier and earlier. Depending on snow and budgets, the highway is routinely open by the middle of March. Call 511 to find out the status of the road at all times of year as the highway has been closed due to wildfires, as well as snow.

MORE ADVENTUROUS? Alpine ridges extend for miles both north and south from the summit. Take a poke around if

Mount Fairplay as seen from the southwest.

you have the time and energy. If you are looking for more hiking, try Wallcutt Mountain (see Appendix A) just south of Eagle. This trip has hikes of varying lengths and is even more remote. The Fortymile National Wild and Scenic River (Trip 50) and the fabled Yukon River (Trip 51) lie ahead farther up the Taylor Highway. They are floats that should not be missed.

DIRECTIONS: Take the Richardson Highway (Alaska 2) southeast out of Fairbanks. Stay on Highway Alaska 2 in Delta Junction. (The Richardson veers sharply off to the south here.) Highway Alaska 2 is called the Alaska Highway (and also the Alcan) east of Delta Junction. A dozen miles (19.4 km) past Tok, turn left (north) onto Taylor Highway (Alaska 5) at Tetlin Junction. Taylor Highway is paved until milepost 64.3. At milepost 33.2, just after a small creek, park on the side of the road to reach the most direct route to the summit of Mount Fairplay. Park as far onto the shoulder as you can manage. The beginning of this route requires some bushwhacking, but the vegetation is only waist-high and paths with lower brush can be found. You can continue up the Taylor to milepost 34 to reach a place where alpine vegetation reaches nearly to the road. This reduces bushwhacking but slightly lengthens the hike. There is a pullout here.

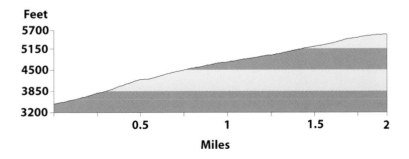

50 *FORTYMILE RIVER*

ONE-WAY DISTANCE: 10–170 miles (16–274 km)

DURATION: Depends on route and water conditions (see below)

HIGH POINT: 1,850 feet (564 m)

TOTAL ELEVATION CHANGE: Up to 1,000 feet (305 m)

DIFFICULTY: Easy to moderate

ROUTE TYPE: Float (class I, a few class II–III rapids), suitable for canoes, rafts, or kayaks (motorized allowed)

BEST SEASON: Late May to September

USGS MAPS: Eagle A-1, A-2, B-1, B-2, C-1, C-2; Tanacross D-2, D-3; CANADIAN: Cassiar 116C/8, Fortymile 116C/7, Mount Gladman 116C/10, Shell Creek 116C/9

LAND MANAGER: Bureau of Land Management (Fairbanks), 907-474-2200

The Fortymile National Wild and Scenic River offers many floating options that take you through the heart of gold mining country, both historic and current. The river was named in 1886 because its mouth was that many miles from Fort Reliance, which is on the Yukon just downstream from Dawson City. Abandoned town sites and active suction dredges can be found along the river. Despite the mining activity, the Fortymile is a very scenic float that can provide solitude and a sense of the wild as it takes you by large cliffs and through fun rapids.

Perhaps the most popular road-to-road section of this river is from the South Fork bridge (milepost 75; about 7 road miles [11 km] past Chicken) to the Fortymile River bridge (milepost 112). This float covers 38 river miles (61 km), flowing past beautiful bluffs and the abandoned town of Franklin (about 11 miles [17.6 km] downstream of the South Fork bridge). The North Fork of the Fortymile River comes into the South Fork about 24 miles (38.4 km) downstream of the South Fork bridge and at this point the river is simply called the Fortymile. (Boaters that fly into the Joseph

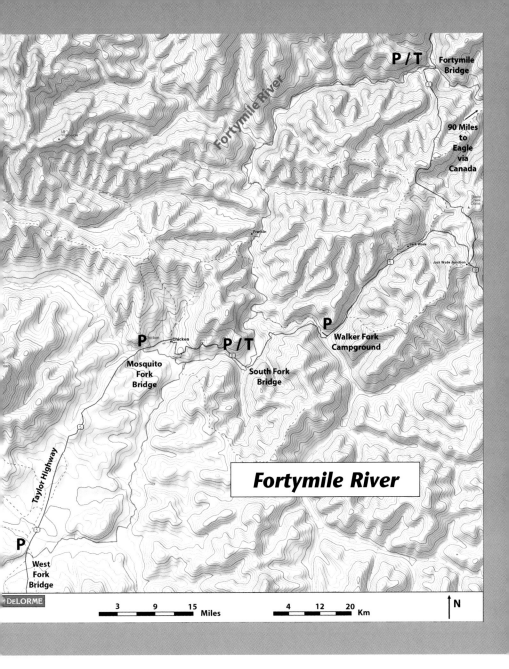

Fortymile River

P / T Fortymile
      Bridge

90 Miles
to
Eagle
via
Canada

Walker Fork
Campground

P / T

Mosquito
Fork
Bridge

South Fork
Bridge

Chicken

Taylor Highway

P

West
Fork
Bridge

• DeLORME

| 3 | 9 | 15 | Miles |
| 4 | 12 | 20 | Km |

↑ N

airstrip would reach this point by coming down the Middle and North forks, a trip
that is 50 miles [80 km] longer than this one, with more severe rapids.)

Some 36 miles (57.6 km) downstream of the South Fork bridge is a set of rapids
called "The Falls," which is generally between class II and III. Canoeists and less
experienced rafters may want to portage on the right (south) side. At high water,

The river is suitable for both rafts and canoes (May).

there are a couple of bends that have class II water. Also at high water, camping sites are more difficult (but not impossible) to find. Gravel bars are usually available at more normal water levels. Traveling times vary greatly depending on water levels, wind, and the amount of paddling you like to do, but generally the float takes between ten and sixteen hours on the river to complete this section.

Shorter floats can be made by putting in upstream of the South Fork bridge at the West Fork bridge (milepost 49.2) or the Mosquito Fork bridge (milepost 64.3). Both should be run at higher water levels and take boaters right by Chicken. The West Fork of the Fortymile flows into the Dennison Fork and reaches the South Fork bridge after 30 miles (48 km). Allow eight to ten hours for this stretch. The Mosquito Fork of the Fortymile runs into the Dennison Fork, which creates the South Fork. The float from the Mosquito Fork bridge to the South Fork bridge is 10 miles (16 km) and takes from three to five hours. These two options can be combined with the South Fork bridge to Fortymile bridge option to make for longer floats.

At very high water, experienced boaters may want to attempt putting in at the Walker Fork Campground (milepost 82). This put-in (as opposed to the South Fork bridge) increases the distance to the Fortymile bridge only by about 2 miles (3.2 km), but the river is rocky and shallow until it reaches the South Fork after about 6 miles (9.7 km). Smaller crafts, such as kayaks or packrafts, have a better chance of making it through. An option is to meet up with larger crafts that start at the South Fork.

For those with more time, floating all the way down to the Yukon River in Canada and west back to Eagle is a great option. You could start at any of the put-ins described or start at the Fortymile bridge, but be sure to check in with customs on both sides (see Appendix B). The trip is 101 miles (163 km) from the Fortymile bridge to Eagle, though it is possible to take out at Clinton Creek, which shortens the float to 48 miles (77 km). Before the Clinton Creek bridge are two serious rapids. The first, "Deadman's Riffle," is about 15 miles (24 km) below the Fortymile bridge. The rapid can be class III water and can be portaged on the right (south). The second, "Canyon Rapids," is a couple miles before the Clinton Creek bridge and is generally class II or III. The rapid can be lined or portaged on the right (south), but at extremely high water the shore is flooded, making this a very dangerous section.

About 6 miles (9.7 km) past the Clinton Creek bridge, you will reach the silty waters of the Yukon. Though not technical, the Yukon is huge and should not be taken lightly. Beware of high winds. Allow eighteen to thirty-four hours of river time to cover the stretch from the Fortymile bridge to Eagle or ten to sixteen hours to reach the Clinton Creek bridge.

BE AWARE: All boaters heading into Canada (those using either Clinton Creek or Eagle as a take-out) must check in with both U.S. (in Eagle) and Canadian customs. There is also a customs agent at Boundary, just before entering Canada on the Top of the World Highway. Call ahead to check for any specific requirements.

The Fortymile area is gold country, so expect to see both historic and active gold mining operations. Early season boaters may avoid most mining activity (and bugs), as high-water levels are not good for mining. The drawback of higher water is fewer campsites. The river can also be busy in the fall with hunters.

The river has frequent rapids that can be class I–II at high-water levels. "The Falls" is the only significant set of rapids upriver of the Fortymile bridge (not including fly-in trips down the Middle and North forks which have up to class V rapids like the "Kink" that must be portaged). "The Falls" is class II–III and can be portaged on river right (south) bank. The portage is used mostly by canoeists, but experienced canoeists may want to portage their gear and give the rapids a go. Below the Fortymile bridge are "Deadman's Riffle," which can be class III and portaged on the right, and "Canyon Rapids," which is typically class II–III and can be lined or portaged on the right. At extreme high water this section is very dangerous, as the portage route can be eliminated. Be mindful of sweepers.

There are practically no fish in the river, so you may want to leave your pole at home. Please respect the private property found along the banks associated with mining activity.

MORE ADVENTUROUS? If you could not get enough adventure floating the Fortymile, the Yukon might be calling you to float on by Eagle (Trip 51). On the other hand, if you now need to get out and stretch your legs, try the nearly 3-mile (4.8-km) Lost Chicken Dredge Trail (just past Chicken) or climb up Mount Fairplay (Trip 49). Experts may want to explore Wallcutt Mountain (see Appendix A). Top of the World Highway, leading to Dawson, also provides some good hiking opportunities.

DIRECTIONS: There are numerous put-in and take-out locations for Fortymile River. Take the Richardson Highway (Alaska 2) southeast out of Fairbanks. Stay on Highway Alaska 2 in Delta Junction. (The Richardson veers sharply off to the south here.) Highway Alaska 2 is called the Alaska Highway (and also the Alcan) east of Delta Junction. A dozen miles (19.4 km) past Tok, turn left (north) onto Taylor Highway

Bluffs line many stretches of the river.

(Alaska 5) at Tetlin Junction. Taylor Highway is paved until milepost 64.3, at the Mosquito Fork bridge. The town of Chicken is at milepost 66. At milepost 95.7 on the Taylor Highway, there is a "Y" intersection called Jack Wade Junction. Veer left (north) to stay on the Taylor Highway. The road east is the Top of the World Highway and will take you to Dawson, Canada.

Put-ins for the Mosquito Fork (bridge at milepost 64.3) and West Fork (bridge at milepost 49.2) are before Chicken. These put-ins should be used only when the water level is higher. For the Mosquito Fork, turn right (east) just before (south of) the bridge and go about 100 yards (meters) to reach the steep launch. For the West Fork, park just past the bridge. Gear must be carried a short way. The campground is about a quarter mile (0.4 km) to the south before the bridge.

The rest of the put-ins and all the take-outs are past Chicken. The put-in for the Walker Fork is at milepost 82. It is at Walker Fork Campground, near the end of the campground loop. This put-in should be used only at very high water or with river kayaks and packrafts.

The South Fork bridge (milepost 75) can used as a put-in to float to the Fortymile bridge (milepost 112) or as a take-out for floats from the West Fork and Mosquito Fork put-ins. The parking area and launch is on the left (north) side, just before the bridge.

The Fortymile bridge at milepost 112 can be used as a take-out for the previous put-ins or as a put-in to float to Clinton Creek or all the way to Eagle. A very steep launch is on the right (east) side and parking on the left (west side).

To get to the Clinton Creek take-out, take the Top of the World Highway east for 41.5 miles (67 km) into Canada. Turn north on the Clinton Creek road, and follow it for 25 miles (40 km) until you reach the Clinton Creek bridge. But if you are going that far, why not float all the way back to Eagle? For those intrepid boaters heading to Eagle, that town is at milepost 160 to the end of the road.

51 *YUKON RIVER*

ONE-WAY DISTANCE: 154 miles (248 km)

DURATION: 5 to 10 days

HIGH POINT: 820 feet (250 m)

TOTAL ELEVATION CHANGE: 220 feet (67 m)

DIFFICULTY: Moderate

ROUTE TYPE: Float (class I), suitable for rafts, canoes, or kayaks (motorized allowed)

BEST SEASON: June to September

USGS MAPS: Charley River A-1, A-2, B-2 to B-6, C-6, D-6; Circle C-1, D-1; Eagle D-1 (though the three 1:250 quads would suffice)

LAND MANAGER: Yukon–Charley Rivers National Preserve (Fairbanks), 907-457-5752

The Yukon has not changed all that much from the days of Robert Service and the Klondike gold rush. If anything, the river is wilder and less populated than in his day. The river still casts a spell on intrepid adventurers, fortune seekers, and their ilk. The grandeur and raw power of the river have not diminished over the years, and, thankfully, the river is still untamed. The same swift, silty waters that carried miners to the Klondike gold fields still can carry you back through history and into spectacular country. The trip from Eagle to Circle is a classic float that takes you through the heart of the wilderness of Yukon–Charley Rivers National Preserve. The size, power, remoteness, and mutability of the river dictates that only seasoned paddlers with wilderness experience should lead a trip down the Yukon.

There are many places to get out and stretch your legs along the river. The first comes before you even start—right in Eagle. Head to the northwest part of town, the road will give way to a trail. You will need to walk across Mission Creek (no bridge) to get to Eagle Bluff, which tops out at just over 2,000 feet (610 m). It is a short but

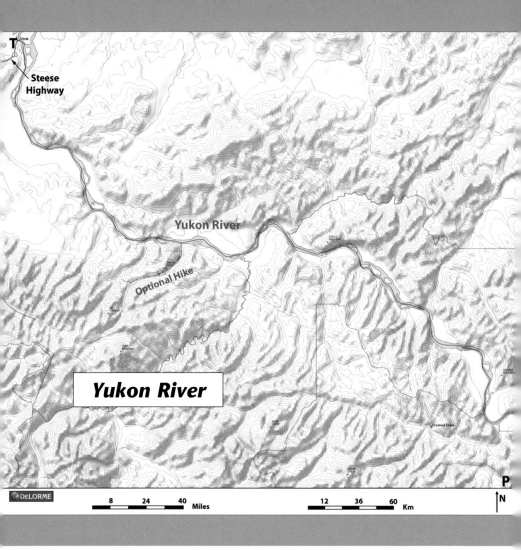

Steese
Highway

Yukon River

Optional Hike

Yukon River

DELORME

| 8 | 24 | 40 |
Miles

| 12 | 36 | 60 |
Km

N

steep climb. From the bluff, you get an excellent view of the town and river. The view is calming and awe-inspiring, but soon the river will call to you to get started.

From the moment you launch, you will have a feeling that something special awaits. The outpost of Eagle and its connection to civilization quickly fades into the distance. The river, zipping along at about 6 mph (9.7 km/h), makes sure of that. It is so silt laden that you can actually hear it grinding against your boat, even rafts. The scouring sound against an aluminum canoe seems deafening in contrast to the silence of the natural environment.

Calico Bluff, about 15 river miles (24 km) downstream from Eagle, marks your entrance into Yukon–Charley Rivers National Preserve. The entire float, save the last 15 miles (24 km), is within the preserve. Calico Bluff, looming 800 feet (244 m) above the river, is an amalgamation of intricate and alternating light and dark layers that are a testament to the pressures that formed it. To the north are the rugged peaks Limestone Hogback, Adams Peak, and McCann Hill.

Seventymile River will enter on your left (south). It was named for its distance from the Klondike gold fields. The area has lots of alder and an island, so the river can be easily missed. Montauk Bluff, about 10 miles (16 km) farther, is the next landmark at river mile 25 (km 40).

Nation River comes flowing in from the north (river right) a dozen miles (19.4 km) past the bluff, river mile 36 (km 58). A mile and a half (2.4 km) past the confluence of the Nation and Yukon rivers, and on the opposite side of the Yukon, is the historic gold rush ghost town of Nation. Many productive claims were established here along Fourth of July Creek and its tributaries. Almost all of the streams in the area flowing north into the Yukon produced gold, while none of the south-flowing streams on the opposite side did. Gold can still be found by panning the south-side streams. Please leave all historical artifacts as you found them.

At only 3,122 feet (951 m), Kathul Mountain, river mile 65 (km 105), certainly is not one of Alaska's big peaks, but it towers above the surrounding region here in the flatter country. The dry soils of the mountain's southern slopes were not glaciated during the last ice age. As a result the mountain still has rare plants, the closest relatives of which are found in Siberia. Although a tempting hike, please avoid these slopes to protect the fragile plants.

The mouth of Kandik River is another 10 or so miles (16 km) past Kathul Mountain. Normally, the river's water is very clear and provides an interesting contrast to the Yukon's muddy color. The force of the Yukon can back the Kandik up in its own channel, creating a pool of clear water that gets warmed by the sun—potentially a good swimming hole.

From the Kandik, Biederman Bluff is in full view. At first it is hard to comprehend that the bluff is more than 6 miles (9.7 km) long and looms a couple thousand feet over the river. The bluff is curved, and by the time you pass it, you are facing south and into the preserve's other namesake river, the Charley. The preserve contains the entire Charley watershed. The river is considered one of the state's premier wilderness floats. The current is slow enough that you can paddle a ways up it from the Yukon. Large white spruce stands along its shores make excellent camping spots. These stands lured pioneers to build cabins near the confluence of the Yukon and Charley. One of these fully stocked cabins saved a life of a World War II airman one winter in the 1940s. His plane had crashed upriver, and he made his way down to this area.

Some 12 miles (19.4 km) from the mouth of the Charley is the historic Slaven's Roadhouse—river mile 95 (km 153). The building has been restored by the National

Historic Slaven's Roadhouse.

Park Service and has interpretive materials. There is also a public-use cabin a short walk from the river. It is available on a first-come, first-served basis and is free. The roadhouse is at the mouth of Coal Creek, from which a dredge pulled more than its share of gold until the 1970s. A road leads from the roadhouse, past the dredge, about 4.5 miles (7.3 km) up to the Coal Creek mining camp, which is now used as an NPS base camp. (There is an upper road that bypasses the dredge. It can be drier but still goes through the camp.) For those looking to stretch their legs and possibly use the public-use cabin, try hiking up 2,340-foot (713-m) high Slaven Dome. Follow the road southwest out of Coal Creek camp for another 4 miles (6.4 km). The road will start climbing a hill. Twisted aspen trees grow on the south slope. Head uphill and to the northeast to reach the summit. You will want to spend a while to enjoy the view of the Yukon River, looking where you have been and where you are heading, before hiking back. You can either backtrack or drop to the east to regain the road. The round trip to the dome from Slaven's Roadhouse and back is about 16 miles (26 km). By staying on the road, rather than heading for Slaven Dome, you will end up at the historic Woodchopper Roadhouse.

Past Slaven's Roadhouse, the river has fewer place-names (as gold was not found there), which adds to the feeling of remoteness. The unnamed bluffs in this area are rugged sandstone and quite stunning. About 20 miles (32 km) downriver of Slaven's Roadhouse is Takoma Bluff, the last bluff you will see on river left (west or south). Smaller bluffs and slopes on river right (east or north) will be visible for another 20 miles (32 km) past Takoma Bluff. As the bluffs and slopes become more indistinct and the river turns northeast (a direction it has not gone since Eagle Bluff), you must get to the left (west) bank. Take the left channels as the main channel of the Yukon avoids Circle altogether. If you miss Circle, the next town is Fort Yukon—a very, very long way away. Additional channels break from the left (west) channel. Stay to the left (west), with the last left (west) turn feeling almost like a 90-degree turn. At this turn, you will see the town of Circle. The boat ramp is the first part of town to which you will come. For most, this is where the Yukon adventure will end.

BE AWARE: The Yukon is a very powerful river; do not underestimate it. Although the river is class I, it has strange and strong currents, undertows, and seemingly out-of-place gravel bars lurking just under the surface. Strong winds can cause waves and dramatically slow travel, especially for rafters. The river is very wide and powerful, so getting from one side to the other can take a long time; plan accordingly. The cold, silty, and swift (6 mph [9.7 km/h]) water can make recovering overturned canoes difficult. Only experienced paddlers with backcountry experience should attempt this trip. The bugs can

Checking maps to make sure he does not pass the town of Circle.

be highly tenacious in spots if the wind dies down. High-water levels can eliminate most gravel bars that are used for camping. Be sure to contact the NPS about river conditions before leaving. Watch for motorboats moving at high speeds, especially near Eagle and Circle.

MORE ADVENTUROUS? Paddlers can continue on the Yukon River all the way to the Yukon River bridge, the river's only road crossing in Alaska. The bridge is on the Dalton Highway. The voyage can take weeks, with insane bugs and slower water downriver of Circle, but the adventure is timeless. Another alternative is to choose a different put-in. Dawson City and Whitehorse in Yukon Territory, Canada, are gold rush towns that helped shape the mystique of the Yukon. Both make excellent starts for a river trip. Dawson to Eagle is about 100 river miles (160 km) and is a popular float.

DIRECTIONS: Take the Richardson Highway (Alaska 2) southeast out of Fairbanks. Stay on Highway Alaska 2 in Delta Junction. (The Richardson veers sharply off to the south here.) Highway Alaska 2 is called the Alaska Highway (and also the Alcan) east of Delta Junction. A dozen miles (19.4 km) past Tok turn left (north) onto Taylor Highway (Alaska 5) at Tetlin Junction. The Taylor Highway ends in Eagle, some 160 miles (258 km) from Tetlin Junction. Follow the highway to First Street and turn right. Head southeast for less than a quarter mile (0.4 km), then turn left on Fremont. A quick right and then left, and you will be at the public boat launch.

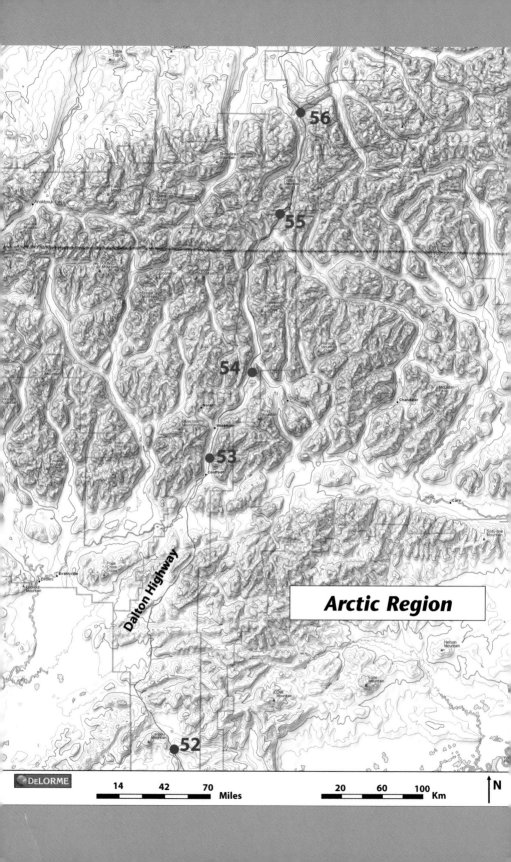

Arctic Region

Arctic Region

As you head north in Alaska, trees become smaller and sparser, eventually disappearing altogether. Arctic Alaska certainly has a different ecosystem than interior Alaska; however, the Arctic Circle lies well within the bounds of the Interior. The last three adventures in this book lie in and north of the Brooks Range, which is out of my definition of the Interior. I included them because they are popular with Interior residents and because most Brooks Range explorers will gear up in Fairbanks, or at least pass through there. The arctic region is the most remote area described in this guidebook, and only more experienced users should attempt backcountry travel there. I provide fewer details to promote self-reliance. Travel possibilities in the Brooks Range are endless. I hope I have supplied enough trips to whet your appetite. This area also has plenty of road-to-road float opportunities; however, most stay close to the Dalton Highway or Trans-Alaska Pipeline, or both, so I have chosen not to include them.

52 FINGER MOUNTAIN

R/T DISTANCE: Up to three-quarters of a mile (1.2 km)

DURATION: 30 minutes to 2 hours

HIGH POINT: 2,000 feet (609 m)

TOTAL ELEVATION CHANGE: Less than 50 feet (15 m)

DIFFICULTY: Easy

ROUTE TYPE: Established or social trail (nonmotorized)

BEST SEASON: June to September

USGS MAPS: Bettles B-1

LAND MANAGER: Bureau of Land Management (Fairbanks), 907-474-2200

Just driving the Dalton Highway can be an adventure. It has expansive scenery, is remote, and has few amenities. One of the first places after the Yukon River bridge to get out, stretch your legs, and take in the views is at the Finger Mountain BLM Wayside (milepost 98). Finger Mountain, which is not much of a mountain, was named after a large outcropping that looks like a fist with a finger pointing into the air. At about 25 feet (8 m) high, it really stands out in the tundra and is fun to climb on. Besides the social trail to this outcropping, the views are great to the north along a very short established nature trail.

The nature trail starts on the north side of the parking lot. It has sweeping views of tundra and rocky hills to the north and east. The trail is about an eighth of a mile (0.2 km) round trip and its loose gravel path is obvious. Not as obvious is the social trail out to Finger Rock. It starts off from the southeast corner of the parking lot. The path is obscured in many places because of a recent wildfire, but it should get more obvious with time. Stick to the trail when you can see it. Finger Rock is visible from the parking lot, so you should not get lost as long as your route is not obscured by fog or a whiteout. Some sections of the path offer boulder hopping, which can be fun, but lichens make them slick when wet. The trip to the rock and back is about three-quarters of a mile (1.2 km).

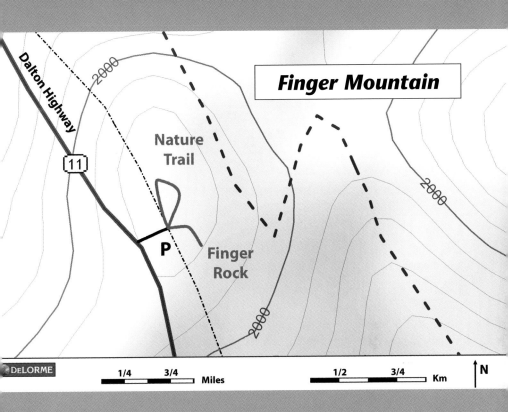

Finger Mountain

Nature Trail

Dalton Highway

[11]

P

Finger Rock

2000

2000

2000

DeLORME

1/4 3/4 **Miles**

1/2 3/4 **Km**

↑ **N**

BE AWARE: The Dalton Highway is often in rough shape and has large, fast trucks. Drive slow and be alert. These trails are not far off the highway, so expect road noise. Rock climbing and bouldering are inherently dangerous; know your skills and limits, and always use the proper safety gear. Be aware of weather conditions before taking a trip on the Dalton. Spring comes much later and winter much sooner here than south of the Yukon River.

MORE ADVENTUROUS? More bouldering can be done in the area. To get to more places, park just down the hill at milepost 99.5—the boulders can be seen from the road. Gobbler's Knob, farther north up the road, is another good place to stretch your legs and admire the view. It is promoted as a nice spot to camp and enjoy the midnight sun. Park at milepost 132 on the right (south) side of the highway, across the road from the turnout with the placard. At the southwest corner of the gravel pit is a dirt road that heads south, then turns east. A half-mile (0.8-km) hike takes you to the top of a butte with lots of good camping sites and nice views of the Brooks Range to the north. You can cut through the gravel pit for a steeper but shorter route.

DIRECTIONS: Take the Steese Highway (Alaska 2) north out of Fairbanks to the town of Fox, 11 miles (18 km) away. In Fox, go straight, which puts you on the Elliott Highway (but still Alaska 2). Continuous pavement ends at milepost 73,

Finger Rock, which gave this mountain its name.

past Livengood. Stay on the road heading north and you will automatically be on the Dalton Highway (Alaska 11, also known as the "Haul Road"). A left turn here would keep you on the Elliott, which you do not want. Park at milepost 98, Dalton Highway, at the Finger Mountain BLM Wayside on the right (east) side of the highway.

53 MARION CREEK FALLS

R/T DISTANCE: 4 miles (6.4 km)

DURATION: 1 to 3 hours

HIGH POINT: 1,750 feet (533 m)

TOTAL ELEVATION CHANGE: 350 feet (107 m)

DIFFICULTY: Easy to moderate

ROUTE TYPE: Social trail (nonmotorized)

BEST SEASON: June to September

USGS MAPS: Wiseman B-1

LAND MANAGER: Bureau of Land Management (Fairbanks), 907-474-2200

Marion Creek tumbles out of the jagged Brooks Range, creating a series of cascades before plunging about 20 feet (6 m) in a scenic waterfall. The creek winds its way through wet black spruce stands and dry lichen-and-spruce woodlands before spilling into the Koyukuk River. A social trail leads to the falls. It is easy to follow in most places but easy to lose in others. Only hikers with some route-finding skills should try the trip.

The trail starts from the northeast corner of the Marion Creek Campground—next to the outhouse, of course. Climbing a small hill to the east, the trail leads to an open lichen-and-spruce woodland. The ground here is covered with *Cladina stellaris*, an old-growth lichen that is a favorite food of caribou. The lichen is sensitive to foot traffic, as will be obvious, so try to stick to the most used trail. The trail follows the bank high above Marion Creek. The creek is eroding the bank, so do not get too close. After about three-quarters of a mile (1.2 km), the easy walking of the lichen-and-spruce terrace abruptly ends, and the trail forks. The left fork heads lower and is difficult to follow. Take the right fork, which continues on through damp tussock-and-spruce forest. Less than a mile (1.6 km) farther, the trail intersects a mining road. Note landmarks where the trail meets the road so you can find the trail when you return.

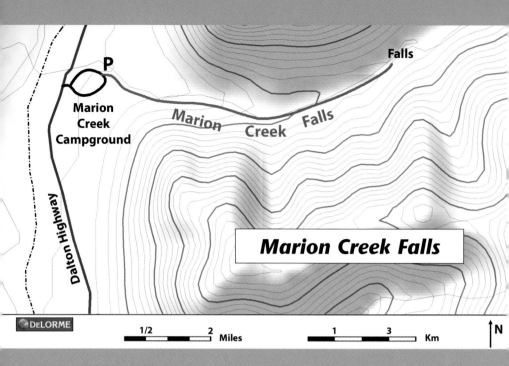

Marion Creek Falls

1/2   2   **Miles**   1   3   **Km**   ↑N

Follow the road east for less than an eighth of a mile (0.2 km). It is open enough to provide great views of the mountains in all directions. The social trail will reappear on the left (north) side of the road and may have flagging. The falls will be audible from here. Follow the trail about 75 yards (meters) to a viewpoint of the 20-foot (6-m) high falls. Do not get too close, as the creek is eroding this bank. The falls are quite scenic, as are the cascades just above the falls. Return the same way you arrived.

If, on your return, you miss where the first part of the trail intersects the road, the road will drop down, taking you to the creek. The road crosses the creek and does not return to the campground. Backtrack on the road to find the trail. You can

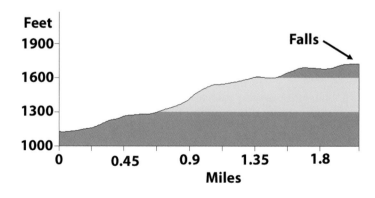

bushwhack uphill from the creek crossing to the trail, but that route is not pleasant.

Marion Creek.

BE AWARE: The Dalton Highway is often in rough shape and has large, fast trucks. Drive slow and be alert. Be aware of weather conditions before taking a trip on the Dalton. Spring comes much later and winter much sooner here than south of the Yukon River. This is a social trail, which you can easily lose. Route-finding abilities are required. Part of this trip is along a new (2006) mining road. Expect changes to the route. Fees are required to stay at the campground.

Marion Creek Falls.

MORE ADVENTUROUS? There are not many other trails in these parts, so more adventurous trips get very adventurous quickly. If you are ready to tackle the vast expanses of the arctic wilderness, many opportunities await you just off the Dalton Highway. Try Trips 54–56, or better yet, chart your own adventure.

DIRECTIONS: Take the Steese Highway (Alaska 2) north out of Fairbanks to Fox, 11 miles (18 km) away. In Fox, go straight, which puts you on the Elliott Highway (but still Alaska 2). Continuous pavement ends at milepost 73, past Livengood. Stay on the road heading north and you will automatically be on the Dalton Highway (Alaska 11, also known as the "Haul Road"). A left turn here will keep you on the Elliott, which you do not want. On the Dalton, a few miles past Coldfoot, turn right (east) at milepost 180 into Marion Creek Campground. The trailhead is at the northeast corner of the campground next to an outhouse. Parking is available there.

54 SUKAKPAK MOUNTAIN

R/T DISTANCE: 4–5 miles (6.5–8 km)

DURATION: 3 to 5 hours

HIGH POINT: 4,459 feet (1,358 m)

TOTAL ELEVATION CHANGE: 6,500 feet (1,980 m)

DIFFICULTY: Expert

ROUTE TYPE: Route (nonmotorized)

BEST SEASON: June to September

USGS MAPS: Chandalar C-6

LAND MANAGER: Bureau of Land Management (Fairbanks), 907-474-2200

Words do not do justice for Sukakpak Mountain. One of the icons of the Dalton Highway, it is simply awesome. Its rugged 3,000-foot (914-m) high cliff face is nearly 2 miles (3.2 km) long. This mountain is imposing, yet it is possible to do this trip without technical gear. The views from the top are unsurpassed.

From the turnout at milepost 203.1, head east. Aim for an obvious, large landslide on the southeast corner of the mountain. The ground can be a bit wet at first, but with the proper route choice it is not bad. The undergrowth is relatively low and open, which makes for fairly good hiking. Follow the landslide or its edge up the side of the mountain. Use caution, as the landslide may still be active. After an

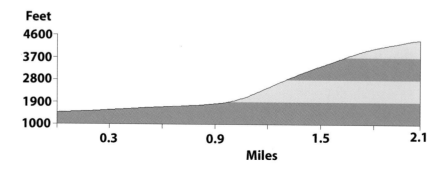

222

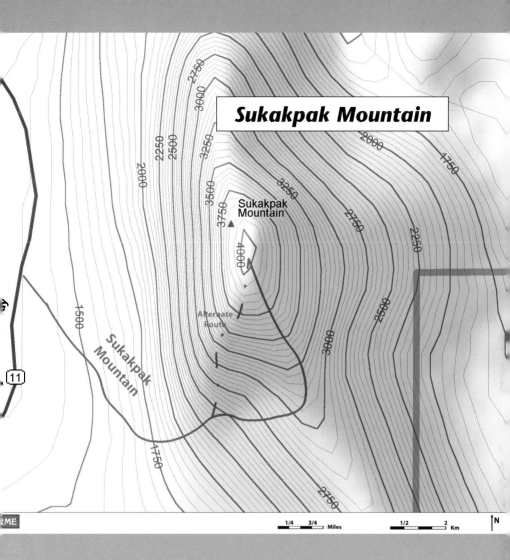

Sukakpak Mountain

Sukakpak Mountain

Alternate Route

Sukakpak Mountain

11

ME

1/4   3/4   Miles

1/2   2   Km

↑N

unrelenting climb, you will reach the ridgetop and be above tree line. You can try for the summit by heading north here, but the climb is very steep and treacherous in places. For a less hair-raising climb to the summit, continue east, first dropping down then ascending to the larger north-south ridge about a half mile to the east. The views of the Bettles and Koyukuk river valleys from here are stunning. Gather your nerve and peer over the edge to admire the sheer face of the mountain from above. Rest your legs for the steep climb down.

BE AWARE: The Dalton Highway is often in rough shape with large, fast trucks on it. Drive slow and be alert. Be aware of weather conditions before taking a trip on the Dalton. Spring comes much later and winter much sooner than south of the Yukon River. This is a route, not a trail—you must be adept at route finding. This climb

The face of Sukakpak looking north.

has very steep pitches, rugged and loose terrain, and a 3,000-foot (914-m) cliff. You should have extremely sure footing or climbing gear if you are going to try to reach the summit. This is sheep country. Please do not disturb them, and restrain your dog if you bring one.

MORE ADVENTUROUS? If you are ready to tackle the vast expanses of the arctic wilderness, many opportunities await you just off the Dalton Highway. Try Trips 55 or 56, or better yet, chart your own adventure.

DIRECTIONS: Take the Steese Highway (Alaska 2) north out of Fairbanks to the town of Fox, 11 miles (18 km) away. In Fox, go straight, which puts you on the Elliott Highway (but still Alaska 2). Continuous pavement ends at milepost 73, past Livengood. Stay on the road heading north and you will automatically be on the Dalton Highway (Alaska 11, also known as the "Haul Road"). A left turn here will keep you on the Elliott, which you do not want. Park at milepost 203.1. The turnout is narrow, so get as far to the right (east) side as you can. You may want to cover your front and back windows with cardboard to protect them from rocks kicked up by passing vehicles.

55 *CHANDALAR–ATIGUN TRAVERSE*

ONE-WAY DISTANCE: 25–30 miles (40–48 km)

DURATION: 2 to 4 days

HIGH POINT: 4,950 feet (1,508 m)

TOTAL ELEVATION CHANGE: 3,800 feet (1,157 m)

DIFFICULTY: Expert

ROUTE TYPE: Route (nonmotorized)

BEST SEASON: June to September

USGS MAPS: Philip Smith Mountains A-5, B-4, B-5

LAND MANAGER: Bureau of Land Management (Fairbanks), 907-474-2200

Once you have been surrounded by jagged 6,000-foot (1,827-m) peaks, walked across open alpine tundra, and floated down remote arctic rivers, you may never want to see a trail again. The Chandalar–Atigun traverse takes you from the south side of the Brooks Range up and over the Continental Divide, and down onto the North Slope. This country is truly wild and remote. This trip can be completed with either of two modes of travel. Packrafting the West Fork of the Atigun River down to the Dalton Highway is the most expedient (and fun) way, but hikers can follow the river out as well. However, that mode of travel requires crossing Atigun River, which can be very difficult.

From the parking area at milepost 242, head west, either along the creek or up on the tundra. The creek is harder on the feet but more level, whereas the tundra bench has more ups and downs but is gentler on the joints. After a couple of miles, the creek turns northwest (not north). Follow it to a pass, which is about 5,000 feet (1,524 m) high and is part of the Continental Divide. Drop off the divide, heading west. Use your route-finding skills to pick a good path down to the valley floor. The creek in the valley is the beginning of the West Fork of the Atigun River. Follow it north. Once it gets deep enough, packrafters can start floating, letting the current take

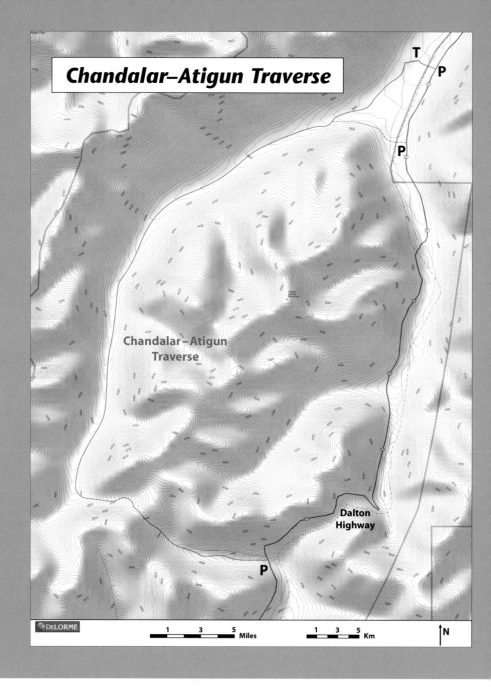

Chandalar–Atigun Traverse

Chandalar–Atigun
Traverse

Dalton
Highway

1	3	5		1	3	5	
		Miles				Km	

DELORME

N

them to within a mile (1.6 km) of the Dalton Highway on the North Slope—where they can hike out to their shuttle vehicle. Sections of the river should be scouted and some areas should be portaged, depending on where you put in, water conditions, and your own abilities. Hikers should stay on the east side of the West Fork and cut east as the valley opens. Hikers will have to cross the Middle Fork of the

Atigun River, which can be treacherous. Only experts should attempt this trip.

BE AWARE: The Dalton Highway is often in rough shape with large, fast trucks on it. Drive slow and be alert. Be aware of weather conditions before taking a trip on the Dalton. Spring comes much later and winter much sooner than south of the Yukon River. This is a route, not a trail—you must be adept at route finding. This climb has very steep pitches and rugged and loose terrain. Packrafting should be attempted only by experienced paddlers. Scout questionable sections of the river before running them. Attempting to cross the

The treeless terrain of the upper Chandalar.

Atigun River without a raft can be very dangerous. Be confident of your river-crossing skills before attempting to hike this trip. This is sheep country. Please do not disturb them, and restrain your dog if you bring one.

MORE ADVENTUROUS? If you are ready to tackle the vast expanses of the arctic wilderness, many opportunities await you just off the Dalton Highway. Try Atigun Gorge (Trip 56) or chart your own adventure!

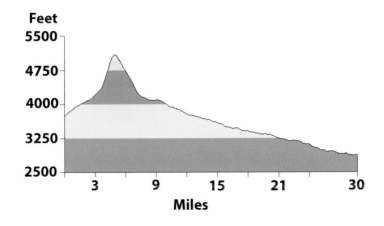

DIRECTIONS: Take the Steese Highway (Alaska 2) north out of Fairbanks to the town of Fox, 11 miles (18 km) away. In Fox, go straight, which puts you on the Elliott Highway (but still Alaska 2). Continuous pavement ends at milepost 73, past Livengood. Stay on the road heading north and you will automatically be on the Dalton Highway (Alaska 11, also known as the "Haul Road"). A left turn here will keep you on the Elliott, which you do not want. Park in the turnout on the left (south) side of the highway at milepost 242, just before the bridge over the West Fork of the North Fork of the Chandalar River. Packrafters can park a shuttle vehicle at milepost 257. Those hiking only can park a shuttle vehicle a couple miles sooner, where the West Fork of the Atigun River valley becomes visible to your left (west).

56 *ATIGUN RIVER GORGE AND SAGAVANIRKTOK RIVER*

ONE-WAY DISTANCE: 50 miles (80 km)

DURATION: 3 to 5 days

HIGH POINT: 2,800 feet (853 m)

TOTAL ELEVATION CHANGE: 2,600 feet (792 m)

DIFFICULTY: Expert

ROUTE TYPE: Route (nonmotorized)

BEST SEASON: June to September

USGS MAPS: Philip Smith Mountains B-4, C-4, D-4

LAND MANAGERS: Bureau of Land Management (Fairbanks), 907-474-2200; Arctic National Wildlife Refuge (Fairbanks), 907-456-0250

The hike along the southern bank of Atigun River starts off serenely. The wide, U-shaped valley is carpeted with soft tundra, and the river quietly meanders through its bottom. The rugged peaks are distant enough so that you do not feel hemmed in. But the valley changes quickly as it narrows and becomes the Atigun River Gorge. The river roars through the gorge, and cliffs rise up its sides. The gorge can be hiked as a pleasant day trip or as an overnight backpack. Intrepid adventurers can hike through the gorge and packraft Sagavanirktok River (also known as the Sag River) back to the Dalton Highway, some 50 miles (80 km) distant.

From the parking lot off milepost 270.8, cross the road and head east. Stay on the south side of Atigun River. The going is easy for the first couple of miles, and the river could even be packrafted. But the valley quickly tightens, and the cliffs become larger. Rafters should exit the river here, before it gets too fast and wild. As the valley tightens the hiking gets more difficult, so day-trippers may want to turn back around here, making for a round trip of about 10 miles (16 km). However, the scenery gets more spectacular the farther you go, so turning back may be hard to do.

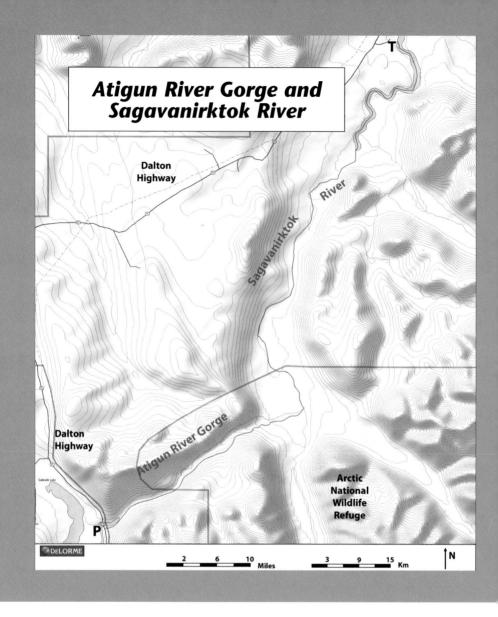

Atigun River Gorge and Sagavanirktok River

Dalton Highway

River

Sagavanirktok

Dalton Highway

Atigun River Gorge

Galbrath Lake

P

Arctic National Wildlife Refuge

DELORME

2   6   10
Miles

3   9   15
Km

↑N

Route-finding skills are more important the farther you go, as there are problematic sections through the gorge. After about 11 miles (17.6 km), Atigun River spills out of the gorge into the wide Sag River valley. The views of the North Slope, including part of the Arctic National Wildlife Refuge, are hard to beat. Packrafters can float the Sag some 40 miles (64 km) north to regain the Dalton Highway.

BE AWARE: The Dalton Highway is often in rough shape with large, fast trucks on it. Drive slow and be alert. Be aware of weather conditions before taking a trip on the Dalton. Spring comes much later and winter much sooner than south of the

The wide valley at the entrance of Atigun Gorge.

Yukon River. This is a route, not a trail—you must be adept at route finding. This climb has very steep pitches and rugged and loose terrain.

Packrafting should be attempted only by experienced paddlers. Scout questionable sections of the river before running them. Do not attempt to packraft the Atigun River Gorge. It is very dangerous. Expert white-water kayakers may relish the challenge. Strong north winds can greatly impede your progress on the Sag. Plan for them. This is sheep country. Please do not disturb them, and restrain your dog if you bring one.

MORE ADVENTUROUS? Sounds like you are ready to tackle the vast expanses of the arctic wilderness; the Dalton Highway has all sorts of opportunities for you. Try the Chandalar–Atigun Traverse (Trip 55) or chart your own adventure!

DIRECTIONS: Take the Steese Highway (Alaska 2) north out of Fairbanks to the town of Fox, 11 miles (18 km) away. In Fox, go straight, which puts you on the Elliott Highway (but still Alaska 2). Continuous pavement ends at milepost 73, past Livengood. Stay on the road heading north and you will automatically be on the Dalton Highway (Alaska 11, also known as the "Haul Road"). A left turn here will keep you on the Elliott, which you do not want. Park on the left (west) side of the Dalton at milepost 270.8, just before the Atigun River bridge (signed #2). The terminus of the trip is at milepost 309.5, where there is parking. The Sag River also comes close to the road at milepost 311, near Trans-Alaska Pipeline Pump Station 3, for those who want to put a few more miles on their boat.

Appendix
Expert Interior Favorites to Discover on Your Own

Black Rapids to Denali Park

This is an Alaska Mountain Wilderness Classic race route that starts from Black Rapids on the Richardson Highway. Most people doing this trip traverse the northern flanks of the Alaska Range to reach Denali Park over 100 miles (160 km) away.

Chena Hot Springs to Circle Hot Springs

The winter route takes travelers up Harrison Creek and Birch Creek to the North Fork of the Chena River and into Chena Hot Springs. You will want a soak at the end of this one! In summer, pack raft down Birch Creek.

Circle to Fairbanks Historic Trail

This trail is part of a route used by miners and others during the gold rush era. The trail, which roughly parallels the Steese Highway, runs for about 55 miles (88 km) from Cleary Summit to Twelvemile Summit, and is almost all on ridges. A pamphlet is available at the Alaska Public Lands Information Center or from the Department of Natural Resources (see Appendix B).

Hutlinana Hot Springs

These hot springs are off Elliott Highway, past Tolovana Hot Springs Trail, at milepost 130. The trip is only 6–8 miles (10–13 km) each way, depending on your route, but the trail is often difficult to find. The latitude and longitude for the hot springs are at 65°12'33" N and 149°59'33" W, and the temperature is about 106°F (41°C). The trip is usually done in the winter, as the trail can be wet before freeze-up.

Kanuti Hot Springs

These 131°F (55°C) hot springs are about 11 miles (17.6 km) to the west of the Dalton Highway. Begin your adventure at milepost 103. Snowmachines are not allowed in the Dalton Highway corridor, which extends 5 miles (8.1 km) to each side of the highway. The trail, often difficult to find, should only be done in winter as it can be very wet at other times of the year. The latitude and longitude for the hot springs are at 66°13′09″ N and 149°33′10″ W.

Nabesna to McCarthy

This is another Alaska Mountain Wilderness Classic route. Most adventurers float the Nabesna River to Cooper Creek and then head over the pass at Blue Lake to reach Chisana. They then turn south, heading through Skolai Pass and over the Goat Trail to the Chitistone and Nizina rivers. Finally, they follow a road to McCarthy.

Nabesna to Northway

This is mostly a float but starts as a hike. Follow the winter trail that heads to the east just before Nabesna. The trail is boggy, but after 5 miles (8 km) you will reach a point on Jack Creek where you can put in to float Nabesna River all the way to Northway. This float has stunning views of the Mentasta and Nutzotin mountains!

Nugget Creek Trail

Wintertime crossings of the Chena River and the South Fork of the Chena River can be treacherous. Otherwise this is a relatively easy 6-mile (9.7-km) trip into the 10 x 12-foot (3 x 4-m) Nugget Creek Cabin. Turn right (south) at milepost 31.4, Chena Hot Springs Road, and follow the green markers.

Wallcutt Mountain

Just south of Eagle, on American Summit, head southwest from the gravel pits. Heading over Peak 4410 you can reach 5,593-foot (1,704-m) high Wallcutt Mountain. The mostly alpine route is 13 miles (21 km) oneway. It has great views of the Fortymile country and rugged mountains to the west. The ridge system can be followed to Glacier Mountain and beyond, but even the shorter hike to Peak 4410 is enjoyable.

B Appendix
References, Contact
Information, and Suggested
Reading

Agencies

ALASKA DEPARTMENT OF FISH AND GAME (State Wildlife Refuges)
Physical address: 1300 College Road, Fairbanks
Phone: 907-459-7213
Web address: http://www.wildlife.alaska.gov/index.cfm?adfg=refuge.main

ALASKA DEPARTMENT OF NATURAL RESOURCES
Physical address: 3700 Airport Way (corner of Airport and University),
Fairbanks
Phone: 907-451-2705
Web address (for undesignated state lands): http://www.dnr.state.ak.us/pic

DIVISION OF PARKS AND OUTDOOR RECREATION
Phone: 907-451-2695
Web address: http://www.dnr.state.ak.us/parks/index.htm

ALASKA DEPARTMENT OF TRANSPORTATION (road condition information)
Phone: 511
Web address: http://511.Alaska.gov

ALASKA FIRE SERVICE
Phone: 907-356-5511
Web address: http://fire.ak.blm.gov/afs/

ALASKA PUBLIC LANDS INFORMATION CENTER
Physical address: 250 Cushman Street, Suite 1a, Fairbanks
Phone: 907-456-0527
Web address: http://www.nps.gov/aplic/center/

BUREAU OF LAND MANAGEMENT
Alaska web address: http://www.blm.gov/ak/

FAIRBANKS OFFICE
Physical address: 1150 University Avenue
Phone: 907-474-2200

GLENNALLEN OFFICE

Physical address: Mile 186 Glenn Highway

Phone: 907-822-3217

CANADIAN CUSTOMS, BEAVER CREEK, YUKON TERRITORY

Phone: 967-862-7230

FISH AND WILDLIFE SERVICE, ARCTIC NATIONAL WILDLIFE REFUGE

Physical address: 101 Twelfth Avenue, Room 236, Fairbanks

Phone: 907-456-0250

Web address: http://alaska.fws.gov/nwr/arctic/index.htm

FORT GREELY VISITORS' CENTER

Phone: 907-873-3660

GEOPHYSICAL INSTITUTE MAP OFFICE (for USGS quad maps)

Physical address: 903 Koyukuk Drive (208 Elvey Building), University of
  Alaska Fairbanks

Phone: 907-474-6960

NATIONAL PARK SERVICE (Fairbanks office)

Physical address: 4175 Geist Road, Fairbanks

Phone: 907-457-5752

Web address (Gates of the Arctic National Park and Preserve):
  http://www.nps.gov/gaar/index.htm

Web address (Yukon–Charley Rivers National Preserve):
  http://www.nps.gov/yuch/

UNITED STATES CUSTOMS AND BORDER PROTECTION (Fairbanks office)

Phone: 907-474-0307

Web address: http://www.cbp.gov

Groups and Businesses

ALASKA ALPINE CLUB (Fairbanks mountaineering club)

Web address: http://www.uaf.edu/aac/fairbanks.html

ALASKA SATELLITE COMMUNICATIONS (Anchorage; satellite phone sales
and rentals)

Phone: 907-868-1782

Web address: http://alaskasatellitecommunications.com

ALASKA SKIJORING AND PULK ASSOCIATION (Fairbanks)

Phone: 907-457-5456

Web address: http://www.sleddog.org/skijor/

ALASKA TRAILS (non-profit advocacy group based in Anchorage)

Phone: 907-334-8049

Web address: http://www.alaska-trails.org

ALASKAN ALPINE CLUB (Fairbanks mountaineering club)
  Phone: 907-479-2149
  Web address: http://www.alaskaalpineclub.org
ALPACKA RAFT COMPANY (Anchorage packraft manufacturer)
  Phone: 907-929-8255
  Web address: http://www.alpackaraft.com
CHENA HOT SPRINGS RESORT
  Phone: 907-451-8104 or 800-478-4681
  Web address: http://www.chenahotsprings.com
FAIRBANKS AREA HIKING CLUB
  Phone: 907-455-7557
  Web address: http://www.fairbankshiking.org
FAIRBANKS CYCLE CLUB
  Phone: 907-459-8008
  Web address: http://www.fairbankscycleclub.org
FAIRBANKS PADDLERS
  Phone: 907-457-6723
  Web address: http://www.fairbankspaddlers.org
FRIENDS OF CREAMERS FIELD
  Phone: 907-452-5162
  Web address: http://www.fairnet.org/agencies/creamers/index.html
NORDIC SKI CLUB OF FAIRBANKS
  Phone: 907-474-4242
  Web address: http://www.nscfairbanks.net
NORTHERN ALASKA ENVIRONMENTAL CENTER (Fairbanks)
  Phone: 907-452-5021
  Web address: http://www.northern.org/artman/publish/index.shtml
RUNNING CLUB NORTH (Fairbanks)
  Web address: http://www.runningclubnorth.org
TOLOVANA HOT SPRINGS
  Phone: 907-455-6706
  Web address: http://www.tolovanahotsprings.com
UNIVERSITY OF ALASKA FAIRBANKS OUTDOOR ADVENTURES
  Phone: 907-474-6027
  Web address: http://www.uaf.edu/outdoor/
UNIVERSITY TRAILS CLUB (UAF)
  Web address: http://www.uaf.edu/trails

Books and Articles

Abou-Donia, M. 2002. "Use Caution When Using DEET." Duke University Medical Center. http://dukemednews.duke.edu/news/healthtipp.php?id=5656.

Alaska Atlas & Gazetteer, second edition. Yarmouth, ME: DeLorme. 156 pp.

Daffern, T. 1992. *Avalanche Safety for Skiers and Climbers*, second edition. Seattle, WA: The Mountaineers Books. 192 pp.

Fredston, J. and Fesler, D. 1994. *Snow Sense*. Anchorage, AK: Alaska Mountain Safety Center, Inc. 116 pp.

Herrero, S. 2002. *Bear Attacks: Their Causes and Avoidance*, revised edition. Guilford, CT: The Lyons Press. 304 pp.

Jettmar, K. 1993. *The Alaska River Guide: Canoeing, Kayaking and Rafting in the Last Frontier*. Seattle, WA: Alaska Northwest Books. 302 pp.

Justice, S. 2003. *Fairbanks Area Climbing Guide*. 50 pp.

Justice, S. 2001. *Mount Prindle Area Climbing Guide*. 37 pp.

Kost, D. 2000. *Hiking in Wrangell–St. Elias National Park*. Anchorage, AK: Danny Kost. 68 pp.

(the) *Milepost: All-the-North Travel Guide*. Updated annually. http://www.themilepost.com

National Geographic. 1990. *Denali National Park and Preserve, Alaska, USA. Trails Illustrated Map*. Revised 1999. Evergreen, CO: National Geographic.

Nienhueser, H. D. and Wolfe, J. 1994. *55 Ways to the Wilderness in Southcentral Alaska*, fourth edition. Seattle, WA: The Mountaineers Books.

Paton, B. C. et al. 1998. *Wilderness First Aid*. Sudbury, MA: Jones and Bartlett Publishers. 350 pp.

Shepherd, S. and Wozniak, O. 2001. *50 Hikes in Alaska's Chugach State Park*. Seattle, WA: The Mountaineers Books. 205 pp.

Troyer, W. 2005. *Into Brown Bear Country*. Fairbanks: University of Alaska Press.

Vos, C. 1999. *The Yukon Hiking Guide*. Whitehorse (Yukon Territory), Canada: Borealis Books. 182 pp.

Waits, I. 2005. *Denali National Park: Guide to Hiking, Photography, and Camping*, second edition. Anchorage, AK: Wild Rose Guide Books. 256 pp.

Waterman, L. and Waterman, G. 1993. *Backwoods Ethics: Environmental Issues for Hikers and Campers*. Woodstock, VT: Countryman Press. 280 pp.

Zimmerman, J. 1994. *A Naturalist's Guide to Chugach State Park*. Anchorage, AK: A. T. Publishing and Printing, Inc. 258 pp.

Please be aware that web page addresses, phone numbers, and physical addresses change. The information listed here was current at the time this book was written. If the information is no longer current, use a search engine for the agency, group, or topic information to locate the current web page. Please e-mail me at outside-interior@hotmail.com about any changes so I can make updates.

Appendix C
Trip Locator Table

D o you know what kind of trip you want to take but are not sure where to go? This matrix can help. The first column contains different types of activities, while the first row shows the different levels of difficulty. Each cell contains the trip numbers (see table of contents) that correspond to the activity and level of difficulty you are interested in.

	Easy	Moderate	Difficult	Expert
Hike	1, 2, 3, 4, 5, 6, 9, 11, 17, 19, 20, 23, 26, 33, 35, 38, 43, 46, 52, 53	2, 4, 5, 6, 14, 16, 17, 18, 19, 20, 23, 24, 28, 30, 32, 33, 34, 35, 36, 37, 40, 41, 42, 46, 49, 53	12, 14, 21, 24, 27, 28, 29, 32, 34, 41, 42	24, 54, 55, 56
Bike	1, 2, 3, 4, 5, 9	2, 4, 5, 6, 16, 28, 34, 46	4, 5, 6, 16, 18, 28	
Ski	1, 2, 3, 5, 6, 8, 9, 11, 17, 22, 23	2, 4, 5, 6, 8, 16, 17, 18, 22, 23, 34, 35, 37, 41	4, 5, 6, 8, 34, 41	4, 8, 34
Classical	1, 2, 3, 5, 6, 8, 9, 11, 17, 22, 23	2, 4, 5, 6, 8, 16, 17, 18, 22, 23, 34, 35, 37, 41	4, 5, 6, 8, 34, 41	4, 8, 34
Skate	1, 2, 8, 9, 11	2, 4, 8, 34	4, 8, 34	4, 8, 34
Skijor	1, 3, 8, 9, 11	8, 34	8, 34	8, 34
Float	7, 8, 9, 10, 13, 38, 39, 43, 44, 50	13, 15, 25, 31, 39, 44, 45, 47, 48, 50, 51	27	41
Raft	7, 8, 13, 39, 43, 44, 50	13, 15, 25, 31, 39, 44, 45, 47, 48, 50, 51	27	13, 44
Canoe	7, 8, 9, 10, 13, 38, 39, 43, 44, 50	13, 15, 25, 31, 39, 44, 45, 47, 48, 50, 51	27, 45	
Kayak	7, 8, 9, 10, 13, 38, 39, 43, 50	13, 15, 25, 39, 47, 48, 50, 51		13, 41, 56
Packraft	7, 10, 13	13, 15, 25, 47, 48, 50	27	41, 55, 56
Rock Climbing	19, 20, 29, 36	19, 20, 29, 36	19, 20, 29, 36	19, 20, 29, 36

Index

Note: *Italicized* page numbers indicate illustrations.

A

Ace Lake, 12
Alaska Bird Observatory, 2
Alaska Mountain Wilderness Classic, 157, 232
Alaska Range, xiii, 97, 169–70, *177*
American Creek valley, 121
Amphitheater Mountains, 178
Anderson River Park, 49
Angel Creek Trail, 66, 83, 85, 88–90
Angel Creek Valley, 13
Angel Rocks, 144
Angel Rocks to Chena Hot Springs Trail, 79–80, 81
Angel Rocks Trail, 58, 61, 81, 92
Ann Creek take-out, 181
Arctic Region, overview, 214–15
Atigun River, 225–28
Atigun River Gorge, 229–31
ATVs, improper use of, 62
aurora borealis, xx
avalanches, xxvi

B

backcountry travel, xx–xxi
Bear Creek Trail, 143
Bear Paw Butte, 82, 91, *93*
bears, xiv, xvi–xviii, xxii, 54–55, 190
Beauty Dome, 129
Beaver Creek, 101, 106, 109–14, 148
beaver fever (*giardia lamblia*), xxiv
Beggar's Canyon, 150
berry picking, 21, 23
Biederman Bluff, 211
Big Bend Trail, 111–12, 141–42, 143, 148

bikers, and trail etiquette, xxvi–xxvii
biking trip locator, 238
Birch Creek, 97, 101, 127–30
Birch Hill, 13, 15–17
Birch Lake, 158, 160
Bison Gulch, 43–45
Black Rapids Glacier, 181
Black Rapids to Denali Park, 232
blueberries, and bears, 54
Bluff Cabin Lake, 160
Bluff Cabin Trail, 160
Bluff Point Trail, 159
boreal forests, xiii, 2, 88, 202. *See also* taiga
boulder fields and bouldering, 53, 81, 82, 149, 201–2, 217
Brooks Range, xiii, 215
Byers Lake, 51, 53, 55

C

cabins, historic, 128, 182, 211
cabins, private, 152, 154
cabins, public-use. *See also* shelters; yurts
    Angel Creek, 85, *86*
    Angel Creek Trail, 88–89
    Bluff, 160
    Borealis-LeFevre, 111, 113, 141, 145, 147, 148
    Byers Lake campground, 51
    Cache Mountain, 142
    Caribou Bluff, 112, 142
    Charley River, 212
    Chena Dome Trail, 89
    Colorado Creek, 65–66, 142, 143
    Crowberry, 142
    Eleazar's, 141
    Fielding Lake, 175, 177
    Glatfelder, 159

    Lee's, 140, 143, 148
    Moose Creek, 141, 148
    Nugget Creek, 233
    Quartz Lake, 159
    Richard's, 108, 142
    Stiles Creek, 71
    White Mountains National Recreation Area, 140–43
    Windy Gap, 142
    Wolf Run, 112, 142, 143
Cache Creek Trail, 12
Cache Mountain Loop Trail, 142
Calico Bluff, 210–11
campfires, xxii
campgrounds
    Byers Lake, 51, 55
    Cripple Creek, 104
    Granite Tors, 59
    Lake Park, 34
    Marion Creek, 219
    Marion Creek Falls, 221
    Mount Prindle, 123
    Ophir Creek, 114
    Paxson Lake, 185
    Rosehip, 59, 60, 61
    Sourdough Creek, 185
    Walker Fork, 206, 208
campsites, set up, xxii
canoe trip locator, 238
Canwell Glacier, 173
Canwell Peak, 173, 174
caribou, xv, 131, 179, 201–2, 219
Castner Creek, 170
Castner Glacier, 196–98, 270
Cathedral Rapids, 197–98, 200
cell phones, xxi
Chandalar–Atigun Traverse, 225–28
Charley Dome Trail, 93, 99
Charley River, 211

Chatanika River, 102–5
Chena Dome Trail, 83–87, 89
Chena Hot Springs, *56,*
 79–80, 81, 97, 232
Chena Hot Springs Resort,
 57, 81–82, 91–94
Chena Hot Springs Winter
 Trail (Road Trail), 64, 67,
 70, 72–73, 82, 88
Chena Lake, 32–35, 38
Chena Lake Recreation Area,
 35, 38, 39
Chena River, 24–27, 57,
 58–61, 97
Chena River Recreation
 Area, 62–63, 65–66, 70
Chena Slough, 36–38, 39
children, traveling with,
 xxvi
Chisana River, 196, 200
Chulitna River, 52
Circle, 209, 212
Circle–Fairbanks Trail, 126,
 135, 232
Circle Hot Springs, 232
Clearwater Creek Trail, 188
Clearwater River and Lake,
 161–62
Clinton Creek bridge, 206,
 208
clothing, xvi
Coal Creek, 212
Colorado Creek Trail, 62–66,
 112, 143
communication facilities, 22
Compeau Trail, 62–65, 66,
 68, 69, 85
Continental Divide, 225
Crazy Mountains, 136
Creamer's Field, 2–3
Cummings Landing, 198

D

Dall sheep, 43–44, 112, 117,
 122, *122*
Dalton Highway, 216–17,
 221, 223–24, 227, 230–31
Dawson City, 204, 213
daylight, xix–xx, xxv
DEET, xvi
Delta Junction Region,
 156–57
Delta River, xiii, 178–81
Denali National Park, ix, 43
Denali State Park, 50, 232
Dickey Lake, 185

difficulty ratings, xi
dogs and dog mushing
 teams, xxvi–xxvii, 4, 90
dominance displays, xviii–
 xix
Donnelly Dome, 165–67
driving directions, xii–xiii
duration estimates, x–xi

E

Eagle, 187, 189, 208, 209–10
Eagle Bluff, 209
Eagle Summit trailhead, 131
Eagle to Circle float, Yukon
 River, 209
Eagle Trail, 187, 188–91
Eielson Air Force Base, 38
Eldorado Creek Trail, 11
Eldridge Glacier, 52, *54*
elevation change, overview,
 xi
Elliott Highway, 143, 221
emergency personal locator
 beacon (EPRB), xxi
Equinox Marathon, 8, 18
Ermine Hill trailhead, 53, 55
Ester Dome, *13,* 18–20
ethical use, ix–x
etiquette, xxvi–xxvii
Eureka Creek, 181

F

Fairbanks area, overview, 1
Falcon Rocks, 150
Far Mountain Trail, 93,
 95–97, *98*
Far Mountain Traverse, 93,
 95–99
Fielding Lake, 175–77
Finger Mountain, 216–18
firebreaks, 64–65, 85
fires, xxii
floats, xxiv, 209, 215, 238
 See also specific trips
flooding, spring, xxv
fog, xxv
food storage, xxii
forests, xiii, xiv, 2, 88, 202
Fort Egbert, 187, 189
Fort Greely, 157, 166–67
Fort Reliance, 187, 204
Fort Wainwright, 167
Fortymile Region, 131, 186–
 87, 204–8
Fortymile River, 187, 204–8
Fort Yukon, 212

Fossil Creek Trail, 142
Fossil Gap Trail, 112, 142
14-Mile Trail, 23, 104–5
Fox, 217

G

garbage, xxii
geographic positioning
 system (GPS), xxii–xxiii
Gerstle River, 199
giardia lamblia (beaver fever),
 xxiv, 54
glacial rivers, xxiii
Gobbler's Knob, 217
gold mining, 187, 204, 207,
 211, 232
gold rush, 128, 178
Goldstream Valley, 8, 10–14
Goodpaster River, 163
Gorilla's Head, 149
Graehl Park, 24, 26–27
Granite Tors, 74–78
Grapefruit Rocks, 149–51
gravel bars, ownership of,
 198
Gulkana River, 181–85

H

Harding Lake, 158
Harrison Creek, 128
Haul Road. *See* Dalton
 Highway
Herrero, Stephen, xix
Highway Lakes, 158–60
hikers, and trail etiquette,
 xxvi–xxvii
hiking trip locator, 238
horses, xxvi–xxvii
hot springs, 82, 105, 232. *See
 also* Chena Hot Springs;
 Tolovana Hot Springs
Hutlinana Hot Springs, 232
hydration, xxv
hypothermia, xxv

I

Indian Peak, 55
interior, defined, xiii
Isberg Recreation Area,
 40–42

J

Jeff Studdert Trails, 3
Jim Whisenhant Cross
 Country Ski Trails, 15
Johnson River, 198, 200
Justice, Stan, 150

K

Kandik River, 211
Kanuti Hot Springs, 232
Kathul Mountain, 211
kayak trip locator, 238
Kesugi Ridge, 1, 50–55
Ketchum Dome, 138
kill sites, xix, xxii
Koyukuk River, 219

L

Lake Park, 32, 34, 35
land managers, xii
Large Animal Research
  Station (LARS), 9
Lavelle Young (stern-wheeler),
  24
leave no trace, xxi–xxii
lichens, xv, 219
Limestone Gulch, 142
Little Champion Creek, 117
Little Champion Creek pass,
  123
Little Chena Dozer Line,
  64–65, 85
Little Coal Creek, 51, 55
Little Tok River, 192–, *194*
loop trails, 5, 34–35, 67,
  139–40, 142–43, 146
Lost Chicken Dredge Trail,
  207
Lost Lake, 158–59
Lower Chatanika State
  Recreation Area (LCSRA),
  105
Lower Chena Ditch Trail, 41
Lower Chena River, 24–27,
  61
Lower Nome Creek Trail, 142
Lowest Rock, 149

M

Manley Hot Springs, 105
maps and map reading, xi,
  xii–xiii, xxii–xxiii, xxv
Marion Creek, 219
Marion Creek Falls, 219–21
Mastodon Dome, 136–38
McKay Creek Trail, 142, 143
McKinley Village, 48
McManus Mountain, 124–26
Middle Tanana River, 28–31
military facilities, 22, 23
mining roads, 98
Minto Flats, 12, 105
Montauk Bluff, 211
Monument Creek, 93, 95, 97

Moon Lake Recreation Area,
  160
moose, xv, xix, 130
Moose Creek, 113
Moose Creek Dam Bikeway,
  32, 34, 35
Moose Creek Trail, 141
Moose Pond, 159
morel mushrooms, xv
mosquitoes, xvi
mountain bikers, xxvi–xxvii
Mount Fairplay, 201–3
Mount Healy, 43–45
Mount Healy Overlook Trail,
  45
Mount Prindle, 106, 115,
  119–23
Mount Silvertip, 169–70
Murphy Dome, 20, 21–23
muskegs, xiii–xiv

N

Nabesna River, 196, 233
National Wild and Scenic
  Rivers, 101, 110–11, 113,
  187, 203, 204
Nation River, 211
nature trails, 34, 67–68,
  158–59, 190, 216
Nenana River, 46–49
Nome Creek, 110, 111, 119,
  142
Northway Village, 196, 200,
  233
no trace wilderness travel,
  xxi–xxii
Nugget Creek Trail, 19, 233

O

O'Brien Creek, 111, 142
overflow conditions, xxiv

P

pace, overview, x
packrafting trip locator, 238
packrafts and packrafting,
  xxiii, 111, *194*, 225
Pavaloff, Pitka, 128
Paxson Lake launch, 182
Pearl Creek Nordic Park, 5, 9
peregrine falcons, 112
permafrost, xiv
Pike's Landing, 25, 27
Piledriver Slough, 36, 37,
  38, 39
Pinnell, Robert, 132
Pinnell Mountain, 97

Pinnell Mountain Trail, 97,
  101, 126, 131–35
Pioneer Park, 27
Pitka's Bar, 128
Porcupine Dome, 132, *134*
preparedness, xx–xxi
Pumphouse bar and
  restaurant, 25–26, 27

Q

Quartz Creek Trail, 115–18,
  122–23
Quartz Lake, 158–60,
  159–60

R

raft trip locator, 238
Rainbow Mountain, 174
Rainbow Ridge, 171–74
rapids, xxiv. *See also specific
  rivers*
Recreational Access Permit
  (RAP), 166–67
Reindeer Hills, 47–48
Richardson Highway lakes,
  158–60
riparian corridors, xiv
river crossings, xxiii–xxiv
River Park Nature and Ski
  Trails, 32, 34–35
river rapids classification
  system, xxiv
rock climbers and rock
  climbing, 74, 77–78, 81,
  82, 121, 122, 149, *151*
rock-climbing trip locator,
  238
route types, xi
runners, xxvi–xxvii

S

safety, xxii–xxiii, xxv. *See
  also* bears
Sagavanirktok River, 229
Sag River, 231
Salcha Elementary School
  trails, 8, 13
Salcha River, 97
satellite phones, xxi, xxv
Serpentine Slide Research
  Natural Area, 113
Seventymile River, 211
shelters. *See also* cabins;
  specific trips
  Angel Rocks, 81
  Granite Tors, 77, 78
  Pinnell Mountain, 133, 135

Rainbow Ridge, 173
Summit Trail, 111, 145, 147
yurts, 93, 99
Shooting Range, 73
shortcuts, xxi
shrub habitat, xiv
Skarland Trail, 5, 9
skate skiing trip locator, 238
skiers, and trail etiquette,
xxvi–xxvii
skijoring, ix, xxvi–xxvii, 238
ski loop trails, 34–35, 67,
139–40, 142–43, 146
ski trip locator, 238
Skyline Ridge Trail, 8
Slaven Dome, 212
Slaven's Roadhouse, 211–12
sledding, 152, 153
Smith Lake, 5
snowmachines, ix, xxvii, 232
snowpack structure, xxvi
snowshoers, xxvi–xxvii
snowstorms, xx
social trails, xi
solifluction lobes, 132
spring flooding, xxv
Standard Creek area, 12
Steese Highway, 102, 143
Steese National
Conservation Area, 101,
115, 127
Steese-White Mountains
Region, 100–101
Stiles Creek Trail, 64, 70–73
storms, xxiv–xxv
Sugarloaf Mountain, 181
Sukakpak Mountain, 222–24
summer hikes, 7, 148
Summit Trail, 109, 111, 114,
141, 143, 144–48
Swamp Saddle, 133
sweepers, xxiv

T

Table Mountain, 134
Table Top Mountain Trail,
106–8
taiga, xiii–xiv
Takoma Bluff, 212
Talkeetna Mountains, 46

Tanacross, 197–98
Tanana River, 28–31, 161–
64, 196–200
Tangle Lakes, 178–80, 185
Tangle Mountain, 181
Taylor Highway, 201, 203,
208
temperatures, xix–xx, xxv
tents, placement of, xxii
Tetlin National Wildlife
Refuge, 197
thunderstorms, xxv
Tok River, 187, 188, 190, 191,
192
Tolovana Hot Springs, 101,
152–53, 155
Top of the Dome, 153
Top of the World Highway,
207, 208
tors, 74–78, 121, 122
Trail Creek Trail, 111, 140,
141, 142
trail etiquette, xxvi–xxvii
trails, groomed, 5
trails, overview, ix, xxi
transition zones, ecological,
xiv
traplines, 66
travel plans, xxi
trees, xiii–xiv, xv
Triangle Peak, 169–70
trip descriptions, overview, x
trip locator table, 238
trip narratives, overview, xii
Troublesome Creek, 54, 55
Troyer, Will, xix
tundra, xv, 138, 146
Twelvemile Summit, 94, 126,
134
Twin Bears Camp, 63, 67, 69
Twin Bears trails, 64–67
Twin Towers, 149, 150
Two Rivers Elementary ski
trails, 8, 13, 17

U

University of Alaska
Fairbanks (UAF) trail
system, 4–5, 8, 9
Upper Chatnika River State
Recreation Site, 102, 104

Upper Chena River, 58–61,
97
Upper Tanana River, 196–
200
U.S. Creek Road, 108, 113

V

VABM Golog (USGS marker),
54, 55
Valdez-Eagle Trail, 189
Victoria Creek, 110

W

walkers, xxvi–xxvii
Wallcutt Mountain, 233
Washington-Alaska Cable
and Telegraph System
(WAMCATS), 189–90
waste disposal, xxi–xxii
water supply, xxiii–xxv
White Bear Trail, 16, 17
Whitehorse, Yukon
Territory, 213
White Mountains, 101, 115,
118, 139–43
Wickersham Creek Trail,
111, 140, 141, 148
Wickersham Dome, 112,
143, 144–48
wildfires, xv–xvi, 108
wildflowers, 136–37
wildlife, xiv, xix, 112. See
also individual species
wind, xxiv
Windy Arch, 142
winter, and outdoor
activities, xx, xxv
Woodchopper Roadhouse,
212

Y

Yukon-Charley Rivers
National Preserve, 97,
209–10
Yukon Flats National
Wildlife Refuge, 113
Yukon River, 111, 113, 129,
187, 207, 209–13
yurts, 93, 99